W9-CCZ-212

AFTER THE NEW TESTAMENT

AFTER THE NEW TESTAMENT

ROBERT M. GRANT

FORTRESS PRESS

PHILADELPHIA

Library of Congress Catalog Card Number 67-17402

4065L66 *Printed in U.S.A.* 1-361

ACKNOWLEDGMENTS

I am grateful to the following for permission to reprint the substance of articles which have previously appeared: the American Academy for Jewish Research for chapter 7 (*Harry Austryn Wolfson Jubilee Volume*, 1965); the *Anglican Theological Review* for chapter 1 (1962); the *Catholic Biblical Quarterly* for chapter 3 (1963); *Church History* for chapter 14 (1954); the *Harvard Theological Review* for chapters 4, 10, and 11 (1948, 1947, and 1949); the *Journal of Biblical Literature* for chapter 8 (1964); the *Journal of Theological Studies* for chapters 2, 9, and 15 (1960, 1956, and 1964); the *McCormick Quarterly* for chapter 12 (1965); the Deutsche Akademie der Wissenschaften zur Berlin and Akademie-Verlag for chapter 6, which first appeared in *Studia Patristica*, 7 ("Texte und Untersuchungen zur Geschichte der altchristlichen Literatur," 92 [1966]), pp. 462-72; and *Vigiliae Christianae* for chapters 5 and 13 (1959 and 1961).

ABBREVIATIONS

Ad Autol.	–	Theophilus, *Ad Autolycum*
Adv. haer.	–	Irenaeus, *Adversus haereses*
Apol.	–	Justin Martyr, *Apologia*
CSCO	–	*Corpus Scriptorum Christianorum Orientalium* (Paris, Rome, *et al.*, 1903-).
Dial.	–	Justin Martyr, *Dialogus*
Dox.	–	*Doxographi Graeci*, H. Diels, editor (Berlin, 1879).
GCS	–	*Die griechischen christlichen Schriftsteller der ersten drei Jahrhunderte* (Leipzig and Berlin, 1897-).
H.E.	–	Eusebius, *Historia Ecclesiastica*
LXX	–	Septuagint
Or.	–	Tatian, *Oratio ad Graecos*
Pan.	–	Epiphanius, *Panarion*
PG	–	*Patrologia Graeca*, J. P. Migne, editor (Paris, 1857 ff.).
PL	–	*Patrologia Latina*, J. P. Migne, editor (Paris, 1844 ff.).
RE	–	*Realencyclopadie der classischen Altertumswissenschaft* (Stuttgart: Metzler, 1894-).
Ref.	–	Hippolytus, *Refutatio omnium haeresium*
Str.	–	Clement of Alexandria, *Stromata*
SVF	–	*Stoicorum veterum fragmenta*, H. von Arnim, editor (Leipzig, 1903-1905).
TU	–	*Texte und Untersuchungen zur Geschichte der altchristlichen Literatur*, O. Gebhardt *et alii*, editors (Leipzig, 1882-).
Vorsokr.	–	*Die Fragmente der Vorsokratiker*, H. Diels, editor (6th ed., revised by W. Kranz; 1951-52).

CONTENTS

INTRODUCTION[1]

THIS BOOK consists of fifteen essays on early Christian life and thought published in various journals and volumes over the last twenty years, some of which I have revised here for the sake of either accuracy or clarity. They are primarily concerned with historical continuities, between the New Testament and the early church, "orthodox" and "heretical" alike, and between early Christianity and the Greco-Roman culture into which it was moving. This is to say that they reflect an effort to relate both the New Testament and, especially, early Christianity to their historical contexts. The principal element lacking in them, as far as I can see, is an emphasis upon the close relations between early Christianity and Judaism, but to some extent this relation is indicated in the essays on Ignatius (chap. 3 below), on the book of Wisdom (chap. 6), and on Theophilus of Antioch (chap. 10).

Like any other document or collection of documents, the New Testament is not self-interpreting. It is easy enough to say that it speaks directly to a modern interpreter or that he asks it questions which it then answers, and to a certain degree this rather naive notion is justifiable. As is the case with any literature which transcends its immediate historical setting (and therefore is valued and preserved), there is something "immediate" about the New Testament, something with which the modern interpreter, like his predecessors, finds an existential relationship. Sometimes, however, the existential relationship is with what the interpreter imagines is there rather than with what he may find under other circumstances or with what other contemporaries believe they can find. One needs certain checks and balances, at

[1] This introduction is based on a John XXII Memorial Lecture delivered at St. Xavier College, Chicago, in 1965.

the very least in order to minimize the possibility of self-delusion. One hopes that what one finds in the New Testament is, to a considerable extent, actually there rather than in the interpreter's imagination.

It seems important to recognize that the New Testament did not come into existence suddenly, like Athena sprung from the mind of Zeus. The creation of the canon was the consequence of an extended historical process. Though historians disagree as to the precise extent of the process, they agree that it existed and that even at the end of the second century, not to mention any later times, different usages were in existence in various Christian churches. This is not to say that there was much doubt about the major books or clusters of books in the New Testament. It is to say that as a whole the church only gradually recognized quite a few of the books as representing the life and thought of the classical Christian period, the apostolic age. The gradualness of this process seems to imply that in interpreting the New Testament the interpreter must view the books historically as well as theologically; he must see them in the light of the whole early Christian movement in which and for which they were written.

Again, it is fairly obvious that behind the written documents lies a situation (or group of situations) out of which and for which the documents were written. Apart from the Pastoral Epistles and the letter to Philemon, the letters of the apostle Paul are addressed to churches. They deal with the problems which these churches, obviously already in existence, are facing. (It may be added that the exceptions are not fully exceptions since they too are concerned with church problems.) The letters therefore presuppose the existence of churches and, I should add, of "the church" as well. In addition, the letters are like the gospels in that they reflect Christian traditions in existence before the documents were composed. The apostle Paul explicitly refers to prior traditions which he has received and has transmitted; the gospels could not have been composed apart from the prior existence of such traditions. To be sure, it has often been argued that John, going beyond the synoptic evangelists, freely created some of the materials used in his gospel. But one may reply that for the early Christians tradition was not merely something transmitted; it was also something to be interpreted, under the guidance of the Holy Spirit; and the extent to which John made use of earlier traditions, not necessarily synoptic, has not yet been adequately analyzed, though a substantial beginning has been made by C. H. Dodd in his *Historical Tradition in the Fourth Gospel.*[2]

To the historical fact of the process of canonization we therefore add the historical fact of the process of transmitting and interpreting tradition; and the consequence, I believe, is that a historical interpretation of the New Testament becomes absolutely necessary. It is demanded by the nature of the materials with which we deal. By "historical interpretation" I mean not simply arranging the documents chronologically and looking for some kind of causal/developmental explanation for the sequence. I mean an interpretation of the documents, thus arranged, in relation to the historical environment (or groups of environments) in which they were first written and first read. This environment, I suggest, is provided by the Christian church or churches in the first century of our era.

At this point a certain difficulty arises, for as we try to determine what Christianity was during the first century there are two obvious problems. (1) Almost all our information about the first-century church comes from the New Testament documents themselves. Practically nothing of any value is contributed by the few notices, Greco-Roman or Jewish, found in documents outside the New Testament. This means that our interpretation may go in a circle. From the New Testament we draw our picture of the church; from our picture of the church we interpret the New Testament. (2) The whole study of church history suggests that the church is not a static entity to be logically defined and, so to speak, put on a chart. It was a living, ever changing movement with which we can compare the Judaism of the first century, both before and after the fall of Jerusalem. Just as it would be rash to assume that Judaism before 70 can be fully understood only from documents written after

[2] Cambridge, England, 1963.

70, so it would be rash to assume that Christianity was absolutely the same at the end of the first century as it was toward the beginning. Indeed, the presence of diversity among the later books of the New Testament, not to mention the Apostolic Fathers, proves that it was not completely uniform. The historical approach, therefore, is hampered by these two difficulties, one methodological, the other related to the nature of the materials—and of history itself.

The first difficulty does not seem insuperable. If we bear in mind the fact that the apostle Paul, for example, was endeavoring to communicate meanings to the recipients of his letters, it is possible that by careful analysis of what he said to his correspondents we can recover a good deal of what they may have had in their minds, even though our reconstructions must remain largely conjectural. In order to understand the church at Corinth, for example, we read not only what the apostle urges its members to believe and do but also what he says or implies they are actually believing and doing. A picture of the Corinthian church can therefore be developed in which to some measure we can highlight the Corinthians themselves and thus for historical purposes—the rediscovery of Corinthian Christianity—go a little beyond the Corinthian letters themselves. Conjecturally we can also make attempts to envisage how their notions hung together and, perhaps most conjecturally, why they thought and did what they thought and did. In the light of such a reconstruction we may well be able to understand more fully why the apostle said what he said. We thus break out, if only partly, from a circular argument.[3]

The second kind of difficulty can perhaps be overcome if we extend the range of our study of the New Testament to include some of the Christian literature almost contemporary with it—indeed, fully contemporary if we accept J. P. Audet's arguments on the early date of the *Didache*. In any case, the writings of Clement of Rome and Ignatius of Antioch are so close in time to the New Testament documents that one would suppose that they provide reliable testimony to the life and faith of the

[3] See now J. C. Hurd, Jr., *The Origin of I Corinthians* (New York, 1965).

church in the time immediately subsequent to the later New Testament documents. They show how the process of Christian life and faith continued, at least at Rome and Antioch and in various communities in Asia Minor. Therefore, in my opinion, one is justified on historical grounds in making use of the writings of the Apostolic Fathers as guides to what the Christian faith was just after the apostolic or subapostolic age, and in viewing the life and thought of the church as moving along lines to be drawn from the New Testament toward these Fathers.[4]

It can be said, and by some critics it has been said, that this principle is theological, not historical, and that when I call it historical I am trying to camouflage theology as history. In my opinion such a criticism is mistaken. (1) In my view theology is not totally separable from history, just as faith is not totally separable from historical fact. I should not deny that one's theological viewpoint tends to influence one's historical judgments, but I should never concede that my historical judgments, or anyone else's, are or can be made *sola fide*. There is a kind of dialogue between the historical data and the historian, an "I-thou" relationship, if one will, in which the historian, no matter how much under the spell of his theology, tries to let the data say something to him instead of doing all the talking himself. (2) It is possible that many of us tend to lay too much emphasis on the continuities present within the Christian churches of the first and second centuries. On the other hand, I cannot say that I am greatly impressed with the evidence intended to show that the history of early Christianity consists of nothing but one crisis after another or that Clement, Ignatius, or Justin would have found apostolic Christianity totally different from that of their own times. The fact that Clement and Ignatius knew I Corinthians practically by heart (see chap. 3) does not suggest that the Corinthian conflicts would have disturbed them much if they had suddenly encountered them at first hand. My own investigations in the history of the Eucharist indicate (to me, at least) that while the rite was slightly modified in the course of the first two or three centuries its essential shape remained con-

[4] Chapter 3 attempts to do this with respect to Ignatius.

stant. Much of our literature emerges out of early Christian controversy. There were matters about which most believers, I am convinced, never thought argument was necessary—and among these I should count the most fundamental matters of doctrine, discipline, and worship.

I continue to claim, therefore, that the primary historical environment in relation to which the New Testament is to be interpreted is that provided by the Christian church of the first two centuries or so, when the New Testament documents were written, transmitted, interpreted, and canonized; and I claim that this judgment, while it may be theological, is certainly historical. Chapter 2 shows how difficult it was for the church to maintain its grasp of historical reality; chapter 6 gives an example of the relation between canonization and theology.

To me the most serious objection against this view is one which arises in the area of historical study. This is one which has been known for a long time but has arisen with greater force in modern times partly because of fresh arguments and partly because of fresh information. This is the argument based on the existence of diversity within early Christianity so great as to suggest that one cannot speak of "the church" or "the common faith" or "the tradition" but only of "churches," "expressions of faith," and "traditions." The chief proponent of this view in modern times was the great lexicographer Walter Bauer;[5] the principal accretions to our knowledge have been provided by the Gnostic library found at Nag Hammadi in Egypt in 1946. It should be said, however, that there are a good many items that point in similar directions. Our picture of Judaism in Hellenistic and Roman times has been remarkably expanded by the Dead Sea Scrolls, by continuing study of the thought of Philo of Alexandria, and by the late Erwin Goodenough's work on *Jewish Symbols in the Greco-Roman Period*, culminating in his analysis of the paintings in the Dura synagogue and crowned by a final volume of synthesis. We may also add an unpublished letter by Clement of Alexandria, to be edited by Morton Smith,

[5] In his *Rechtgläubigkeit und Ketzerei im ältesten Christentum* (Tübingen, 1934; 2nd ed., edited and with an appendix by Georg Strecker, Tübingen, 1964). A translation of this volume is in preparation.

which clearly shows that Alexandrian Christianity was even more "irregular" than has previously been supposed.

Diversity was characteristic of Judaism and Christianity alike in the period which we have proposed to treat as classical—as Père Daniélou has rightly claimed in his *Théologie du Judéo-Christianisme* (Tournai, 1958) and elsewhere. But is diversity all there was? The problem for the historian who deals with early Christianity or, it would appear, any religious movement is that of giving a balanced account in which he does justice both to the centripetal forces within it and to the centrifugal ones. Conceivably, without the centripetal forces there would not be much movement or even life; without the centrifugal ones there would be nothing which could be described as moving or living. During the first two centuries of our era the most effective challenges to the unity of Christian life and thought were presented by various groups which we call Gnostic. To analyze their attitudes is extremely difficult and, as might be expected, some modern scholars have emphasized the varieties of Gnostic experience while others, especially Hans Jonas, have tried to depict the underlying unity. In general the Gnostics somehow related to Christianity insisted that the unknown, hidden God had revealed himself to their spiritual essences through the Christ-power, whom they alone understood; this God had had little to do with the origin of the material universe, which had been directly created by a power hostile to him, the God of the Old Testament. Through knowledge—essentially divine self-knowledge—the Gnostic could escape from this prison-world and return to the God above, from whom he had fallen. Some Gnostics emphasized their rejection of the Old Testament more; some ventured into extreme asceticism, others into promiscuity; still others came very close to common Christian theology, especially as interpreted at Alexandria. Now it is this closeness to Christian theology which justifies us, to a considerable degree, in calling some of the Valentinians "Christian Gnostics" (see chaps. 12, 13, and 15). But it is very difficult, if we lay any emphasis on centripetal forces in Christianity and in Gnosticism, to avoid differentiating them. When Ignatius of Antioch tells us that some of his opponents abstain from Eucharist and prayer because they do not acknowledge that the Eucharist "is the flesh of our Savior Jesus Christ, which suffered for us, which the Father raised up in his goodness" (*Smyrn.* 7), it may be that he is identifying the Eucharist a little too crudely with the flesh of Jesus (presumably he is going along the line of John 6:51-58 but interpreting Johannine thought overliterally). But when we also read that these opponents denied that Christ actually suffered and was crucified, it is hard to see how their opinion can ultimately be regarded as Christian except in some sense so marginal as to become nonsense.[6]

Am I smuggling later theological interpretations, such as my own, into my assessment of the evidence? Perhaps I am, but I think what I am trying to say is that when viewed as a distinctive historical phenomenon early Christianity includes a good deal of diversity, but not quite so much diversity as to involve the denial of the passion and the crucifixion. The fact that Ignatius' opponents regarded themselves as Christians does not necessarily mean that they were Christians. I am not trying to impose later credal or conciliar norms upon the thought of second-century Christians, although, insofar as ancient Christianity can be regarded as a long-continued process rather than just a series of isolated snapshots such an imposition is partly valid; I am trying to see what early Christianity essentially was, not only "in relation" to movements contemporary with it but also "in opposition" to or "in distinction" from such movements.

In other words, the writings of an early bishop like Ignatius show us how the theological ideas expressed in the New Testament came to be interpreted and developed by Christians in the period just after the New Testament books were written. To be sure, such early Christians were writing in specific historical circumstances, for particular purposes, just as the New Testament writers themselves had written. If we take historical-environmental study seriously we cannot absolutize the teaching of the early Fathers as it stands any more than we can absolutize particular historically conditioned texts of the New Testament. But in both kinds of cases we can search in the texts for the basic

[6] For a system based on Jewish, pagan, and Christian ideas see chap. 14.

theological intentions of the authors and find what the Anglican historian A. V. G. Allen (1884) called *The Continuity of Christian Thought.*

Too many students of the New Testament, under the spell of the quest for origins which was especially prominent in the late nineteenth century and the early twentieth, have concentrated their attention upon the New Testament books alone or exclusively in relation to the life and thought of late Judaism or of the Greco-Roman world. The New Testament has thus been isolated from the church which produced it and in which it was transmitted and interpreted. No one can deny the importance of studying the New Testament by itself or of setting the New Testament documents and, for that matter, the early church itself in the wider historical environments in which they came into existence. But what we may call the segregation of the New Testament from the continuing historical life of the church is, like most instances of segregation, harmful for all the parties involved. Some kinds of New Testament study give the impression that Christianity came to an end in the last quarter of the first century, if not with the death of the apostle Paul. In turn, a study of church history which neglects Christian beginnings and passes abruptly from sacred texts to the profane church Fathers without clearly indicating both sameness and difference makes both the first century and the second incomprehensible.

The study of the New Testament has to be combined with the study of the early church. But in what way is the study of the early church to be conducted so that it possesses relevance to the New Testament? It is difficult to go all the way with G. Ebeling, who views the history of Christian doctrine as the history of biblical interpretation, although Ebeling's own work clearly shows that he takes institutional and cultural factors into consideration. To a very considerable extent, however, the writings of the early Fathers can be regarded as interpretations either of biblical documents or of traditions either underlying the documents or parallel to them. H. Koester has argued, in his *Synoptische Überlieferungen bei den Apostolischen Vätern* (1957), that most of the Apostolic Fathers relied not on New Testament gospels but on oral traditions underlying them. If he is right, and in many instances I believe he is right (chap. 3 indicates exceptions), some of the Apostolic Fathers, as transmitters and editors of such traditions, are nearly as close to the original sayings of Jesus as the synoptic evangelists are. To my mind the same observation cannot be made in regard to the sayings of Jesus as transmitted in the Gnostic *Gospel of Thomas*, but I should not consider it absolutely impossible that light on the process of transmission, or even on the form of the original sayings, can come from this peculiar document. St. Jerome suggested that there is some gold in the mud of the apocryphal gospels (see chaps. 13 and 15).

Another aspect of continuity which is being given more emphasis in modern study is that to be found in the church's ongoing worship. Epistolary materials are being traced back to church sermons, to semi- or proto-credal confessions, or to catechetical elements (e.g., by O. Cullmann in *The Earliest Christian Confessions*[7] and P. Carrington in *The Primitive Christian Catechism*[8]). Analogies are being discovered between New Testament expressions and Jewish prayers, benedictions, and doxologies (cf. E. Bickermann in *Revue Biblique*, 69 [1962], 524-32). New studies are enriching our understanding of the developments in early Christian baptism and the Eucharist, not to mention the use of psalms and hymns in worship; there are fresh analyses of the hymn-style. Beyond these types of literature lies the whole modern recovery of what rhetoric meant to early Christian writers, for example to Theophilus of Antioch, whose theology not only was expressed by means of rhetoric but came to fruition in the rhetoric itself (see chap. 5). In other words, form and content cannot be completely divorced, either in early patristic literature or in the New Testament. The forms were used to convey the content.

When one mentions worship (see chaps. 4, 12, and 13) one naturally moves on to the question of the ministers of worship, and we need relatively impartial study of the ways in which the second-century ministers were continuous with, but different from, those in apostolic times. Again one must lay emphasis on

[7] London, 1949.
[8] Cambridge, England, 1940.

the historical nature of this study. There is no special reason at this point to revive the controversies of the sixteenth or the seventeenth century or, for that matter, the nineteenth.

Certainly we need further study of the history of Christian doctrine. The whole direction of the argument thus far suggests that while it is highly important to study what is called New Testament theology—and, indeed, in the context of "biblical theology" as a whole—such study remains isolated (I should even say "truncated") unless it is combined with at least the early history of Christian doctrine. The church did not come to an end; theologians did not stop thinking. To understand "New Testament theology" one must view it in the context of Clement, Ignatius, Justin (see chap. 9), Irenaeus, and others, not to mention some of the Gnostics, if only for the purpose of defining what the alternatives were.[9] In my opinion a philosophical conception of God clearly underlies what Ignatius says about Christ as God. When Ignatius speaks of Christ as the impassible one who for us became passible, he is using terminology strictly theological in order to set forth the paradox of the incarnation. Terminology which points in this direction is already present in the Pauline epistles (see chap. 8) and becomes explicit in II Peter 1:4: "so that you may become participants in the divine nature [*theia physis*], escaping from worldly perishability. . . ."

In addition, the ways in which early Christians interpreted New Testament texts are often significant both historically and theologically. In his study of *The Powers That Be*,[10] Clinton Morrison has rightly treated Romans 13 as a "communication" from Paul to his readers. The apostle expected that first-century Roman Christians would understand what he meant. Morrison then analyzes first- and second-century Jewish and Hellenistic conceptions of demonic or angelic powers standing behind and above the state and concludes that Paul had such powers in mind, not officers of the state as such. I do not agree with this conclusion. Among the ancient writers to be examined in reconstructing the ideological background one should first consider

[9] Cf. my study of *The Early Christian Doctrine of God* (Charlottesville, Va., 1966).

[10] Naperville, 1960.

early Christians; then one finds that all early Christians interpreted "the powers that be" not as demonic or angelic but as the officers of the state. The only exception is provided by some Gnostics mentioned by Irenaeus, and they found spiritual beings everywhere. Therefore, I should claim, Paul was probably speaking directly of the Roman state—in particular historical circumstances which were different from those known to the author of Revelation. I should also claim that this is not only a theological judgment, related to a form of the *consensus patrum*, but also a historical judgment, based on the fact that Polycarp, Theophilus, Irenaeus, and Origen represent not only church tradition but also the Greco-Roman world in which Paul's readers lived.

Study of the Greco-Roman background of early Christianity seems to undergo cycles of attention and neglect, but perhaps given the contemporary problems in systematic theology it is again coming into its own. If one is going to denounce early Christian philosophical theologians one should have some clear conception as to what they were trying to do and why they were doing it. In this regard chapters 4-11 may be of some service. Chapter 4 ("Pliny and the Christians") is an attempt to show that in dealing with Christians a Roman governor did not start *de novo* but relied on his own tradition. Chapter 5 suggests that rhetoric as well as philosophy had a role to play in the formation of Christian thought. Chapter 6 shows how a key passage in the Book of Wisdom influenced Alexandrian theologians. Chapters 7-9 contain reflections on the use of philosophical (and not so philosophical) ideas among early Christians, while chapters 10 and 11 deal with the cultural backgrounds of two Christian leaders toward the end of the second century. In most of these essays I have tried to indicate not only that philosophical ideas are often present in unexpected areas of Christian thought but also that what philosophy there was, was the vehicle of a faith which remained Christian.

The study of early Christian life and thought does not and cannot provide absolute norms for Christian theology (see chap. 1). It does, however, illuminate the history of the Christian tradition in regard to its maintenance and reinterpretation in the church. It shows us that it is possible to be rather fully at home in the world without losing grasp of the tradition, even though sometimes the limits of diversity (see chaps. 12-15) seem to have been transcended. In this sense, I believe, these essays, explicitly historical, are implicitly theological as well.

ROBERT M. GRANT

I

THE STUDY OF THE EARLY FATHERS

1

THE STUDY OF THE EARLY FATHERS IN MODERN TIMES

THROUGHOUT THE seventeen or eighteen centuries that separate modern Christians from the early Fathers there has tended to be an appeal to them in times of crisis or of fairly rapid transition. The Fathers can provide support for conservatives and for radicals alike, for clearly they lived close to the apostolic age—closer, at any rate, than men later than them!—and yet their writings are different in form and in content from the New Testament books. Conservatives who value tradition can appeal, and have appealed, to the patristic tradition (see chap. 2 below); more radical historians can point to the diversity among them and to the difference between them and the New Testament.

The crisis of the Reformation was a crisis which necessitated a fresh look at the history of the Christian church. The publication and the renewed study of ancient Christian documents meant that it was both possible and necessary to explain the differences between the New Testament and the Fathers, as well as the differences within the New Testament and within the patristic writings. Sometimes the differences were explained as due to the rapid falling away of the church from its primitive purity; in the *Church History* of Eusebius there are some early quotations which point toward such a view. Sometimes the Fathers as a group were compared with the New Testament, to the advantage of the latter. A few scholars, among whom we may mention the Catholic reformers Lefèvre d'Étaples and Erasmus, occupied themselves with the publication of the writings of the early Fathers in order to show that the church did not immediately lose its radiance. They were aware of the possibility that the church could become corrupt, but they did not believe that *sola scriptura* provided the norm for reform.

During the course of the sixteenth century two trends in patristic study became evident. First, scholars were eager to publish the writings of the early Fathers in order to provide a foundation for the study of early Christianity. The most prominent among those who published such texts were Robert Étienne of Paris and the Swiss humanist Conrad Gesner. In general, the new documents were published at Paris or at Rome, for the most valuable of the manuscripts were to be found in the libraries of those centers. No early Christian writing was published in England during this period. Second, scholars had become aware that not every writing ascribed to a Father was necessarily written by him, though very little work of a genuinely critical nature supported or confounded their doubts. Again, what critical work there was was produced in France and Italy, and to some extent in Germany and Switzerland.

A. ENGLISH PATRISTICS

The first major contribution of English patristics was made, as one might expect, in a situation in which political and religious factors were inextricably combined. Cyril Lucar, orthodox patriarch of Constantinople, was grateful to the English ambassador for his help in a struggle with the Jesuits, and to show his gratitude he presented him with the famous biblical manuscript now known as Codex Alexandrinus. The manuscript, which reached England in 1628, contains at the end the early epistle known as *I Clement*, as well as part of the homily called *II Clement*. Five years later these documents, virtually unknown for many centuries, were published at Oxford by Patrick Young, librarian to Charles I. Because of the growing political tension in England—not to mention the continuance of the Thirty Years' War on the continent—the documents did not at first receive the attention they deserved. One may doubt that a careful perusal of *I Clement* would have prevented the religious wars of Charles and his opponents; but it would at least have modified the claims which both sides made in regard to the ministry of the early church. Ultimately the publication of *I Clement* also provided an authentic document in relation to which the fictitious character of the later Clementine literature could be demonstrated.

Meanwhile James Ussher, who had left Cambridge for the Anglican archbishopric of Armagh in Ireland, had made an equally significant discovery. In the library of Gaius College he had found a manuscript of the thirteenth-century Latin translation of Ignatius by Robert Grosseteste, bishop of Lincoln. It contained the letters which, reflecting fourth-century church life, were coming to be regarded as forgeries. More important, it contained the seven letters mentioned by Eusebius but in a version quite different from that set forth in the sixteenth-century editions of Ignatius. Ussher concluded that this version was the authentic one, and he proceeded to make a detailed comparison so that he could free Ignatius' letters from the late interpolations. His task was impeded by his other scholarly and controversial efforts, as well as by the civil war; but his *Ignatius* finally appeared in 1644. A fire at Oxford destroyed most of the sheets of the edition of Barnabas which he had also prepared; otherwise he would receive credit for yet another *editio princeps*.

Opponents of episcopacy immediately denied that Ussher's reconstruction had any greater validity than the Greek manuscripts of the late version of the letters, but his theory was manifestly confirmed in 1646, when the Dutch classical scholar Isaac Voss (encouraged by the archbishop) published the text of the one Greek manuscript which actually contains nearly all of the genuine letters.

In little more than a decade, then, English patristic scholarship made up for lost time. The work of Young and, especially, of Ussher produced a genuine revolution in patristic studies and for the first time made possible a valid historical and theological picture of the earliest Christianity outside the New Testament. Among their successors in the seventeenth century we should mention above all John Pearson, bishop of Chester, with his *Vindiciae Ignatianae*, and John Fell, dean of Christ Church and bishop of Oxford, whose wide-ranging patristic studies remain highly valuable. By the end of the century it was universally recognized that England, and especially Oxford, was the center of early patristic research.

During the eighteenth and early nineteenth centuries English work was not so important. There is no British edition of the Greek apologists, for example, which can be compared with that of the Benedictine Prudentius Maran (1742). The nineteenth century, however, witnessed the tremendous scholarly endeavors of the great triad from Cambridge: Westcott, Hort, and—especially for patristic studies—J. B. Lightfoot, bishop of Durham. The discovery of a Syriac abridgement of the Ignatian letters made it necessary for Lightfoot to recapitulate and expand the work of Ussher, and his five massive volumes on Clement, Ignatius, and Polycarp will remain a permanent achievement of patristic scholarship. His studies provided the setting in which the most important discovery of the nineteenth century could be placed.

This discovery was made by Philotheos Bryennios, Orthodox metropolitan of Thyatira, who found in Constantinople a manuscript of the year 1056 which contained not only the complete text of *I* and *II Clement* but also a document previously unknown, the *Teaching of the Twelve Apostles* or *Didache*. The publication of the *Didache* in 1885 resulted in excitement comparable only to that which attended the finding of the Dead Sea Scrolls. Obviously this little manual reflects a kind of Jewish Christianity which is either very early or is trying to look as if it were early. The ministers known to the community are prophets and teachers and itinerant apostles, while its readers are instructed to appoint for themselves bishops and deacons. The fact that the *Didache* is very hard to date has meant that a great deal of speculation has surrounded it. Indeed, it cannot be said that even today the "riddle of the *Didache*" has been solved, although the work is increasingly located well before the end of the first century. Lightfoot too placed it fairly early.

As for other discoveries of early patristic writings and of materials related to them, the international character of patristic study today means that they cannot easily be assigned to any particular country or ecclesiastical group. The homily on the passover by Melito of Sardis was published by Campbell Bonner, professor of Greek at the University of Michigan; another Greek papyrus of the same work has appeared in Switzerland; and a Coptic version belongs to the University of Mississippi. The Gnostic documents found at Nag Hammadi in Egypt are being published at Cairo, but some of them have appeared under international auspices. Professor Morton Smith of Columbia University is preparing an edition of a new and important letter of Clement of Alexandria which he discovered near Jerusalem. The journal *Vigiliae Christianae* is published at Amsterdam but has an international board of editors.

One of the most important links among patristic scholars is provided at Oxford by the quadrennial Patristic Conferences, organized by Professor F. L. Cross. These conferences have greatly facilitated communication in the field, and have done much to promote the renaissance of patristics which is actually occurring.

Thus far we have concentrated our attention primarily on the discovery and discussion of the new documents which have restored, or even recreated the early Fathers in the period since the Renaissance and the Reformation. Even more important is the question of the historical and theological significance of the early patristic writings. This kind of question was raised from the classical side by Guillaume Budé in his famous treatise *De transitu Hellenismi ad Christianismum* (1535). It was obviously less significant to men like Ussher and Lightfoot, more concerned with the preliminary and necessary analysis of literary problems (though both dealt with history as well) than with creating syntheses.

B. THE PROBLEM OF CONTINUITY AND SYNTHESIS

The kind of assumption prevalent among many of the pioneers in patristic studies is exemplified in the Preface to the Anglican Ordinal (1550). "It is evident unto all men, diligently reading

Holy Scripture and ancient Authors, that from the Apostles' time there have been these Orders of Ministers in Christ's Church —Bishops, Priests, and Deacons." To be sure, something like these orders can be found in the New Testament, and the "ancient authors" studied in 1550 included Irenaeus and Eusebius; one can readily observe the orders in their writings. At any rate, one can see that bishops, presbyters, and deacons are named. The assumption was therefore made that the names corresponded to the functions and that the functions had always remained essentially the same. Since the genuine writings of Clement and Ignatius, not to mention the *Didache*, were not available, the element of continuity was somewhat exaggerated and the historical development of the ministry remained unknown. The basic idea of patristic authority was almost what it had been since the fifth and sixth centuries (see chap. 2 below).

What has been more characteristic of modern study is an emphasis on the lack of continuity between the New Testament and the Fathers and, for that matter, between Jesus and the church. Probably the most important early work along these lines was the *Traité de l'emploi des saints pères* published by the French Protestant theologian Jean Daillé in 1632; an English translation, *A Treatise concerning the Right Use of the Fathers in the Decision of the Controversies that are at this day in Religion*, appeared at London in 1651. Daillé's ideas have become so much a part of the common stock of critical thought that they seem almost self-evident today; but they were not self-evident when he wrote. First he discussed literary questions. There is, he said, little Christian literature from the first three centuries, for much has been lost or suppressed and there are many forgeries and interpolated texts. The subjects discussed often have little to do with modern controversies, and the style of the Fathers is often rhetorical and obscure. Daillé's second group of criticisms may be called historical. The Fathers often expressed private opinions, whether their own or those of others; they changed their minds; they did not often differentiate necessary beliefs from those merely probable. We need to know the mind of the whole ancient church, not just the views of individuals. Finally comes criticism more basically theological. The

Fathers are not always reliable witnesses to Christian belief. They were often self-contradictory and made mistakes and oversights even in matters of faith; they also contradicted one another. Indeed, neither the church of Rome nor the Protestants really acknowledge them as judges in disputes. Their only value lies in their testimony to the Christian life and to the fundamental principles acknowledged by all.

It is clear that to use the Fathers rightly is to use them historically, as witnesses to the early history of Christianity, since they have no real theological authority. The studies of patristic scholars after Daillé have almost always implicitly recognized this point.

By the end of the nineteenth century a "new wave" of detailed critical studies had made it possible to look for new syntheses in which the "mind of the whole ancient church" could be set forth, as well as the history of the church as a corporate body. The most important studies, continuing on into the first third of the twentieth century, were undoubtedly those made by Harnack, Duchesne, and Lietzmann. In turn, reactions to their views were expressed by Walter Bauer in his *Rechtgläubigkeit und Ketzerei im ältesten Christentum*, an attempt to prove that "heresy" was always prior to "orthodoxy," and Martin Werner in *Die Entstehung des christlichen Dogmas* (1941; English translation, *The Formation of Christian Dogma*, 1957), a treatment of church life and thought as based upon the loss of primitive apocalyptic eschatology.

It cannot be said that any of these syntheses has proved tenable, partly because their authors have usually been trying to prove some special thesis about the goodness or badness of early Christianity and partly, it would appear, because they have too often neglected the complexity of the relations between early Christianity and its environment. Today no great synthesis commands anything like universal assent. Shaken by the rise and fall of the great schemes of the nineteenth and twentieth centuries, most scholars are hesitant to claim that they possess the only key to the understanding of early Christianity. Their caution is certainly justified by the collapse of one synthesis after another. But it may be suggested that the lack of a single key does not justify the avoidance of a more modest effort to use whatever means are available while recognizing the limitations of these means.

The situation is not unlike the one which is said to exist in cultural anthropology. There have been so many special studies of primitive or not so primitive communities that there is no lack of materials with which to deal. What is needed is not more field work but more and better analysis of reports already available. Similarly, the study of the early Fathers does not require more documents. It requires more and better analysis and synthesis of the materials now known, including not only the patristic texts themselves but also the texts of ancient non-Christian writers which illuminate the environment of the early church. We need to know (*a*) what the Fathers said, (*b*) to whom they said it, (*c*) why they said it, and (*d*) what they meant. This task involves considering them in their double context, that of the church and that of the world.

C. TATIAN AS AN EXAMPLE

Perhaps our statements can be made more precise if we consider an actual case. For many years, indeed for centuries, the Greek apologists have been discussed as if they reflected a single movement and a roughly unified point of view. But such is not the case. The viewpoints (theological and apologetic alike) of these authors are rather different, as are the circumstances under which they wrote. Aristides, Justin, Melito, Tatian, Athenagoras, and Theophilus share the conviction that Christianity is superior to all of pagan culture and, especially, to pagan religion; but they set forth different attitudes toward the state and the relation between Christian revelation and Greco-Roman philosophy, as well as toward the relation between the Logos or Son of God and the world. Again, all of these writers have long been viewed in relation to the philosophical currents of their times. Only recently has it been recognized that they owe much to the rhetorical teaching of their day, and that their theological outlooks are better understood if the scope of rhetorical training is borne in mind.

Thus the thought of Tatian, who explicitly states that he had been trained in rhetoric, deserves analysis in relation to what is known of contemporary study of grammar and rhetoric. It also needs to be treated as a logical and theological whole—as has recently been done in the study of M. Elze (1960).

Only after such analysis can one proceed to ask questions about the relation of Tatian to the Greco-Roman culture he professed to despise. But at this point one must make a distinction between what Tatian says about the culture and what the culture actually included. Too often historians and theologians alike are content with a rather simple picture of the Greco-Roman world; they neglect the tremendous diversity which is as characteristic of the second century as of the twentieth. Generalizations about "the ancient world view" are no more valid than those about its modern counterparts.

If we then look at the *Oration* of Tatian in order to find out what his relations to his contemporaries actually were, we find that he begins with a claim that the more obvious features of the culture were all borrowed from barbarians. Does this claim make him non-Greek? Not at all; he is simply employing a treatise or two "on discoveries" of the sort well known to his contemporaries. For many centuries Greek writers oscillated between claiming that everything good was Greek and claiming that everything good was ultimately barbarian. Tatian says he is a barbarian; but he expresses Greek thoughts in Greek for Greeks. Similarly his piquant anecdotes about the lives, teachings, and deaths of Greek philosophers are commonplaces of his time, as one can see from the work of Diogenes Laertius. His attacks upon Stoic doctrines about God and the cosmic conflagration and astrological fatalism are not attacks on Greek thought as such; his point of view was shared by many other writers, especially Platonists and Skeptics.

It is especially important to notice that Tatian's attacks upon public spectacles, including pantomimes, boxing, gladiatorial combats, and the drama would have met a friend at court had they reached him. Indeed, the court was the highest. We know from the life and the *Meditations* of Marcus Aurelius that he shared Tatian's hostility to all these shows. Is Marcus Aurelius a representative of the culture? Perhaps not; but then we should probably aim at a new definition of culture, and a more inclusive one.

At one point Tatian states that "there ought to be one common polity for all." Exactly the same view is described by the emperor as "the idea of a polity in which there is the same law for all, a polity administered with regard to equal rights and equal freedom of speech" (*Meditationes* 1:14).

What one should actually say about Tatian is not that he viewed Christianity as hostile to culture, even though this view is what lies on the surface of his *Oration*, but that as a representative of a minority group in the heterogeneous culture of the empire he adopted the views held by others, sometimes those of minorities, sometimes not. More theologically, one should say that he advocated views which seemed to him to be in harmony with the Christian revelation. The unfortunate feature about his advocacy is that he does not seem to have had a very firm grasp upon either Christian or Greco-Roman thought.

Our purpose in briefly discussing Tatian has been to indicate the necessity for fresh historical studies which will actually relate the writings of an individual author, or of groups of authors, to the environment, as a necessary preliminary for the synthetic studies of early church history which are not yet available. Early Christian theology, however, is equally important, and perhaps needs even more correction from study of the actual texts, examined in relation to the cultural currents of their times.

I have elsewhere (see chap. 7 below) touched upon the use of pre-Socratic philosophy by early Christian writers and have tried to assess the significance of a line from Xenophanes for the theology of Irenaeus. No early Christian writer was a strictly biblical theologian in spite of the claims made by some of them.

While much remains to be done in the way of relating early Christian writers to the philosophers whom they did or did not mention, the study of specifically theological themes also offers great opportunities.

D. THE QUESTION OF CHRIST AS GOD

As an example of the kind of theme I have in mind, I propose a brief consideration of the early Christian teaching about Christ as God. Naturally we shall not expect to find in the second century the subtlety of the fourth or the fifth, but in view of the paucity of New Testament statements on this subject it may be worthwhile to see what the early Fathers had to say. First, it might be worth observing that no such statements are to be found in writings which are generally considered witnesses to "Jewish Christianity," writings such as *I Clement*, the *Didache*, and the *Shepherd* of Hermas. Christological doctrine is differently expressed in these documents. Second, the other writers of the second century are practically unanimous in speaking of Christ as God. The best known example is provided by Ignatius of Antioch, who frequently refers to "Jesus Christ my God" and even speaks of "the passion of God" and "the blood of God"—to the regret of later writers, including the unknown author who created the Pseudo-Ignatian letters in the fourth century. The homily known as *II Clement* begins with the exhortation to think about Jesus Christ as about God. Sixth-century Monophysites, with obvious historical justification, quoted such passages against adherents of the Chalcedonian formula. But already in the third century the author of the *Little Labyrinth* (Eusebius, *H. E.* 5:28) listed second-century writers who spoke of Christ as God (Justin, Miltiades, Tatian, and Clement) and as God and man (Irenaeus, Melito). Wherever his claims can be checked (five-sixths of the references) they are correct.

Difficulties arose when the view of Christ as God was interpreted in relation to the incarnation and, especially, the crucifixion. Some writers followed the line taken by Ignatius (and perhaps already present in Acts 20:28), simply speaking of Christ as "the God who suffered" (Tatian, Clement of Alexandria). The difficulties to which this view led are reflected in two statements made by Zephyrinus of Rome.

> I know one God, Christ Jesus, and apart from him no other, generated and passible.

It was not the Father who died, but the Son.

As Hippolytus remarks, vigorously criticizing these statements, Zephyrinus was no theologian. But Zephyrinus was obviously trying to maintain the deity of Christ (a doctrine clearly traditional) and to differentiate the Father from the Son. Attempts of this sort were not based upon philosophical analysis but upon problems inherent in what G. L. Prestige has called "the religious data of Christianity." The more fully developed doctrine of the Trinity represents an attempt to face these problems.

Similarly the christological problem as such was not philosophical in origin. It was evident from scripture and tradition that Christ was both God and man. But what was the relation between what came to be called the two natures? Once more we find Ignatius trying to express the paradox of the Incarnation. He calls Christ "the invisible one visible for our sake, the intangible, the impassible passible for our sake" and says that in him "God was manifest in human fashion [*anthrōpinōs*]."

A little later both Gnostics and more orthodox Christians encountered great difficulties at this point. Justin is willing to speak of Jesus as having come either "of Mary" or "through Mary," and he says that his blood was not human but derived from "divine power." The Gnostics usually spoke of the Savior as having come simply "through Mary," since they did not regard him as in any way human. Indeed, the Valentinian Theodotus insisted that when the Savior spoke of the suffering of the Son of Man he was speaking of someone other than himself, for the body could not have died with the Life present in it, nor could death have overcome the Savior. Clement of Alexandria claimed that because of Mary's virginity she did not nurse the infant Jesus, and Jesus himself "ate not because of the body, which was maintained by holy power," but simply so that observers might not regard him as unreal. Origen too, in his apologetic writing, sharply differentiated "the divine being in Jesus" from his "human aspect." Like Theodotus, he held that it was the divine being which said, "I am the Truth" and "I am the Life." In other words, starting from the basic assumption that God cannot suffer, these writers held that God cannot become fully incarnate.

The more paradoxical view of Ignatius is once reiterated by Irenaeus: "the impassible one became passible"; and Irenaeus also argues that the sufferings of the incarnate Lord were experienced in his human nature, derived from Mary (blood, soul, and flesh). At one point he says that Christ was "man that he might be tempted, Word that he might be glorified," and adds that he was able to suffer when "the Word was quiescent." This idea seems to be based on the silence of Jesus in the presence of those who crucified him (Mark 14:61; 15:5 and parallels; Isa. 53:7; also Justin). But it is also related to Irenaeus' analysis of thought-processes. From mind (divine or human) proceed concept, consideration, thought, implicit reason (*endiathetos logos*), and finally expressed reason or word (*prophorikos logos*). The quiescence of the Word seems to mean that Christ did not speak when he suffered. He remained divine for the divine element within him was essentially the mind of God.

Irenaeus' analysis (if we have properly reconstructed it) does not seem very satisfactory, and part of the difficulty may be due to (1) his picture of God as essentially Mind—a view seemingly based primarily on a line from the philosopher Xenophanes —and (2) his belief that God is impassible, though this belief has very little importance in his theology.

We should also note that in his *Commentary on Matthew* Origen was willing to say that "as being philanthropic, the impassible one suffered by being compassionate."

The question then arises whether or not those early Fathers who sharply differentiated the divine and the human in Christ were unduly influenced by the philosophical notion of the impassibility of God (Philo, Justin, Athenagoras, Clement, Origen part of the time). Should not this philosophical notion be qualified by the expression of God in Christ? Prestige claims that the idea of impassibility is logically derived from the idea of God's dependability and immutability. But it may be argued that dependability is the primary notion, and that it does not necessarily involve their immutability or impassibility. When we see Clement stating that one must allegorize biblical passages which ascribe emotion to God or even speak of his will, we may wonder whether enough attention is being paid to the Bible.

At this point we should mention a highly important passage in Origen's *Homilies on Ezekiel* (6:6). Certainly in the early treatise *De principiis* Origen, like Clement, held that God is impassible. But in the homily he is willing to state not only that the Savior suffered but also that the Father suffers. He provides biblical support for this view by quoting Deuteronomy 1:31 and combining it with echoes from Exodus 34:6. By taking these passages literally, Origen definitely rejects the allegorism of Philo. In addition, he states that love is a *passio* and that because of us the Father undergoes emotions (*humanas sustinet passiones*).[1]

A passage like this, unusual though it is, suggests that students of the Fathers should not uncritically accept the conventional sketches of the history of doctrine. If Christ was regarded as God, the revelation of God in him is surely more significant than definitions of God even when regarded as axiomatic in antiquity. If it could be said that he who has seen him has seen the Father (John 14:9), it is hard to suppose that the "detached insights" of Ignatius and Origen are not valid. The true difficulty with modalistic monarchianism or patripassionism does not lie in the ascription of suffering to the Father; it lies in too precise an identification of the Father with the Son.

E. THE NEED FOR SYNTHESIS

Thus far we have been chiefly concerned with the more "positive" theological aspects of patristic studies. It should be recognized, however, that both New Testament studies and patristics have something rather negative to say to certain kinds of apologetics. Thus, for example, there is no historical basis for the kind of prayer which invokes Christ as having promised to be with ministers of apostolic succession to the end of the

[1] On Origen's thought see now my book on *The Early Christian Doctrine of God* (Charlottesville, 1966), pp. 28-32.

world. The scriptural passage which underlies these words is Matthew 28:20, addressed to "the eleven disciples," not to their successors; and a clear picture of apostolic succession is to be found nowhere in the New Testament (the case of Matthias, Acts 1:15-26, provides no exception). When we go forward to the writings of the Apostolic Fathers, it is significant that Clement, who provides a clear picture of apostolic succession, has no idea of the monarchical episcopate; and—more important—Ignatius, who militantly defends the monarchical episcopate, has no notion of apostolic succession. At Rome, after Clement's time, Hermas can still speak of "the presbyters who are in charge of the church." Obviously there *was* a succession from the apostles, but it was not at first an episcopal succession (compare II Tim. 1:6 with I Tim. 4:14), and it was not at first related to a promise of Christ. A more general idea of the value of apostolic succession must be based on a theological conception of the work of the Spirit in the church.

A similar conclusion can also be drawn from the history of the transmission of *I Clement* and the letters of Ignatius. Among all the quotations from these documents provided by later Fathers and ecclesiastical writers from the second century to the fifteenth there seems to be none which is related to the ministry or to apostolic succession. The reason for this silence is probably that there was little, if any, controversy over these questions. Perhaps one could also conclude that the questions did not arise because they were not as important as they have seemed to be since the seventeenth century, and especially since the rise of a rather naive "appeal to history."

What, precisely, is the significance of what the Apostolic Fathers did or did not say? Obviously their historical significance is very great. One way or another, they cast practically the only light we have on the crucial period between about A.D. 90 and about 140. They alone can tell us what church life and thought came to be after the close of the apostolic age. But if we are concerned with what the church came to be, we are necessarily concerned not so much with the church as crystallized in any particular period (even our own) as with the *process* of the church's life and thought. This process did not come to an end in 140, or at Nicea or Chalcedon, or at Trent, or—one may suppose—at any other point. To be sure, it is often argued that there was a kind of golden age after which decline-and-fall set in. Marcion held that Jesus' Jewish disciples corrupted his gospel; Mani later agreed with him. Modern scholars have sometimes traced similar processes of deterioration. But unless one holds that the function of the church was simply to reiterate the gospel without interpreting its universal implications, it is hard to see why the first expressions—with all their diversity—had to be the final ones.

The nineteenth Article of Religion of the Church of England states that "as the Church of Jerusalem, Alexandria, and Antioch, have erred; so also the Church of Rome hath erred, not only in their living and manner of Ceremonies, but also in matters of Faith." This is a modest enough statement, and by inference it applies to the Church of England as well. In the life of all churches there is a mixture of truth and error; as a whole the church is *semper reformanda;* and in the ongoing life of the church a look backward is sometimes useful. What is needed is not only detailed analysis of biblical and patristic writings to determine their differences but also a more synthetic kind of study which, while recognizing variety, goes on to set forth the common elements of faith and life (perhaps especially as reflected in liturgy).

Admittedly the task of synthesis is difficult, and in many respects it is uncongenial to the task of teaching and research, with which it has to be held in tension. It also has its own risks. The synthesizer may come to believe that he has found an "essence of Christianity" in some doctrine which was a commonplace of ancient philosophy, or the Christian way of life in what was merely a *modus vivendi.* On the other hand, he may try to show that true Christianity consisted or consists simply of what Christians did *not* share with others, thus reviving the heresy of Marcion.

In sum, then, the future of patristic studies seems to lie with those who will combine a detailed knowledge of individual authors with an awareness of the whole process of church history and Christian thought. Such students will have a qualified reverence for the past but will remain awake to the situation of Christianity in the present. Like the ideal scribe who is a student of the kingdom of heaven, they will bring forth from the treasure of patristic studies things both new and old (Matt. 13:52).

2

THE USE OF THE EARLY FATHERS, FROM IRENAEUS TO JOHN OF DAMASCUS

If you had been a student of theology, or even a theologian, during the millennium between 400 and 1400, or 500 and 1500, you would undoubtedly have been accustomed to the appeal to the Fathers. The Bible contained the revelation recorded by prophets, apostles, and apostolic men; the writings of the Fathers contained the inspired reflections of the mind of the church. When you heard of the Fathers, you would ordinarily think of the great theologians of the fourth and fifth centuries; but you would be aware that behind these theologians stood the "Apostolic Fathers"—to use the phrase of Severus of Antioch—who were links in the chain of tradition which bound together the New Testament and patristic theology.

These Apostolic Fathers had been bishops of the Catholic church, appointed by the apostles themselves or, in one instance, by their immediate successors. They had been prolific writers, and most of their writings had been preserved by the church. Clement of Rome had written a good many letters, but his most significant works had been the *Apostolic Constitutions* and the story of Peter contained in the *Recognitions* and *Homilies*. Ignatius of Antioch had written twelve letters which revealed that his doctrine was almost Chalcedonian. Polycarp of Smyrna had not written so much, but one could read the Acts of his martyrdom, as well as the biography by his admirer Pionius. (There were also martyr-acts of Clement and Ignatius.)

By 500 one might prefer to remember the achievements of these early Fathers in the field of philosophical theology. In this area the supply was quite equal to the demand. Not only were there many writings of Justin, philosopher and martyr, in circulation, but the treatises of Dionysius the Areopagite, convert of

Paul and first bishop of Athens, were also available. Along with the treatises went ten letters, including one to Polycarp, one to Titus, and one to the apostle John. It was obvious that Dionysius had been closely related not only to the apostles but also to their successors.

One would probably pay little attention to such reflections of rather crude theology as were to be found in the writings of Barnabas, Hermas, and Papias. These authors, even though they lived in apostolic times or close to them, were insignificant when compared with the other, more impressive theologians whose writings seemed much more relevant. On the other hand, one might read the treatise of Irenaeus of Lyons, disciple of Polycarp and firm defender of the apostolic tradition against all heresies. While, of course, Irenaeus' writings contained regrettable errors, on the whole they were in harmony with contemporary orthodoxy. As for the Greek apologists of Irenaeus' day, there was no reason to read them, since the situation for which they wrote was now, happily, in the remote past.

It is really amazing to contrast this attitude to the early Fathers with that which has come into existence since the Renaissance and the Reformation. Today Clement of Rome is recognized as the author of a relatively brief letter to the Corinthians which, practically unknown after the fourth century, was first published in 1633. The genuine letters of Ignatius, largely driven out of circulation by an interpolated version, were recovered and printed in 1646. The authentic writings of Justin were separated from the forgeries with which they were printed in 1551 only in the course of the nineteenth century, when the genuineness of the Dionysian corpus, severely criticized by Lorenzo Valla in the fifteenth century (though the arguments he used were much older), was finally disproved. Barnabas, Hermas, and Papias have been recognized as significant witnesses to the primitive "theology of Jewish Christianity."

One difference between the older view and the more modern one is related to differences in attitudes toward authority, specifically the authority of the church, of the Fathers, and of tradition. In modern times the historical way of looking at things has tended to diminish the relevance of early patristic texts to us.

We tend to think of them in relation to the times in which they were written, in relation to an environment which is not ours. This attitude must have been shared to some extent by those who busied themselves with bringing the early Fathers up to date in the fourth, fifth, and sixth centuries. They presumably believed that the authentic Clement, the authentic Ignatius, and the other authentic early Fathers had not provided authority adequate for later theology, and therefore they proceeded to modify the images of the early Fathers so that they would be usable in theological controversy.

What we propose to examine is the way in which the appeal to the early Fathers arose and the course of its development from the late second century to the time of John of Damascus, who in his *Sacra Parallela* collected patristic texts, ancient and modern, to illustrate orthodox teaching on various subjects.

A. THE EARLY HISTORY OF THE APPEAL

Not unnaturally, Irenaeus of Lyons, himself an early Father, made use of the writings of Fathers still earlier when he was developing his theological system in opposition to Gnostic heretics. In his *Adversus haereses* he referred to the writings of Clement, Polycarp, Papias, and Justin; he also used, without naming their authors, some of the writings of Ignatius, Hermas, and Theophilus of Antioch.[1] The use of early Fathers became especially significant when controversies over the history of doctrine arose. For instance, the followers of Theodotus of Byzantium argued that their own apostolic, and adoptionist, doctrine had first been falsified by Zephyrinus of Rome (199-217). The orthodox author of *The Little Labyrinth* replied that the doctrine of Christ as God had been expressed by earlier apologists such as Justin, Miltiades, Tatian, and Clement of Alexandria, and the doctrine of Christ as both God and man by Irenaeus and Melito.[2]

[1] On Irenaeus' sources cf. E. Vernet in *Dictionnaire de Théologie Catholique,* Vol. 7 (Paris, 1922), cols. 2507-17; M. Widmann in *Zeitschrift für Theologie und Kirche,* 54 (1957), 156-73.

[2] Eusebius, *H.E.* 5:28:3-5.

If a high status was to be accorded to the writings of the apologists, naturally those of the Apostolic Fathers were to be placed higher still. Irenaeus seems to have regarded *I Clement* and the *Shepherd* of Hermas as scripture;[3] Clement of Alexandria so regarded both *I Clement* and the *Shepherd* and, in addition, the *Letter of Barnabas* and the *Didache*.[4] Origen treated all these, except for the *Didache*, in the same way, though he was aware of doubts about Hermas.[5]

On the other hand, the *Shepherd* is clearly rejected by the author of the Muratorian list (*ca.* 190? from Rome?), as well as by Tertullian in his Montanist period.[6] Early in the fourth century Eusebius explicitly denied the canonicity of Hermas, *Barnabas*, and "the so-called *Teachings of the Apostles*," [7] though he was not sure what to make of *I Clement* since it was still publicly read in some churches.[8] In Athanasius' *Festal Letter* of 367 the *Didache* and Hermas are clearly excluded from the canon,[9] though Hermas, at least, was still regarded as "very useful." [10] Athanasius also quoted as authoritative a sentence from Ignatius' letter to the Ephesians (7:2) and referred to him as bishop of Antioch "after the apostles." [11]

Even if the writings of the early Fathers were not generally regarded as canonical, they were still quoted or paraphrased. There are reflections of the *Didache* in the *Catecheses* of Pachomius, early in the fourth century;[12] and Cyril of Jerusalem explicitly refers to *I Clement* and to Irenaeus.[13] Basil of Caesarea, writing *On the Holy Spirit* in 375, appeals to Irenaeus, Clement of Rome, and the Dionysii of Rome and Alexandria; he quotes

[3] *Adv. haer.* 3:3:3 (Harvey ed., p. 11); 4:20:2 (p. 213); but see now A. Rousseau *et al.*, *Irénée de Lyon: Contre les hérésies Livre IV* (Paris, 1965), pp. 248-50.

[4] *Str.* 4:105:1, etc.; 1:181:1; 2:31:2; 1:100:4.

[5] Cf. R. P. C. Hanson, *Origen's Doctrine of Tradition* (London, 1954), pp. 139-40.

[6] *De pudicitia* 10 and 20.

[7] *H.E.* 3:25:4.

[8] *Ibid.*, 3:16.

[9] *PG* 26, 1177D-78A; cf. *PG* 25, 456A.

[10] *PG* 25, 101A.

[11] *PG* 26, 776C.

[12] *CSCO* 160 (*Scriptores Coptici* 24), 1, 6, 8-9, 13, 23, 46.

[13] *PG* 33, 1025B (Clement); 540A, 549A, 561A-B, 925A (Irenaeus).

I Clement 58:2 as "very ancient" and speaks of Irenaeus as one "who lived near the time of the apostles." [14] If the homily *On the Generation of Christ* is his,[15] he also quotes from "one of the ancients" a passage about the virginity of Mary (Ignatius, *Eph.* 19:1).[16]

Also in the late fourth century we find Epiphanius using *I Clement* 54:2[17] (as well as the pseudo-Clementine letters *Ad virgines*[18] and the *Homilies*—or an earlier form of them[19]) and reproducing long passages from Irenaeus; Didymus of Alexandria, too, cites *I Clement*, as well as Hermas.[20]

These examples show that early writings continued to be used by theologians. They do not show precisely what theological authority was ascribed to them. Presumably, however, what Methodius says of Justin could have been said of all the early writers: they were men "remote from the apostles neither in time nor in virtue." [21]

In order to make the authority of the early Fathers more explicit, the emphasis laid on their antiquity had to be combined with the notion that they were really to be included among those who were being called the "fathers" of the church.[22] This term is used by Athanasius[23] and Basil[24] in reference to the delegates to the Council of Nicea, though apparently it is first applied to ante-Nicene writers by Theodoret in a letter written in 449-50.[25]

B. THE DOGMATIC APPEAL

The appeal to the early Fathers entered a new phase in the early fifth century, when the Antiochene representatives at the

[14] *PG* 32, 201B-C.
[15] So H. Usener, *Das Weihnachtsfest* (2nd ed; Bonn, 1911), pp. 249-52.
[16] *PG* 31, 1464C.
[17] *Pan.* 27:6:4.
[18] *Ibid.* 30:15:2.
[19] *Ibid.* 26:16:8.
[20] *PG* 39, 1596C-D, 1141B.
[21] *De resurrectione* 2:18:9.
[22] Cf. H. du Manoir in *Recherches de science religieuse,* 25 (1935), 442-45.
[23] *PG* 25, 225A; 26, 688B.
[24] *PG* 32, 588B.
[25] *PG* 83, 1384D.

Council of Ephesus (431) presented a dossier which included citations from Ignatius (*Eph.* 7:2 and 20:2) and Hippolytus,[26] as well as from Irenaeus and Methodius.[27] In three epistles, as well as in his *Eranistes* of 447, the Antiochene Theodoret listed early orthodox writers. For him they included Ignatius, Polycarp, Justin, Irenaeus, Hippolytus, and Methodius.[28]

Similarly the Constantinopolitan historian Socrates, writing about the middle of the fifth century, argued that the idea that Christ had a human soul was not novel in Athanasius' time; it had been mentioned by Irenaeus, Clement, Apollinaris of Hierapolis, Serapion of Antioch, and others.[29] Unfortunately it appears that Socrates' list is no more than a list; we know that Irenaeus and Clement, at least, were notoriously vague in speaking of Christ's human soul.[30]

What Theodoret and Socrates show us is that in their time there was a lively concern for ancient patristic opinions, and that these opinions were highly regarded as witnesses to early orthodoxy. We are therefore not surprised to find that some of the texts have been modified in the course of transmission. Several quotations from Ignatius are more "orthodox" as reproduced by Theodoret than they are in the manuscripts we possess, and something has gone badly wrong in the quotations from Hippolytus. As Nautin has observed, they bear a variety of titles but seem to come from a single work, and they have been modified in the direction of explicit teaching about Christ's two natures.[31]

Once the Antiochenes had appealed to Ignatius of Antioch in support of their views and in opposition to Cyril of Alexandria, Cyril's Monophysite successors were not slow to find passages

[26] L. Saltet in *Revue d'histoire ecclésiastique,* 6 (1905), 774-76.

[27] *Ibid.,* p. 526 n. 2, and pp. 534-35; probably they are derived from the *Preces Basilii diaconi* (E. Schwartz, *Acta Conciliorum oecumenicorum* 1:1:5 [Berlin, 1927], p. 7).

[28] *PG* 83, 1284C, 1384D, 1440A-C.

[29] *PG* 67, 392A-3A.

[30] J. N. D. Kelly, *Early Christian Doctrines* (London and New York, 1958), pp. 148, 154. It is possible, though of course not provable, that Socrates refrains from mentioning Ignatius because he knows the interpolated version, which states that Christ did *not* have a human soul.

[31] P. Nautin, *Le Dossier d'Hippolyte et de Méliton* (Paris, 1953), pp. 15-32.

in the Ignatian letters which provided authority for their own ideas. Timothy Aelurus, Monophysite patriarch of Alexandria between 457 and 460, compiled a dossier of testimonies which included five selections from Ignatius (of these only one had been quoted by Theodoret), as well as two fragments from Irenaeus and one citation from his work *Adversus haereses*.[32] (We may add that Timothy assigned to Alexander of Alexandria a fragment which was later ascribed to Melito of Sardis.[33])

Timothy's great successor in Monophysitism, Severus of Antioch, gradually developed the argument from the early Fathers to a fuller degree. In his early *Philalethes* (508-11), largely directed against Cyril of Alexandria (though claiming to defend him),[34] the only ante-Nicene writer he mentioned was Paul of Samosata.[35] Soon afterwards, however, when he wrote *Ad Nephalium*, he was ready to quote a sentence from Ignatius (*Rom.* 6:3) and a fragment of Irenaeus, both of which Timothy had already used.[36] About 520, after being deposed from his see, Severus devoted more time to patristic research, as he composed his three books *Contra impium grammaticum*, a grammarian named John who "seems to have been the first notable neo-Chalcedonian." [37] Severus noted that his opponent had cited a passage from Irenaeus "against the Valentinians." This citation, he said, was wrong and, for that matter, the quotation had been interpolated.[38] He then proceeded to give authentic quotations from the "famous and apostolic fathers," in order to show that there was no separation of the two natures of Christ after their union.[39] He cited passages from six of the letters of Ignatius, two from Polycarp, and one from *II Clement*, as well as one

[32] E. Schwartz in *Abhandlungen der Bayerischen Akadamie der Wissenschaften, Philos.-philol. u. hist. Kl.* (1927), No. 6, p. 117; F. C. Conybeare in *Journal of Theological Studies*, 15 (1913-14), 433-36. On the first fragment cf. Nautin, *op. cit.*, pp. 64-72.

[33] Nautin, *op. cit.*, pp. 56-64.

[34] R. Hespel, *Le Florilège cyrillien réfuté par Sévère d'Antioche* (Louvain, 1955).

[35] *CSCO* 134 (*Scriptores Syri* 69), 124.

[36] *Ibid.*, pp. 36-37. For the fragment of Irenaeus see p. 20 n. 4.

[37] Hespel, *op. cit.*, p. 14.

[38] *CSCO* 102 (*Scriptores Syri* 51), 201-3; cf. Nautin, *op. cit.*, pp. 34-40.

[39] *CSCO* 102 (*Scriptores Syri* 51), 205.

from each of Irenaeus' five books against heresies.[40] His dossier was rounded out by quotations from nineteen later Fathers.[41]

Two points are worth adding about Severus' use of the early Fathers. First, he paid attention to textual problems. He was aware that some older codices had "Let me be a disciple of my God" in Ignatius, *Romans* 6:3, though he himself preferred to read "Let me be an imitator of my God." [42] Second, in compiling this dossier he made no use of the recently invented writings of Dionysius the Areopagite, though from an undated letter we know that elsewhere he used them.[43] He was relying upon authorities which he knew his opponent would accept.

Severus' "orthodox" successor at Antioch, Ephraem of Amid, who died about 545, knew that he had to confirm the doctrine of the two natures from early sources; he quoted not only from the New Testament but also from a group of Fathers beginning with Ignatius, and he argued that Ignatius' use of the definite article with the word "God" in *Smyrneans* 1:1 could not be used to show that Ignatius advocated Monophysite doctrine.[44] Ephraem also appealed to the Dionysian writings as authorities.[45] His contemporary, Leontius of Byzantium, who compiled a dogmatic dossier in support of neo-Chalcedonian doctrine, avoided using Ignatius' writings and instead, in order to have some early authorities, relied on what he called Justin's *Expositio rectae fidei*[46]—actually written by Theodoret, as Severus knew[47]—as well as a fragment supposed to come from Justin's treatise *Against the Greeks*,[48] and the treatises of Dionysius the Areopagite, "contemporary with the apostles." [49] The two fragments assigned to Irenaeus and Hippolytus are not genuine.[50]

[40] *Ibid.*, pp. 206-11 (Severus knew all seven letters of Ignatius).

[41] *Ibid.*, pp. 212-49.

[42] *Ibid.*, p. 206.

[43] J. Lebon in *Revue d'histoire ecclésiastique*, 26 (1930), 880-915.

[44] *PG* 103, 961B, 997C.

[45] *PG* 103, 989D.

[46] R. Devreesse in *Revue de science religieuse*, 10 (1930), 558-59.

[47] *CSCO* 94 (*Scriptores Syri* 46), 39, 63, 71, 82; cf. J. Lebon, *op. cit.*, pp. 536-50.

[48] Devreesse, *op. cit.*, p. 570.

[49] *Ibid.*, pp. 569-70.

[50] *Ibid.*, p. 559; cf. Nautin, *op. cit.*, pp. 33-42.

A detailed analysis of the history of doctrine seemed to be needed at this point, and it was provided by Leontius' disciple Theodore of Raithu, who probably wrote the treatise *De sectis* assigned to his master. Here church history is divided into five periods: from Christ's birth to his ascension, from his ascension to the end of Acts and the deaths of the apostles, from that time to the beginning of Constantine's reign, from Nicea to Chalcedon, and after Chalcedon. Since the first period is that of the incarnation and the second is the apostolic age, the third, ante-Nicene period is obviously significant. Theodore lists the authoritative teachers of that time by name. They are Ignatius, Irenaeus, Justin, Clement and Hippolytus of Rome, Dionysius the Areopagite, Methodius, Gregory Thaumaturgus, and Peter of Alexandria. These writers are especially significant since all parties can agree that they are authorities.[51]

Two of these early Fathers are also quoted by Andrew of Caesarea in Cappadocia, who wrote his commentary on the Apocalypse in the first half of the sixth century; they are Justin[52] and the Areopagite.[53] In listing the "more ancient" writers who valued the Apocalypse highly he mentioned three more of them (Irenaeus, Methodius, and Hippolytus), as well as Papias,[54] whose authority he doubtless believed was guaranteed by Irenaeus.

Monophysite anthologists continued to be active in this period, and we possess a Syriac version, produced before 562, of an enlarged dogmatic dossier containing citations from the Fathers who wrote both before and after Nicea.[55] The first group of ante-Nicene quotations consists of three from Ignatius and one from Polycarp (all these had been cited by Severus); one from Clement's letter *Ad virgines* and two from *II Clement;* three from Irenaeus (*Adv. haer.*); three from Hippolytus; two from Methodius; and three from Melito of Sardis—none of which is

[51] *PG* 86[1], 1212C-13A.

[52] *PG* 106, 328B, 408D (perhaps from Eusebius).

[53] *PG* 106, 257B-C, 305C, 356D.

[54] *PG* 106, 220B.

[55] I. Rucker in *Sitzungsberichte der Bayerischen Akademie der Wissenschaften, Philos.-hist. Abt.* (1933), No. 5; from British Museum Addition 12156.

genuine.[56] Another ante-Nicene group includes three more fragments ascribed to Melito and two ascribed to Hippolytus.[57]

It is obvious that this dossier is largely based on the researches of Timothy Aelurus and Severus, but some new materials have been added: to wit, the quotations from Melito, Hippolytus, and Methodius. The use of Hippolytus and Methodius can be explained as related to the list of acceptable writers promulgated in the school of Leontius of Byzantium and, for that matter, earlier used by Theodoret and perhaps by Antiochenes generally. But why Melito? Perhaps the Monophysites, reading Eusebius (we know that Severus did so[58]), noticed that he was an important early witness to the doctrine of Christ as both God and man (see p. 22 n. 2, above), believed that they had found a forerunner, and began the work of research or composition. They might also have found the title of his treatise (*Peri ensōmatou Theou* mentioned by both Eusebius[59] and Theodoret.[60]

The importance of Melito's name in this period is indicated by the ascription to him, about 550, of a form of the *Transitus virginis Mariae* which begins with the words *Melito, servus Christi, episcopus ecclesiae Sardensis,* and goes on to claim that he had heard the apostle John.[61]

In any event forgeries came to be exceedingly popular after the middle of the sixth century. The Areopagite's writings rapidly came to be accepted, and even in dossiers where they were not present other nonauthentic writings were cited. About 570, in the collection of the Monophysite Stephen Gobarus, we find references to the works of Ignatius, Justin, Hegesippus, Irenaeus, Clement of Alexandria, and Hippolytus; but the Ignatius is pseudo-Ignatius and the Justin is the author of the *Cohortatio.*[62]

[56] Nautin, *op. cit.,* pp. 56-64, 73.

[57] One fragment of Melito is clearly not authentic (Nautin, *op. cit.,* pp. 64-72); the others come from the *Homily on the Passover.*

[58] *CSCO* 102 (*Scriptores Syri* 51), 201; cf. E. W. Brooks, *The Sixth Book of the Selected Letters of Severus* (London, 1904), Vol. 2, pp. 169-70, 414.

[59] *H.E.* 4:26:2.

[60] *PG* 80, 113A-B; cf. *PG* 12, 93A.

[61] *PG* 5, 1231D; cf. M. Jugie in *Échos d'Orient,* 25 (1926), 305.

[62] *PG* 103, 1104D, 1100C-D, 1096A, 1100B, and 1104D. Cf. A. v. Harnack in *Harvard Theological Review,* 16 (1923), 205-34; G. Bardy in *Revue des études byzantines,* 5 (1947), 5-30.

There was some concern for genuine writings at the end of the sixth century. Though Pope Gregory the Great used pseudo-Dionysius[63] he thanked Anastasius of Antioch for sending him the letters of Ignatius[64] (probably in the interpolated version) and wrote to Aetherius of Lyons to describe his search for the writings of Irenaeus.[65] In general, however, writings of the early Fathers—except for some of the Clementine literature and the works of the Areopagite—were unknown in the West.[66] In the East early if not always authentic writings were still used. About 600 the Monophysite archimandrite Dorotheus quoted *II Clement*[67] and may even have paraphrased the *Didache*.[68] A few years later the Palestinian monk Antiochus wrote his *Pandectes*,[69] a collection of 130 homilies in which he borrowed extensively from the Areopagite, the two pseudo-Clementine letters *Ad virgines*, all the genuine letters of Ignatius except *Romans*, the letter of Polycarp, the *Shepherd* of Hermas (*Mandates* 2-12 and *Similitudes* 1-9), Clement of Alexandria (cited as Irenaeus), and Eusebius. About 630 the *Paschal Chronicle* made use of the Areopagite, the Clementine *Recognitions*, the interpolated Ignatian letters,[70] Melito of Sardis (once from Eusebius, once in an independent quotation[71]), and Apollinaris of Hierapolis.[72] Evidently the author of the *Chronicle* had available a considerable library of second-century literature. Perhaps it was the library at Caesarea in Palestine, which was destroyed by the Arabs in 637—or that at Jerusalem, dispersed about the same time.[73]

The disappearance of these libraries was disastrous, but many prominent writers had already come to prefer forgeries to au-

[63] *PL* 76, 1254B.

[64] *PL* 77, 764C-5A.

[65] *PL* 77, 1174B.

[66] For the Areopagite's writings at Rome in 649 cf. *Sacrorum conciliorum nova collectio,* ed. G. D. Mansi (Florence, 1759-98), Vol. 10, cols. 975-77.

[67] *PG* 88, 1836B.

[68] *PG* 88, 1661D, 1840C.

[69] *PG* 89; cf. G. Bardy in *Dictionnaire de la spiritualité,* ed. M. Viller (Paris, 1932-), Vol. I, cols. 701-2.

[70] *PG* 92, 540B-C.

[71] *PG* 102, 629C, 632A.

[72] *PG* 92, 80C-81A.

[73] On Jerusalem cf. A. Ehrhardt in *Römische Quartalschrift,* 5 (1891), 217-65.

thentic documents. For example, in the encyclical letters of Sophronius, patriarch of Jerusalem from 634 to 638, the only ante-Nicene authorities quoted are Dionysius and Justin[74]—neither one the real author of the document employed.

Scholia on the Areopagite, traditionally ascribed to Maximus Confessor, who wrote towards the middle of the seventh century, reflect a singular mixture of the authentic and the nonauthentic. It may be that John of Scythopolis is responsible for the reference to a nonexistent letter of Polycarp to the Athenians,[75] as well as for one or two allusions to Papias.[76] But it is probably Maximus who quoted from Hermas[77] and Aristo of Pella,[78] and he certainly quoted spurious fragments from Justin (*To Euphrasius*),[79] Irenaeus (*To Demetrius*),[80] and Pantaenus.[81]

The same situation is found in the late seventh-century *Doctrina Patrum.* Ten quotations apiece come from the Areopagite and from the *Expositio rectae fidei,* attributed to Justin; in addition there is a quotation from the forged letter of Ignatius to the Philippians—cited as *Tarsians.*[82] At the sixth ecumenical council (680) only two authors supposedly ante-Nicene were cited: Dionysius the Areopagite and Justin, as author of the *Expositio.*[83]

A more complete dossier was available to Anastasius of Sinai, toward the end of the seventh century. He wrote his *Hodegos* against the Monophysites and countered their use of Ignatius (*Rom.* 6:3) and a fragment from Melito's paschal homily by claiming that the passages referred to the suffering and death not of God but of the human nature of the Logos.[84] He went on to supply an "orthodox" fragment from Melito (fr. 6 Otto)

[74] *PG* 103, 1089C; *PG* 87, 3177B-C.

[75] *PG* 4, 17D (perhaps a textual error; cf. J. B. Lightfoot, *The Apostolic Fathers,* Part 2: *S. Ignatius, S. Polycarp,* 1 [London, 1885], 555); H. U. v. Balthasar in *Scholastik,* 16 (1940), 16-38.

[76] *PG* 4, 48D, 176C.

[77] *PG* 4, 241D.

[78] *PG* 4, 421B-C.

[79] *PG* 91, 280B-D.

[80] *PG* 91, 276B-C.

[81] *PG* 91, 1085A-B.

[82] F. Diekamp, *Doctrina Patrum* (Münster, 1907), p. 87; for the author see J. Stiglmayr in *Byzantinische Zeitschrift,* 18 (1909), 14-40.

[83] Mansi, 11, 263C-D, 372D, 424B-C.

[84] *PG* 89, 196D, 200C-D.

which seems clearly post-Arian, since it speaks of the two natures of Christ and calls Him "true God" and *proaiōnios*.[85] His own favorite early authorities were the Areopagite, Irenaeus, and Clement of Alexandria.[86] (From the Monophysites he took over the expression "Apostolic Father" and applied it to the Areopagite.[87]) In addition in his commentary on the *Hexaemeron* he referred to Philo, Papias, Justin, and Pantaenus;[88] elsewhere he quoted Hippolytus.[89] Presumably these quotations and references come from a source closer to Antiochene theology than that used in his *Hodegos*.

The end of the seventh century seems to mark the end of creativity in writings ascribed to the ante-Nicene Fathers. To be sure a few forgeries were added later, such as the letter of "Justin" to Zenas and Serenus, but nothing essentially new was provided. From the eighth century onward the Greek church viewed its task as that of transmission rather than creation. Fortunately what was transmitted included genuine writings as well as forgeries. John of Damascus, who compiled his *Sacra Parallela* at Jerusalem in the first half of the eighth century, was fond of Dionysius and of the pseudo-Clementine literature. He also made use of two of the forged Ignatian epistles, and of several writings wrongly attributed to Justin. At the same time, however, he provided quotations from *I* and *II Clement*, from the genuine letters of Ignatius, from Justin's apologies and *Dialogue*, and from Theophilus and Irenaeus.[90] In so far as these quotations are not derived from earlier anthologies, they show that materials were still available for the reconstruction of a true picture of early Christian literature.[91]

[85] *PG* 89, 228D-229B; cf. W. Bauer, *Das Leben Jesu* (Tübingen, 1909), p. 287 n. 2; Nautin, *op. cit.*, pp. 83-85

[86] *PG* 89, 93A.

[87] *PG* 89, 213D, 753D.

[88] *PG* 89, 942A, 956D, 961D—962A.

[89] *PG* 89, 592C-D.

[90] Cf. K. Holl, *TU* 20, 2; on the Damascene, A. Jülicher in Pauly-Wissowa, *RE* 9, 1810-11.

[91] On the other hand, Theodore of Studium (759-826) uses only the interpolated Ignatius (*PG* 99, 677C, 1485A) and a writing falsely ascribed to Justin (1604A), and seems to confuse Clement of Rome with the Areopagite (1701C).

C. CONSEQUENCES OF THE DOGMATIC APPEAL

If we look back over the period from the second century to the eighth, we can identify several clearly discernible stages. (1) First is the ante-Nicene era, when forgeries were relatively rare and often detected. No one in this period made much use of most of the forgeries we later encounter in such quantities. The work of Eusebius of Caesarea marks the high-water point of this period, for Eusebius was remarkably careful in his selection of sources. (2) The century after Nicea saw the production and acceptance of a good deal of forgery. The Father to whom most of it was ascribed was Clement of Rome, now thought to have written "encyclical letters" on virginity, the Clementine *Homilies* and *Recognitions*, and the *Apostolic Constitutions*. Martyr-acts and lives of Clement, Ignatius, and Polycarp obscured the memory of these Fathers. (3) It was not until the fifth century, however, that aggressive forgeries began to force authentic documents into disrepute. After the Council of Ephesus the appeal to early Fathers meant that some of their writings had to be rewritten. Apollinarius of Laodicea had earlier tampered with some patristic writings, but apparently he had not bothered to touch second-century documents. Now, however, the letters of Ignatius were interpolated and forgeries were added. While Monophysites continued to use Ignatius' genuine epistles, they led the way in accepting the new treatises and letters ascribed to Dionysius the Areopagite. In the course of the sixth and seventh centuries we find forgeries ascribed to Justin, Melito, Irenaeus, Pantaenus, Clement of Alexandria, and Hippolytus. Indeed, in the seventh century the whole picture of the early Fathers was corrupted when the favorite early authorities were Dionysius and "Justin."

Under such circumstances the preservation of any authentic texts seems almost miraculous. The needs of dogmatic theology, undisturbed by much historical sense, had resulted in a distortion of the historical materials on which the theology was supposedly built. The absence of any understanding of historical development had led to a situation in which genuine and false documents were so thoroughly mixed that they could not be disentangled for more than a millennium.

Only during the Renaissance and the Reformation could a beginning of analysis be made, and the work of sifting out the wheat from the chaff has continued to the present day. We use the word "chaff" in reference to the historical framework of the spurious documents. The value of the prayers in the *Apostolic Constitutions* is independent of their being ascribed to the apostles or to Clement; the theological significance of Dionysius does not altogether depend on his identification with the first-century Areopagite. But if we are to view the history of the church as a process of life and thought, we must place the links in the process in their proper order. We can do so only by becoming aware not only of the sequence of the early links themselves but also of the sequence of those who in ancient times changed the order of the links. This means that the study of the early Fathers cannot be confined to the writings which we now regard as authentic. A complete picture will be given only when we examine the transmission and use of all the literature ascribed to them.

II
EARLY CHRISTIAN TRADITION

3

SCRIPTURE AND TRADITION IN IGNATIUS OF ANTIOCH

One of the earliest Christian writers outside the New Testament, and among them the most creatively original as a theologian, is St. Ignatius of Antioch, from whom we possess seven authentic letters which he wrote in Asia Minor on his way to martyrdom in Rome. What kind of picture of scripture and tradition can we derive from these letters? If we can reconstruct this picture adequately, it will be important in other regards; it will help us to determine the extent to which Ignatius modified or developed New Testament conceptions and the extent to which he was under the influence of non-Christian factors such as mystery-religions and Gnosticism.

A. SCRIPTURE

There are only two quotations in Ignatius' letters which are introduced by the formula, "It is written." These are the quotations, both from the book of Proverbs (3:34; 18:17), in *Ephesians* 5:3 and *Magnesians* 12. The first of them, "God resists the proud," is shared by Ignatius with other early Christian writings (I Pet. 5:5; Jas. 4:6; *I Clem.* 30:2); the second, "the righteous man is his own accuser," is not quoted by others, and may have been a favorite verse for Ignatius himself.

It is important to observe that these quotations from Proverbs are the only ones he provides. The point may suggest that he found the Wisdom literature especially congenial and that Wisdom ideas may underlie other parts of his letters. We shall return to this subject later.

Elsewhere he uses the expression "It is written" only in reporting a debate between himself and certain Christians, apparently Judaizers, in Philadelphia. They had said, "If I do not find it in the charters [*archeia*], I do not believe it in the gospel." He had replied, "But it is written." They said to him, "That is the question." Ignatius then proceeds—in Pauline fashion (cf. Gal. 2:14-15)—to pass from past debate to present argument and to state that for him "the charters are Jesus Christ, the inviolable charters are his cross and death and resurrection and faith through him" (*Philad.* 8:2). His account seems to make sense only if we assume that the Judaizers wanted proof of some theological point from the Old Testament (charters) and Ignatius said that he could provide it; they expressed their doubt that he could, and Ignatius then said that the true foundation of Christian faith is not the Old Testament as such but Jesus Christ, to whom the Old Testament points (*Philad.* 5:2; 9:2; *Smyrn.* 7:2).

This means that, at least in arguments with heretics, Ignatius did not find the quotation of texts very satisfactory. He preferred to appeal to cardinal revelatory events of Christian history, not to the Old Testament. With his attitude we may compare that of his contemporary, Papias of Hierapolis: "I did not suppose that information from books would be of as much value to me as information from a living and surviving voice" (Eusebius, *H. E.* 3:39:4). One might even say that Ignatius, though he did not use the word *paradosis*, valued tradition more highly than scripture.

But before drawing such a conclusion we should observe that he seems to refer to scripture at points where he does not say he is doing so. Something like Isaiah 52:5 is quoted in *Trallians* 8:2, in a form close to that reflected in *II Clement* 13:2. Again, there seem to be allusions to Isaiah 5:26 in *Smyrneans* 1:2 and to Psalm 32:9 in *Ephesians* 15:1. Taken together, these allusions suggest that Ignatius knew something of the Old Testament though it cannot be said that his mind was steeped in it.

The book related to the Old Testament in which his mind does seem to have been steeped is IV Maccabees, as O. Perler has pointed out in an article still not sufficiently well known.[1] This Hellenistic Jewish sermon on martyrdom and particularly on the

[1] *Rivista di archeologia cristiana,* 25 (1949), 47-72.

Maccabean martyrs exercised considerable influence not only on Ignatius' style but also on his thought. The fact that he never refers to it should make us watchful for other books he does not mention.

When we turn to the books of the New Testament we find—not surprisingly—that Ignatius was influenced by some of them more than by others. It is very clear that he knew I Corinthians practically by heart. It would appear that there are no fewer than forty six allusions to it in his letters. Some of them, as might be expected, are clearer than others. There can be little doubt about a passage like this:

> Why are we foolishly perishing, ignoring the gift which the Lord has truly sent? My spirit is devoted to the cross, which is a stumbling block to the believers but salvation and eternal life to us. Where is the wise man? Where is the debater? Where is the boasting of the so-called intelligent?

Here (*Eph.* 17:2—18:1) Ignatius is obviously following I Corinthians 1:18-20 with remarkable care. But he also quotes isolated phrases from the epistle—for example, in *Trallians* 12:3 and in *Romans* 5:1.

> I need your love, so that I may be judged worthy of the lot which I am set to obtain, "lest I be found a castaway" [I Cor. 9:27].

> I become more of a disciple because of their wrongdoing, "but not by this am I justified" [I Cor. 4:4].

This is to say that he can take Pauline expressions and use them in contexts of his own. Such usage is hardly surprising. Ignatius, in fact, could not have used Pauline expressions in Pauline contexts.

We should also point out that he feels quite free to paraphrase Paul's words. According to I Corinthians 6:9-10, "the unrighteous" will not inherit the kingdom of God; the unrighteous are defined as those who practice certain kinds of sins. When Ignatius uses this passage he rewrites it thus: "Do not be deceived, my brothers; those who corrupt families [*oi oikophthoroi*] will not inherit the kingdom of God." He is laying emphasis upon only one of several points which Paul was making, though upon the one which in the context of I Corinthians was the most important. In *Philadelphians* 3:3 he is concerned with another point. "Do not be deceived, my brothers; whoever follows a schismatic will not inherit the kingdom of God." Interestingly enough, these two paraphrases contain Ignatius' only references to the kingdom of God. And he further paraphrases the second of them in this way: "whoever walks in accordance with an alien opinion is not in agreement with the passion." The relation of passion and kingdom of God is ultimately based on synoptic doctrine about suffering as prior to Christ's entrance into glory (cf. Luke 24:26; Mark 10:37-40, etc.). What is significant here is that Ignatius does not restrict himself to Paul's words or to exact exegesis of what Paul said; he synthesizes New Testament teaching as he paraphrases.

He can also take Paul's words as referring to himself, as we have already seen. It may seem rather surprising that he can thus use words in which Paul speaks of himself as an apostle; but such is the case. In *Ephesians* 21:2 Ignatius speaks of himself as the last or least of the Syrian Christians, judged worthy to serve for God's honor. This might seem to be a simple, straightforward statement. But in *Magnesians* 14 and *Trallians* 13:1 the thought recurs, expressed thus: "I am not worthy to be called a part of them [the Syrian Christians], since I am the least of them." The words "not worthy to be called" now show us that "least" is derived from I Corinthians 15:8, and in *Romans* 9:2 the word *ektrōma* confirms the point. Here Ignatius is using what we may call "allusive quotation." Of course we cannot prove our point, but we should suggest that in every instance, not just the last, he had I Corinthians in mind.

Now what does this use of I Corinthians show? It shows that Ignatius used the letter in several different ways and that sometimes he quoted, sometimes he alluded, sometimes he allusively quoted, and sometimes he quotingly alluded. Any idea of exactness in analyzing his usage must be read in by the analyst. It does not exist in Ignatius' own writings.

We may add that the fact we can detect allusions to all the other Pauline epistles may reflect scholarly ingenuity but is more likely to show that Ignatius had read the letters.

Now we turn to the question of the gospels. Few topics have been more militantly debated, at least as far as Ignatian studies are concerned. It is hard to see why this has been so. Perhaps it has been felt that if Ignatius did not know Matthew and John his letters could be regarded as unchristian or at any rate unbiblical. The most important recent works on the subject are those by C. Maurer on Ignatius and John, *Ignatius von Antiochien und das Johannesevangelium* (Zurich, 1949), and H. Koester on the synoptic gospels, *Synoptische Ueberlieferungen bei den Apostolischen Vätern* (Berlin, 1957). Maurer makes his case by (1) showing that other second-century writers quoted from or alluded to John in ways not very different from the manner of Ignatius, (2) indicating that Ignatius used other sources in a fashion much like that in which he may have used John, and (3) comparing John with Ignatius at key points where ideas and/or language are similar. This method of argumentation may not be absolutely conclusive, but the thesis that Ignatius used the Gospel of John seems highly probable. I should be willing to admit that perhaps Ignatius knew its author instead of, or even in addition to, the book itself.

Koester's case in regard to Ignatius and the synoptic gospels does not seem so conclusive. He classifies the materials common to Ignatius and to the synoptics (especially Matthew) in a rather schematic way: "kerygmatic tradition," "mythological expressions," "paraenetic formulas and similarities in terminology," "free tradition," and "special relationship with a single gospel." By arranging the materials in this way he is able to place last the passage which, one might suppose, would go at the beginning of his study: Matthew 3:15 in relation to *Smyrneans* 1:1 (Jesus was baptized by John "so that all righteousness might be fulfilled by him"). But since Koester has already disposed of all other echoes of Matthew he can now take care of 3:15 as well. Since Ignatius himself was interested only in the sacramental meaning of baptism, not in the problem to which Matthew refers, he would not have read Matthew. "Would not have" soon becomes "did not"; in Koester's view the passage in *Smyrneans* 1:1 reflects a kerygmatic formula composed by someone else—who did read Matthew!

Again, there are two passages in Ignatius' *Letter to Polycarp* (2:1-2) which might suggest that he knew the gospels.

If you love good disciples it is no credit to you.	If you love those who love you, what credit is it to you? (Luke 6:32)
Become wise [sing.] as a serpent in everything and guileless forever as the dove.	Then become wise [pl.] as the serpents and guileless as the doves (Matt. 10:16).

Here, one might suppose, is evidence for the use (presumably from memory) of one synoptic gospel and then another synoptic gospel. But no—the first quotation could have arisen in the "free tradition" as a variant form of Matthew 5:46; and if this is so, then the second quotation could have come from "free tradition" too. Here Koester states his principle clearly: "it is more probable that both logia come from the free tradition than that one is derived from Matthew, the other from Luke." Why is it more probable? Koester goes on to state that "today words of Jesus are adduced by men who have never read a gospel." Undoubtedly this is so. Is it relevant? Arguments of this kind make the use of texts unnecessary. The analogy controls the argument and provides the conclusion.

Let us try a different analogy. Modern New Testament critics would certainly avoid combining materials from various gospels in the way in which (it would appear) Ignatius combined them. Was he a New Testament critic? Was he using books at the time he wrote his letters? Was he really concerned with keeping the gospels separate?

Actually, in almost every case (except, we should hold, the ones cited above) it is possible to hold either that Ignatius was relying upon memories of what he had read (scripture) or that he was relying upon memories of what he had heard (oral tradition). To make a decision is very difficult. Analogies inevitably enter into consideration. The kind of memory ascribed to Ignatius tends to be the kind of memory possessed by the scholar discussing his work. Thus Koester would say that Ignatius had an excellent memory and used oral tradition; I should incline to say that his memory was not that exact and that he may have remembered books. (He certainly remembered a book in the case of I Corinthians.)

Another analogy which is worth mentioning, in view of Ignatius' relation either to the Fourth Gospel or to the Fourth Evangelist, is that between his use of his sources and the use found in John. First there is John's use of his own writings. T. F. Glasson[2] has listed fifteen instances in which there are "inaccurate repetitions in the Fourth Gospel," and he asks the question, "Could the writer tell us more plainly that he is not concerned with literal exactness but with the essential meaning?" This is not exactly parallel to the usage of Ignatius, who does not quote from his own works. But the conclusion, in regard to Ignatius' use of scripture, may well hold good. Second there is John's use of the Old Testament. C. Goodwin[3] has dealt with his methods in an article entitled "How did John treat his sources?" The only *known* source of John is the Old Testament, which is treated occasionally, loosely, confusedly, with conflation, distortion, the concealment of context, the introduction of alien elements, and tricks played by memory. This judgment is rather severe and could be expressed differently; but in any event it indicates clearly enough that John did not use the Old Testament "scientifically." His use of it seems to have been not unlike Ignatius' use of Old Testament, gospels, and epistles.

We conclude that there is no reason to suppose that Ignatius did not know the Pauline epistles and the gospels of Matthew and John. At the same time, we should agree with E. Flesseman-van Leer[4] that "Ignatius attaches little importance to the authority of scripture as such (though he nowhere denies this importance)." In fact, we should be inclined to go a little beyond this conclusion and to suggest that for him apostolic doctrine, as interpreted in the church (or as foreshadowed in the Old Testament), is of primary importance. It makes little difference to him whether the doctrine has been transmitted in oral or in written form. Perhaps the best example of the difficulty is provided in *Smyrneans* 3:1-3.

[2] *Expository Times,* 57 (1946), 111-12.

[3] *Journal of Biblical Literature,* 73 (1954), 61-75.

[4] *Tradition and Scripture in the Early Church* (Assen, Holland, 1954), p. 35.

> I know and believe that even after the resurrection he was in the flesh. And when he came to those with Peter he said, "Take, handle me and see that I am not an incorporeal demon." And immediately they touched him and believed, being mingled with his flesh and spirit. Therefore they despised death and were found to be above death. After the resurrection he ate and drank with them as a being of flesh, though spiritually he was united with the Father.

Where do the words ascribed to Jesus come from? According to Origen, they come from a *Doctrina Petri* (an inference from the mention of Peter here?); according to Jerome, from the Gospel according to the Hebrews. Eusebius says he does not know their source. There is no reason to suppose that any of these Fathers had considered Ignatius' manner of citation as carefully as modern scholars have done, and we therefore venture to suggest that Ignatius is simply paraphrasing Luke 24:39 ("Handle me and see, for a spirit does not have flesh and bones such as you see that I have")—especially since eating and drinking with the risen Lord is mentioned in Luke 24:30, 35, 41-43, as well as in Acts 10:41 (in a speech by Peter).

We should not regard it as absolutely impossible or unsuitable for Ignatius to have made use of an apocryphal gospel. But it seems just as likely that he was using Luke in the way in which, as we have seen, he used other written sources—from memory.

Finally, we submit that the question "Scripture or tradition?" is not as clearcut as it looks, when we are considering the writings of a Christian who almost certainly was not using books at the time he wrote, whether or not he had used them earlier. Under such circumstances scripture would tend to be treated as tradition, just as at earlier points, even in Ignatius' life, tradition almost certainly came to be crystallized as scripture.

B. TRADITION

It may well be asked what place is now left for tradition in Ignatius' thought when we have argued that in many instances he relied upon written sources of the kind later called scripture. To some extent we have answered this question by refusing to differentiate scripture and tradition. For instance, when he paraphrases the Pauline epistles or the gospels it should probably be maintained that his paraphrases themselves constitute tradition, not apostolic but (at a very early date) episcopal.

One good place to find tradition is, of course, in the credal summaries in which Ignatius sets forth the church's faith against various kinds of heretics. There are three of these (*Eph.* 18:21; *Trall.* 9; *Smyrn.* 1:1-2). And in two of them we find traditions which are not strictly based on the New Testament, although the thought of Ignatius as he expresses the traditions may be so based. In *Ephesians* 18:2 he makes a christological statement which ends thus: "He was born and was baptized in order by his passion to cleanse the water." This interpretation is presumably Ignatius' own, for in his view the material is not pure and therefore stands in need of purifying; purity is attained through suffering (see *Rom.* 4:1; 6:2), and suffering is related to baptism as we see not only in the Pauline epistles but also in Mark 10:38-39. This is to say that as Ignatius hands down credal formulas, whether based on scripture or not, he does not hesitate to add his own—traditional—interpretations. Similarly in speaking of the death of Christ he says that it was "in the presence of beings in heaven and on earth and under the earth" (*Trall.* 9). Nothing precisely like this is to be found in the New Testament, and we must ascribe it to tradition.

Elsewhere in Ignatius' letters there are traces of similar materials. For instance, there is the imaginative description of the appearing of the star of Jesus' birth (*Eph.* 19). This has sometimes been ascribed to Gnostic sources, but the evidence for such an ascription is almost entirely later than Ignatius, and the solution proposed by A. Cabaniss[5] that the Wisdom of Solomon (18:14-15; also 7:29-30) gave impetus to Ignatius' thought is more probable. Again, Ignatius tells us (*Eph.* 17:1) that the Lord accepted ointment on his head in order to breathe imperishability upon the church. Presumably he has in mind Matthew 26:7, the only gospel account in which the ointment is poured on Christ's head; with this he seems to combine John 12:3, where

[5] *Vigiliae Christianae,* 10 (1956), 97-102.

we read that "the house was filled with the odor of the ointment." And these passages are fused with John 20:22, where Jesus breathes the Holy Spirit upon his disciples. The fact that a similar interpretation occurs in Clement, *Excerpta ex Theodoto* 3:2, does not prove that it is Gnostic in origin.

These examples may suffice for showing what kind of detailed, semi-historical tradition Ignatius provides for us. There is, however, a much broader sense in which "tradition" may be used, and it is with this sense that we wish to conclude our discussion. By this we mean that one can speak of "the Christian tradition" as a whole or in general, and can ask the question whether Ignatius remained faithful to this tradition or, instead, introduced dangerous innovations. It would appear that much of the critical literature of the last thirty years has been devoted to showing how Ignatius corrupted primitive Christianity: he was concerned with the unity of the church as episcopal and sacramental; he regarded martyrdom as the highest way for the Christian. In this paper we do not propose to discuss his theology as a whole or in detail. We intend simply to point out that these three points do not mark a break with the New Testament church but continue early Christian tradition.

1) The episcopal unity of the church is, of course, relatively new. In the New Testament we find emphasis upon unity and mention of bishops, but the two ideas are not correlated.

In Ignatius' view the model for the relation between Christians and their bishop is provided by the relation between Jesus and the Father. This relationship is described in terms almost certainly derived from the Gospel of John. (*a*) As Jesus is united with the Father, and the apostles are united with Jesus, so the church must be united with the bishop and presbyters (*Magn.* 7:1; *Eph.* 5:1; in part repeated in *Smyrn.* 8:2). Such a picture is clearly Johannine (17:23, etc.). (*b*) As Jesus was sent by the Father (Ignatius actually says that he came forth from the Father, *Magn.* 7:2), and the apostles were sent by the Lord, so the bishop has been sent (*Eph.* 6:1). We meet Johannine themes again: the Father sent Jesus and Jesus sent the disciples (13:30; 17:18; 20:21, etc.) and Jesus came from the Father (8:42; 13:3; 16:27, etc.). (*c*) As Jesus follows the Father (and the apostles follow Jesus, though Ignatius does not say so), so the church follows the bishop (*Smyrn.* 8:1; *Magn.* 7:1). (*d*) As Jesus is subject to the Father and the apostles are subject to Christ and the Father, so the church is subject to the bishop (*Magn.* 13:2; cf. *Trall.* 2:1). These last two ideas are paralleled in John (5:19, 30; 8:28-29; 10:30).

In addition, "he who honors the bishop has been honored by God" (*Smyrn.* 9:1), for to honor the bishop is to honor the Son and to honor the Son is to honor the Father (John 5:23); "if anyone serves me the Father will honor him" (John 12:26).

This is not to say that Ignatius derives all his ideas from John, even all his ideas about unity. The ideas about discipline and unity which he expresses in *Magnesians* 13:2 are almost certainly derived from Ephesians, a letter which he clearly knew (cf. especially *Polyc.* 5:1). "Be subject to—the bishop and—one another [Eph. 5:21], as Jesus Christ is to the Father and the apostles to Christ [Eph. 5:24] and the Father, so that there may be a union both fleshly [cf. Eph. 5:31] and spiritual." This is to say that Ignatius combines New Testament themes in various ways; he is not a man of one book—or of two, like Marcion.

On what basis can Ignatius assign to the bishop what is usually said in John about the Son? On what basis can he say that the bishop is a "type" or copy of God (*Trall.* 3:1), the bishop of all (*Magn.* 3:1)? He must regard the bishop as somehow equivalent to the apostle in earlier times—and there are no apostles in Ignatius' own time (*Magn.* 6:1; 7:1; *Rom.* 4:3). He can use what Paul said of himself (Gal. 1:1) and apply it to the bishop of Philadelphia (1:1). He can also use the language of the gospels about apostles and apply it to bishops (*Eph.* 6:1; John 13:20). Both passages show that bishops are bishops not because of human appointment but because of divine mission. They somehow replace the apostles, presumably because of the passage of time. As Jesus worked through the apostles (*Magn.* 7:1), so the bishops exist in accordance with his purpose (*Eph.* 3:2; *Philad.* inscr.). To be subordinate to the bishop is to be subordinate to Jesus Christ (*Trall.* 2:1). In all his language about the bishop there seems to be a trace of the Pauline imitation/hierarchy ideas. (*a*) There is a hierarchical structure, as in I Corinthians 11:3.

There Paul describes it by saying that the "head" of a woman is her husband, the "head" of a man is Christ, and the "head" of Christ is God. Similarly in I Corinthians 3:22-23 everything belongs to the Christian community, which in turn belongs to Christ, who belongs to God. (Compare Eph. 5:23: the husband is the "head" of the wife as Christ is the "head" of the church.) Thus for Ignatius the hierarchy consists of God, Christ, apostles (= bishops), church. If we knew—as we do not—that he used II Corinthians, we might suggest that the function of the bishop was like that of the apostle, who "betrothed" the church to Christ (II Cor. 11:2). (*b*) There is a structure involving imitation, as in I Corinthians 11:1, where Paul directs Christians to imitate him as he imitates Christ, and in John 5:19, where we read that the Son imitates the action of the Father. But these New Testament parallels do not fully explain the emphasis on the role of the bishop. In the New Testament itself the bishop is mentioned in the singular only three times (I Tim. 3:2; Titus 1:7; I Pet. 2:25, of Christ, cf. Ignatius, *Rom.* 9:1) and in the plural only twice (Acts 20:28; Phil. 1:1).

Behind the letters of Ignatius there must lie some kind of transition from the New Testament situation toward his own. The best explanation of the factors involved is probably that of A. A. T. Ehrhardt.[6] In the *Didache* (13:3) Christians are instructed to revere the prophets as their high priests but are to appoint bishops who will exercise the same kind of ministry (15:1). This is to say that in the *Didache* the bishop will also be the Christian high priest. And here we note that the office of the Ignatian bishop is remarkably similar to that of the Jewish high priest. Like this priest, he prophesies (*Philad.* 7).[7] Like him he is the center of unity for the community (*Magn.* 7).[8] "He who does not obey the high priest will be punished as if he had uttered blasphemy against God himself." [9]

Now admittedly we do not know that Ignatius explicitly compared the bishop with the high priest. But we do know that he

[6] *Church Quarterly Review,* 140 (1945), 113-26.

[7] Cf. Hecataeus in Diodorus Siculus, 40:3:5; Ehrhardt, *op. cit.,* p. 116.

[8] Cf. Josephus, *Contra Apionem* 2:193.

[9] *Ibid.* 2:194.

compared him with Jesus, and Jesus with the high priest (*Philad.* 9:1). Because of Ignatius' use of imitation/hierarchy ideas, we should believe that he viewed the bishop as the Christian high priest. After all, Christian ministers had already been regarded as high priests in the *Didache* and in *I Clement* 40-41.

The motifs with which emphasis upon episcopacy was combined are also present in Jewish apologetic where the high priest was mentioned. Thus in *Magnesians* 7:1, Ignatius speaks of "one prayer, one supplication, one mind, one hope in love . . . in Jesus Christ"; his language thus recalls the New Testament (Eph. 4:3-6 and John 10:16). But he proceeds at once (*Magn.* 7:2) to speak of "one temple of God, one sanctuary, one Jesus Christ, who came forth from the one Father and is with the one and departed to the one." This language recalls that of John (8:42; 13:3; 14:12, 18; 16:10, 17-18). But the idea behind the terminology was developed in Hellenistic Judaism; there is one temple for the one God.[10]

What we find in Ignatius' discussion of the episcopate, then, is not a development due to personal pride or neurosis, or to factors found in the mystery religions or in Gnosticism, but a development based upon the thought of the New Testament and, to some extent, on ideas present in contemporary Judaism. Daniélou has pointed out that other Jewish ideas are reflected in his letters.[11]

2) In discussing the sacramental unity of the church we do not intend to deal with all aspects of Ignatius' doctrine of the sacraments; we are concerned only with the unity of the church. Two passages about the Eucharist are especially important: *Ephesians* 20:2 and *Philadelphians* 4. In the first, Ignatius speaks of "breaking one loaf, which is the drug of immortality, the antidote to dying." Here his language is almost purely Pauline. "The loaf, which we break, is it not participation in the body of Christ? For we, though many, are one loaf, one body; for we all share in the one loaf" (I Cor. 10:16-17). That the loaf mediates immortality could be inferred from I Corinthians 11:

[10] Josephus, *loc. cit.*

[11] *Théologie du Judéo-Christianisme* (Tournai, 1958), pp. 49-53.

28-30, where Paul states that those who eat it unworthily are likely to be sick or to die. It is also the doctrine of John 6: 51*c*-58. In the second passage, Ignatius says:

> Be zealous to use one Eucharist; for one is the flesh of our Lord Jesus Christ and one is the cup for union with his blood; one is the sanctuary, as one is the bishop together with the presbytery and deacons. . . .

In this passage the unity of the Eucharist is not the point of departure but the goal; however, the base of Ignatius' thought surely lies in the Pauline passage quoted above, where Paul begins with the words, "The cup of blessing which we bless, is it not participation in the blood of Christ?" (I Cor. 10:16), and goes on immediately to mention a "sanctuary" (10:18). Ignatius does not say exactly what Paul said; he uses Paul's thought and language and reinterprets both.

Once more, we should point out that Ignatius not only begins with New Testament terminology but interprets it in language related to Judaism. The kind of Judaism we have in mind is that which underlies the eucharistic prayer of the *Didache* (9:4): "As this broken bread was scattered over the mountains and when gathered became one, so let thy church be gathered together from the ends of the earth into thy kingdom." Here too the unity is eucharistic.

3) Finally, it is claimed that Ignatius' ideas about martyrdom are somehow unchristian. In his view he cannot really be a disciple unless he suffers; he cannot otherwise "attain to God." He wants to become "an imitator of the suffering of my God." It is really very difficult to understand how T. Preiss could devote so much time to comparing Ignatius' ideas with those in Philippians (where the circumstances are quite different) and could totally neglect the resemblance of Ignatius' thought to that expressed in Colossians 1:24 and elsewhere, including Philippians 3:13 ("sharing in his sufferings"). Colossians, of course, is treated as non-Pauline by some recent scholars; but the early Fathers did not share such a view.

Following G. Kittel,[12] we should also note that Colossians 1:24

[12] *Zeitschrift für systematische Theologie,* 18 (1941), 186-91.

echoes the teaching of Jesus in the gospels; it does not express an isolated aberration of the apostle.

The basic idea of Ignatius is therefore derived from the New Testament church. What of the language in which he expresses it? This has been investigated by O. Perler in the article already mentioned; he found many clear traces of the influences of IV Maccabees on Ignatius' style and thought. Once more, then, Ignatius takes New Testament ideas and expresses them in a context in which Jewish influences are important. This context is historically that of Antioch, where Judaism flourished for centuries.

In each of these instances Ignatius has taken an apostolic theme and has expressed it in terminology related to Jewish thought (so also the "myth" in *Ephesians* 19 is Matthean in origin but set forth in terminology from the Wisdom of Solomon). But Ignatius was no Judaizer or sympathizer with Judaism. How can this fact be explained?

C. CONCLUSION

In the first part of this paper we have argued that the evidence about Ignatius' use of the Old and New Testaments is such as to suggest that he knew many of the New Testament books but had not classified them either as scripture or nonscripture. In the second part we have argued that evidence for tradition in his letters is to be found in credal summaries, in imaginative expansions of gospel pericopes, and in some of his basic ideas about episcopal and sacramental unity and martyrdom. We now proceed to indicate why we regard the basic ideas as traditional rather than based on Ignatius' own creativity. To some extent our argument is based upon a remark by Perler (p. 64) to the effect that if Ignatius read and valued IV Maccabees, it must have been written before the break between the church and the synagogue. His remark must be qualified by the continuing close relations between Judaism and Christianity as reflected in late second-century Christianity at Antioch. But this much can be said about Ignatius: had he known that the context of his ideas was Jewish he could hardly have accepted it, in view of the danger of Judaism as set forth in his letters! Therefore his ideas are traditional, not his own. The ideas are simply Christian. What makes them look unique or even unchristian is the stylistic expression which Ignatius provided. He is an exception to the early Christian rule against stylistic vigor. The fact that he could write exciting prose, however, should not force us to regard him as alien to Christianity.

If his basic ideas are traditional what can be said of the relation between scripture and tradition? Here we can only claim that, whatever may be the case in regard to other writers, we must say that for Ignatius, because of his early date, there is practically no difference between scripture and tradition. Indeed, it might be more accurate to say that in the one case where the question seems to come up, Ignatius favors tradition over scripture (*Philad.* 8:2). Best of all, perhaps, would be to say that in his time the question had not been raised in any sense known to modern theologians.

The historical and theological significance of Ignatius lies in the fact that, writing early in the second century, he preserved apostolic tradition as it had been interpreted at Antioch in the generation before him. He is thus a witness to a stage of Christian life and thought which might otherwise have been lost. His own contribution consists primarily of the intensity of emphasis with which he expresses the traditional faith, not of the capacity for innovation with which critics have wrongly credited him.

The principal features of his thought come to him from the apostolic faith as interpreted in the Jewish Christian circles of Antioch. Though Ignatius rejected Jewish Christianity in some regards, he did not endeavor to purge his own thought of the Jewish influence which he cannot have recognized as such. It is when we recognize the presence of this influence that his place in Christian history becomes comprehensible, and the following problems are much closer to solution. (1) Why is Ignatius so different from the other Apostolic Fathers? Actually he shares with them a mixture of ideas and expressions both Jewish and Greek (if we want to use such a differentiation, still *broadly* useful); in this regard he obviously resembles both Clement and Hermas.[13] (2) What is the place of Ignatius in the history of the church of Antioch? Previously it has been impossible to understand how from this advanced "Hellenism"—or whatever it is that characterizes Ignatius' ideas—Christian thought at Antioch could pass on to the more strongly Jewish ideas of Theophilus, bishop there around 180.[14] It has been supposed that Ignatius stood close to the Gnostic Saturninus of Antioch, perhaps his contemporary, not to the "main stream" of Christianity. But when one recognizes that Ignatius' Hellenism is to a considerable degree a matter of style and expression[15] one begins to see links, if not between Ignatius and Theophilus, at least between pre-Ignatian Christianity at Antioch and post-Ignatian Christianity there. We rightly emphasize the diversity present within the early church; we must give equal credit to the continuity of its life and teaching.

[13] On the Jewishness of *I Clement* see Daniélou, *op. cit.*, pp. 53-55; for Greek aspects, W. Jaeger, *Early Christianity and Greek Paideia* (Cambridge, 1961), pp. 12-26; for Hermas, R. Joly, *Hermas: Le Pasteur* (Paris, 1958), pp. 46-54.

[14] See chap. 10 below, and my article in *Harvard Theological Review*, 43 (1950), 179-96.

[15] On this see H. Riesenfeld in *TU* 79, 312-22; I am grateful to the author for a reprint received after this essay was written.

ADDITIONAL NOTE ON EPISCOPACY IN POLYCARP. It has sometimes been suggested that Polycarp's letter to the Philippians shows that Ignatius was exaggerating the importance of episcopacy. This claim is based on the way the letter begins ("Polycarp and the presbyters with him to the church of God sojourning at Philippi") and on the mention of presbyters and deacons (5-6, 11), *not* of a bishop. Any explanation of these facts involves a certain measure of historical imagination. The suggestion we should make is that Polycarp refrains from mentioning a bishop at Philippi because the person, not the office, of the bishop is in question there; he is, we suggest, the Valens mentioned in chapter 11. For this reason—because he has perhaps been deposed—the Philippians are to be subject to the presbyters and the deacons (not the bishop) as to God and Christ (5:3). When Polycarp asks (in regard

4

PLINY AND THE CHRISTIANS

MANY INFERENCES have been drawn by liturgical scholars from the letter of Pliny to Trajan, *Epistulae* 10:96, in the year 112. The purpose of this note is to suggest that such inferences are at least partly invalid.

Pliny states that he has never been present at judicial investigations where Christians have been involved, although earlier in his mission to Bithynia and Pontus he forbade the meetings of associations and must have been prepared to investigate infringements of his order. He is uncertain as to what precise charge is to be brought against them, although he is aware, since he employs torture, that they are lawbreakers. The Roman government was accustomed to intervene in such cases only when there was or seemed to be a threat against public order.[1] But Pliny does not know just how to proceed.

Cicero had pointed out (*De legibus* 2:37) that in a case involving nocturnal rites the significant example was that of the suppression of the Bacchanalia in 186 B.C. (cf. Tertullian, *Apologeticum* 6:7), and Pliny would naturally look for such a precedent. He would find an account of it in the historian Livy, who wrote for practical use by giving examples from the past—so that *tibi tuaeque rei publicae quod imitere capis* (Praef., 10). And we know that like many of his contemporaries Pliny was an ardent admirer of Livy (cf. *Epistulae* 2:3:8), and that at the age of seventeen he had already begun making excerpts from his work (*Epistulae* 6:20:5, written about twenty-five years later).[2]

The parallels between the record of Pliny's examination and the narrative of Livy suggest that Pliny was influenced by his

[1] Cf. H. Last in *Journal of Roman Studies,* 27 (1937), 80-92.

[2] He did not use an epitome like the one mentioned in Martial 14:190 or found fragmentarily in *Oxyrhynchus papyri* 4:668 (including summaries of Books 37-40).

memories of the historian's work, and that his phrasing does not necessarily reflect the Christians' words at every point.

	Pliny		Livy, Book 39
7	*ante lucem convenire*	8	*occulta et nocturna sacra*
	carmen . . . secum invicem	18	*ex carmine sacro praeeunte verba sacerdote precationes fecerant,*
	sacramentum non in scelus		*in quibus nefanda coniuratio in omne facinus ac libidinem*
	cibum promiscuum . . . innoxium	8	*vinum et epulae . . . caedes ut ne corpora quidem exstarent*
9	*omnis aetatis, omnis ordinis, utriusque sexus*	8	*mixti feminis mares, aetatis tenerae maioribus*
	neque civitates tantum sed vicos etiam atque agros superstitionis istius contagio	9	*huius mali labes ex Etruria Romam veluti contagione morbi penetravit*

While such charges are almost commonplace against obscure minority groups, the similarity of language seems to show that Pliny has Livy in mind, and to a considerable extent takes his phrasing from him.

This conclusion supports the interpretation of H. Lietzmann, "Carmen = Taufsymbol," *Rheinisches Museum*, 71 (1916), 281-82 (cf. A. Kurfess in *Zeitschrift für die neutestamentliche Wissenschaft*, 35 [1936], 295-98) as against C. J. Kraemer, Jr., in *Classical Philology*, 29 (1934), 293-300 (carmen a psalm), S. L. Mohler in *Classical Philology*, 30 (1935), 167-69 (carmen the Shema), L. C. Mohlberg in *Rivista di archeologia cristiana*, 14 (1937), 109-22 (carmen the Kyrie), and C. C. Coulter in *Classical Philology*, 35 (1940), 62 (carmen a hymn). It also confirms the observations of A. D. Nock in *Classical Review*, 38 (1924), 58-59 (sacramentum a baptismal oath) as against Mohlberg (not baptismal) and does not contradict the view of Kraemer that the oath is based on the Decalogue.

In a more recent article, "La lettre de Pline à Trajan sur les chrétiens (X, 97)," in *Recherches de théologie ancienne et médiévale*, 31 (1964), 161-74, F. Fourrier independently made the same comparison, added details, and reached similar conclusions.

5

SCRIPTURE, RHETORIC, AND THEOLOGY IN THEOPHILUS

THEOPHILUS OF ANTIOCH has a style which, if not especially exciting, is (as Pierre Nautin has remarked) *toujours clair.*[1] From time to time he seems to devote greater attention to the devices of rhetoric; in his books *Ad Autolycum* there are two passages (1:3 and 3:15) in which he employs the brief cola characteristic of Asian rhetoric and found also in the *Homily on the Passover* probably written by Melito bishop of Sardis.[2] These passages are especially interesting because in them scriptural sources are employed in a rhetorical manner for theological purposes. The method Theophilus here uses is different from that found in his second book, where he quotes long sections of the book of Genesis and then proceeds to provide exegesis for them. In 1:3 and 3:15 his use of scripture is allusive rather than explicit. But the purpose is the same; it is to create scripturally-grounded theological statements.

We shall consider first his method as reflected in these two passages and then his method as it is developed in the passages in the second book in which he is discussing the Logos of God.

A. ATTRIBUTES OF GOD (1:3)

The first passage begins with a list of seven attributes of God (glory, magnitude, height, strength, wisdom, goodness, beneficence), each of which is accompanied by an adjective to indicate that, in relation to the attribute, God is really ineffable and inexpressible. Then Theophilus lists thirteen appellations of God,

[1] *Vigiliae Christianae,* 11 (1957), 214.
[2] Cf. A. Wifstrand in *Vigiliae Christianae,* 2 (1948), 201-23.

along with the aspects of his activity to which they really refer.[3] What Theophilus says is that God is not actually Light, Logos, Mind, Spirit, Wisdom, Strength, Power, Providence, Royal Rule,[4] Lord, Judge, Father, or Fire. Briefer lists of the same kind are to be found in Justin, *Apol.* 2: 5(6): 2 (Father, God, Creator, Lord, Master); Clement, *Str.* 5:82:1 (the Good, Mind, the Self-Existent, Father, God, Demiurge, Lord); *Ad Diognetum* 9:6 (God wants us to regard him as Nurse, Father, Teacher, Counselor, Physician, Mind, Light, Honor, Glory, Strength, Life); and *Corpus Hermeticum* 2:14 (Nock-Festugière ed., pp. 37-38: Mind, Spirit, Light). The theological problem involved is clearly stated by Origen. Literalists think that God is a body because in scripture they read that he is called Fire or Spirit, but the appellation of Light shows that he is not corporeal.[5] Minucius Felix (*Octavius* 18:10) reflects the same difficulty: "if I call him Father you will suppose him to be carnal; if King, you will suppose him to be earthly; if Lord, you will understand him as mortal."

The difficulty seems to have arisen not just among Gnostics, as Prestige claimed,[6] but among rather unphilosophical Christians like Irenaeus, who were willing to express God's transcendence in terms ultimately derived from Xenophanes.[7] Thus Irenaeus says that God can be called "wholly Mind, wholly Spirit, wholly Understanding, wholly Conception, Reason, Hearing, Eye, Light: the source of all good things." [8] Irenaeus thus identifies the transcendent source with that of which it is the source; other theologians make more careful distinctions.

[3] The correct transmission of the text seems to be guaranteed by the parallel list in Novatian, *De trinitate* 2, apparently derived from Theophilus. We should add that a note of J. C. T. Otto (*Corpus Apologetarum Christianorum saeculi secundi,* 8 [Jena, 1861], 11 n. 9) on this passage is erroneous; it reads "ἀγαθοσύνην) Sic codd. msti, non ἀγαθωσύνην, quod exspectaveris." The reading of the Venice manuscript is actually ἀγαθοσύνην.

[4] Theophilus has βασιλείαν; Novatian apparently interprets it as *maiestatem.*

[5] *De Principiis* 1:1:1 (Koetschau ed., pp. 16-17); cf. *In Iohannem commentarius* 13:21 (Preuschen ed., p. 244); *Contra Celsum* 4:13; 6:70, 72.

[6] *God in Patristic Thought* (London, 1936), p. 4; and it is not true that Gnostic theology was always positive (contrast Ptolemaeus' doctrine as analyzed by F.-M. Sagnard, *La gnose valentinienne* [Paris, 1947], index) when contrasted with the negative doctrines of the Fathers.

[7] Cf. C. C. J. Webb in *Journal of Theological Studies,* 40 (1939), 36-37.

[8] See chap. 7 below.

Our problem now is that of determining why Theophilus chose the attributes which he did choose. He probably begins with I John 1:5 (God is Light) and corrects it by Genesis 1:3, where light is created by God. Then he turns to John 1:1 (the Logos was God) and states that the Logos was actually the Beginning (Gen. 1:1; Prov. 8:22) through which God effected his creation. Against Irenaeus and others he denies that God is really Mind; the appellation refers to God's knowing, not to his nature. "Spirit" really means his breath; it is not a definition, in spite of what John 4:24 may seem to mean. "Wisdom" is his offspring (Prov. 8:22), not God himself.

The next two appellations are surprising unless one considers the extent to which Theophilus is working over New Testament words and phrases. "If I speak of him as Strength, I speak of his might; if I speak of him as Power, I speak of his operation." Here Theophilus is probably reflecting the language of Ephesians 1:19: "the surpassing greatness of his *power* toward us who believe in accordance with the *operation* of the *might* of his *strength*." In the New Testament passage the words directly related to God are "power" and "strength" (cf. Eph. 3:7, "the operation of his power"), and these are the words which Theophilus explains in operational terms.

He then explains that providence is to be related to God's goodness, and concludes with five appellations which he may be treating in an anti-Marcionite manner. "Kingdom" or "royal rule" refers to God's glory (cf. Matt. 4:8; doxology added at Matt. 6:13; *Didache* 9:4; 10:5), and is not to be understood as Christ himself, as Marcion believed.[9] To speak of God as Lord means speaking of him as judge; as Father, as "all things" (so Athenagoras, *Legatio ad Graecos* 16; Tertullian, *Adversus Praxean* 5);[10] as Judge, as just. To call him Fire means speaking of his wrath—against Marcion.[11] Thus Theophilus opposes the Marcionite rejection of God as creator and judge and maintains the traditional Jewish-Christian doctrine.

[9] A. v. Harnack, *Marcion: das Evangelium vom fremden Gott* (2nd ed.; Leipzig, 1924), p. 126.

[10] Cf. E. Evans, *Tertullian's Treatise Against Praxeas* (London, 1948), p. 212.

[11] Harnack, *op. cit.*, p. 264*.

We do not agree with the comment of Bardy on this passage. "It would appear that Theophilus himself would have found it hard to interpret this mishmash. Here as elsewhere he is carried away by a mad desire to keep talking."[12] Theophilus' rhetoric is not always adroit, but he has something to say.

B. CHRISTIAN LIFE (3:15)

The other passage consists of the short cola of which Melito was so fond. Theophilus has just been discussing the charges of cannibalism and promiscuity (now called "adultery") made against Christians.

> Far be it from Christians to consider doing any such thing—
> [Christians] among whom
> temperance is present, continence is exercised, monogamy is preserved, purity is guarded;
> injustice is driven out, sin is uprooted;
> righteousness is practiced, law is customary, religion is performed, God is acknowledged;
> truth controls, grace preserves, peace protects;
> holy Logos leads, Wisdom teaches, Life controls, God reigns.

The first four nouns list virtues directly opposed to the accusation of adultery; these virtues are commonly mentioned by Christian writers who deal with monogamy. Thus temperance, continence, and purity occur in a list of virtues in *I Clement* 64; Hermas speaks of preserving or guarding purity (*Mandates* 4:4:3; 4:1:1); Clement of Alexandria commends continence, temperance, and monogamy (*Str.* 3:4:1-3); and in the *Clementine Homilies* (3:26:4) we read that the true prophet "destroys wars, teaches peace, enjoins temperance, eradicates sins, legislates marriage, permits continence [the nonascetic note of the Clementina], leads all to purity." The virtues of Christians are next indicated in a negative way: among them there is neither wrongdoing nor sin.[13]

After this Theophilus proceeds to a description of the Christian religion which is essentially the same, though practically in

[12] G. Bardy—J. Sender, *Théophile d'Antioche* (Paris, 1948), p.65 n. 1.
[13] Perhaps a reflection of I John 5:17, where the two are identified.

reverse order, as the description he has given in *Ad Autol.* 3:9. There he has said that "We acknowledge God . . . we have learned a holy law . . . concerning religion . . . concerning righteousness." In the present passage he is doing no more than insisting on the actuality of this (Jewish or Jewish-Christian[14]) conception. The mention of God is placed last because it is the climax of the section.

Another section then begins, and we hear of truth, grace, and peace probably because grace and truth are associated in John 1:17 and Colossians 1:6 and grace and peace are found together in most of the Pauline epistles.[15] From these divine gifts Theophilus passes to the giver: a (really "the") holy Logos (cf. 3:13), Wisdom, Life, and God. One is surprised to find "life" mentioned between Wisdom and God, but perhaps at this point Theophilus' thought is governed by his verbs rather than his nouns. "Holy Logos leads," and in John 14:6 we read that Jesus (the Logos) is "the way, the truth, and the life." Elsewhere in John, in verses to which Theophilus elsewhere alludes (John 14:26 in 2:33 and 3:11; John 16:13 in 2:38), we learn that the Spirit (identified with the Logos in 2:10) is to "lead" and to "teach." We should suggest that Theophilus has constructed his last section chiefly out of Johannine materials.

Once more, the initial effect of Theophilus' work suggests that it is "merely" rhetorical; but further examination seems to prove that, as in the writings of other early Christian writers, rhetoric and theology cannot be so easily separated. It is not that there is a theology lying underneath the rhetoric; it is instead that through and in the rhetoric the theology comes to expression.

C. THE LOGOS IN SCRIPTURE AND RHETORIC

Once more, if we consider Theophilus' development of the Logos-doctrine we find that his method is, as we have said, to

[14] Cf. my article in *Harvard Theological Review,* 43 (1950), 179-96.
[15] Cf. 3:23, a prayer that readers may be led by God's truth and grace.

use scripture in a rhetorical manner in order to construct theology. Our formula is intended to take into account both the Hellenistic (or, more specifically, Hellenistic Jewish) elements in his thought[16] and those derived from what has been classified as Jewish or Jewish Christian theology.[17]

a. Scriptural Sources

We first encounter God's Word (Logos) and Wisdom in *Ad Autol.* 1:3, where, as we have seen, Theophilus tells us that they are terms used only of God's operations, not of his essence or nature. Theophilus finds confirmation for his doctrine of "the God who acts" when (in 1:7) he says that "God heals and makes alive through the Logos and the Wisdom"; through them he made all things, for the Old Testament says that "by his Word the heavens were established, and by his Spirit all their power" (Ps. 33:2, LXX). "Spirit" means God's "most powerful" Wisdom, and Theophilus quotes Proverbs 3:19-20 to prove that Wisdom was active in creation. In other words, at this point his doctrine is based on Old Testament exegesis.

In his second book many further details are provided. In 2:10 we read that God begot his Logos, previously immanent *(endiathetos)* in his bowels, and emitted him with his Wisdom (based on Ps. 44:1, LXX). The Logos, through whom all things were made (John 1:3, quoted in 2:22), is identified with the *archē* of Genesis 1:1, just as it is identified among Jewish Christian writers earlier in the second century—and later as well.[18] The Logos, says Theophilus, is Spirit of God and Beginning and Wisdom and Power of the Most High. This is to say that he identifies him with the Spirit mentioned as borne over the waters in Genesis 1:2; with the Beginning mentioned in Genesis 1:1; with Wisdom in Proverbs (as we have already seen); and with the Power of the Most High whose coming was predicted to Mary by the angel Gabriel in Luke 1:35. The two middle iden-

[16] Cf. chap. 10 below.

[17] Cf. G. Kretschmar, *Studien zur frühchristlichen Trinitätstheologie* (Tübingen, 1956); J. Daniélou, *Théologie du Judéo-Christianisme* (see above, p. 49 n. 11).

[18] Daniélou, *op. cit.,* pp. 219-22.

tifications have obvious precedents in Justin and in the New Testament. The first and the last, however, require some explanation. It would appear that one could not pass from Logos to Spirit without some middle term; and this is provided in the New Testament when Paul refers to "the Lord" as "the Spirit" (II Cor. 3:17). Similarly the correlation of Logos with Power of the Most High requires an identification of both Logos and Power with Jesus or, to put it differently, an interpretation of Luke 1:35 as fulfilled in John 1:14. This is to say that underneath Theophilus' expressions lies the New Testament. Theophilus, unlike some Jewish Christians, probably does not identify Christ with Gabriel;[19] he is quite reticent on the subject of angels (cf. only 2:28). For his theology the most important correlation is that of Logos with Wisdom. At creation the Wisdom of God was in him[20] and the holy Logos was with him: this is proved by a text from Proverbs (8:27-29) which has Wisdom say that she was with God at creation.

In 2:13 Theophilus explains that "in the Beginning" (Gen. 1:1) means "through the Beginning," and he goes on to explain the literal meaning of Earth, Abyss, Darkness, and Spirit in Genesis 1:2, presumably against Gnostic teachers who found aeons in this verse.[21] The same chapter states that the command (*diataxis*) of God, i.e., his Logos, shone forth as light; God called the light "day." Here Theophilus may well be indicating that the word (verb) of God, "Let there be—light," is imperative in form rather than, as Tatian interpreted it,[22] optative. Theophilus does not proceed to work out the identification of Logos with Day as other early Christian writers do,[23] but such an identification may be in the back of his mind, since from 2:15 we learn that the first three days of creation are symbols of the Triad consisting of God, his Logos, and his Wisdom. The identification can only be latent, however, since, as Daniélou has pointed out, the two lines of symbolic thought (Triad, Day) are radically different.

[19] *Ibid.*, pp. 180-82.

[20] Reading the text with P. Nautin in *Vigiliae Christianae,* 11 (1957), 212-16.

[21] Eg., Marcus in Irenaeus, *Adv. haer.* 1:18:1 (Harvey ed., p. 169).

[22] Cf. Origen, *De oratione* 24:5; he points out that "let there be" is clearly imperative in force in Genesis 1:9, 11, 20, 24.

[23] Daniélou, *op. cit.,* pp. 222-26.

In 2:18 Theophilus tells us that the creation of man was not effected in the same way as was the work done by God before that point in creation. God made everything else by "a word" (not the Word), but he made man with his own[24] hands, i.e., his Logos and his Wisdom. This is not very clear, but it seems to be an attempt to explain the use of the plural hortatory subjunctive in Genesis 1:26 while avoiding Gnostic speculations (similarly Theophilus avoids explaining the "male-female" of Genesis 1:27, since in his view Genesis 2 provides a fuller descripton of part of Genesis 1).

In 2:22 we find a more elaborate discussion of the Logos, continuing the statement made in 2:10. Theophilus explains that it was not God but his Logos who "walked" in paradise; Adam heard his "voice," which is his Logos, who is his Son. Theophilus uses the rhetorical-Stoic-Philonic terms "immanent" and "expressed" to indicate what he is talking about, but they are not his point of departure. Instead, the key phrases of this chapter are found in the New Testament, first in allusions, then in an explicit quotation. For Theophilus refers to the Logos as God's power and wisdom (I Cor. 1:24), as God's Son, and as the firstborn of all creation (Col. 1:15). He says that the Logos was God's pre-creational Counsellor (Prov. 3:20, cited in 1:7 in relation to Wisdom) as his Mind and Intelligence. Counsellor and Mind come from Isaiah 40:13 as interpreted in I Corinthians 2:16-17; "mind" is interpreted as "intelligence" by Theophilus himself in 1:3.[25] These passages show that he has Christ in mind as he writes, and the point is proved when he goes on to give an explicit quotation of John 1:1-3, explaining that *pros* in John 1:1 means *en*, just as previously (2:13) he has said that *en* in Genesis 1:1 means *dia*. He also explains that *theos ēn ho logos* means *ek theou pephykōs*, since in his view the appellation *ho theos* is reserved for the Father.

In view of the meaning of these passages it is almost certain that the expressions *ho hagios logos* and *hē euangelios phōnē*

[24] The emendation *ἰδίων* for the *αἴδιον* of the Venice manuscript goes back to Gesner's edition of 1546.

[25] *Nous* is identified with *phronēsis,* in relation to God, in Stobaeus, *Eclogiae* 1:2:24 (Wachsmuth ed., Vol. I, p. 31, 5).

(3:13) refer not to Christian books but to Christ speaking in them, and the same observation, though less certainly, could be made in regard to *to euangelion* (3:14). The divine Logos speaks in the Pauline epistles (3:14). So among Christians "holy Logos leads the way, Wisdom teaches, Life presides, God reigns" (3:15).

b. Further Use of John

We already know that Theophilus is fond of the Gospel of John (2:22) and that he uses the New Testament allusively. Some light may be shed on his idea of the Holy Spirit if we consider additional passages in which he seems to be alluding to the "farewell discourses" of John 14-16. J. C. T. Otto already indicated an allusion to John 16:21 in 2:23, where Theophilus refers to women's forgetfulness of labor pains. This is not especially significant. More important are the allusions to John 14:26. Christians possess the truth because they are taught by the Holy Spirit (2:33). The prophets (inspired by this Spirit) were sent "to teach and remind" the people of the content of the law of God (3:11). Finally, "Wisdom teaches" among Christians (3:15), just as "holy Logos leads the way" (cf. John 16:13). Similarly there is one obvious allusion to John 16:8 and 13. In 2:38 Theophilus speaks of the revelation given primarily through the Sibyl and the prophets but also through poets and philosophers "concerning righteousness and judgment and punishment"; the latter group spoke unwillingly, but they "were convinced by the Truth." Theophilus is referring to the work of the Spirit of truth (John 16:13) in convincing the world "of sin and of righteousness and of judgment." This is to say that just as in the Gospel of John the work of the spirit is not clearly differentiated from that of the Logos, and indeed continues it, so in the thought of Theophilus it is difficult to differentiate the Spirit from the Logos. At times he identifies them; at times he does not. The reason for this lack of clarity is doubtless to be found in the fact that Theophilus is not a philosophical theologian but an exegete whose training was primarily in rhetoric. In his work we find materials for a system, or materials from several systems. The task of synthesis remained to be performed by men like Irenaeus and Origen.

The content of Theophilus' doctrine, then, seems to be based on the Old and New Testaments. The form, however, is supplied by a mixture of Greek philosophy and Greek rhetoric.

c. A Parallel in Aelius Aristides

For the form in which Theophilus expresses his doctrine we may look at some of the works of the famous rhetorician Aelius Aristides, his contemporary. Like Theophilus (2:9), Aelius Aristides attacks the notion that poets are "alone loved by God" and claims that "the prophets of the gods" are more evidently inspired (*Orationes* 45, Keil ed., p. 354, 14-17). Following Homer (*Ilias* 2:489) he states that ten mouths and ten tongues would be inadequate for the praise of Sarapis (*Orationes* 45, p. 357, 4) or Asclepius (*Orationes* 47, p. 376, 6); Theophilus, like some of the Latin writers cited by Courcelle, multiplies by a thousand.[26]

In his relatively early *Oration to Zeus* (Keil ed., no. 43), Aristides states that one cannot speak of Zeus' coming into being, for he was from the beginning and always will be, self-engendered (i.e., not the son of Kronos) and greater than one who is produced from another (p. 340, 18). Zeus made the universe. "He begins from the foundations and makes earth in order to establish everything upon it" (p. 341, 6; cf. Theophilus 2:13, who points out the superiority of the Genesis narrative, in which God begins from above). Then he set firm the sea, the air, and finally the fire above, called aether. He adorned the whole heaven with stars just as he adorned the sea with islands. Next he made animals suited to each type of environment. The gods dwell in the heaven, men on earth, marine animals in the sea, and birds in the air. All are governed by harmony and providence (cf. Theophilus 1:6-7). While the gods' "first native land" is heavenly, they govern air, sea, and earth as "satraps" of Zeus. The philosophical-rhetorical monotheism of Aristides is close to that of Theophilus.

In another oration (Keil ed., No. 37) Aristides shows us that

[26] P. Courcelle in *Revue des études latines,* 33 (1955), 231-40; cf. also E. Norden, *Aeneis Buch VI* (Leipzig, 1903), p. 286; A. Höfler, *Der Sarapishymnus des Aelios Aristeides* (Stuttgart, 1935), p. 45.

even the Logos-doctrine of Theophilus can be paralleled in contemporary paganism. Following the traditional Stoic interpretation of Athena as the Wisdom of Zeus, Aristides states that she is "the only child of the sole Fashioner and King of all" (p. 304, 8). Zeus had nothing out of which to fashion her, but by himself he generated and bore her, so that she is the sole genuine (legitimate) offspring of the Father. She was born from his head fully armed, as the sun rises with its rays, "adorned from within by the Father." Because of the mode of her generation she can never abandon the Father but is always with him as his companion. She is united with him; she "breathes toward" him and is alone with him, mindful of her generation and giving a suitable repayment for the pangs of birth (p. 305, 3). She is the eldest of the gods, and "Zeus would not otherwise have bound various elements together had he not set Athena beside him as his companion and counsellor" (p. 305, 9; cf. Wisdom in Theophilus 2:22). Athena is a "power" of Zeus (cf. Theophilus 2:22); one can describe the acts of Athena as the common actions of Zeus and Athena (p. 312, 16). Pindar rightly says that she sits at the right hand of the Father and receives his commandments for the gods. But she is greater than a messenger (*angelos*); she herself gives commands which she has received from the Father, "taking the place of any exegete or introducer for the gods when there is need of one" (p. 305, 21-26). In relation to mankind she inspires right action and prevents wrong. Led by Athena men never act sinfully, and "they will never do any good deed without Athena" (p. 312, 7; 306, 27).

The resemblance of this doctrine to that of Theophilus is very remarkable. We find in it the same emphasis on the generation of Logos-Sophia that Theophilus lays, and the functions of the hypostases in Aristides and in Theophilus are substantially identical. The resemblances are probably to be explained not only by the probability that Aristides and Theophilus addressed similar audiences, but also from the existence of patterns for *Götterreden* in rhetorical schools. Once more we are led back to the notion that, beginning with scripture, Theophilus developed his theological doctrines by means of liberal use of the rhetorical training he must have possessed.

D. APPENDIX: THEOPHILUS AND NEW TESTAMENT ETHICS

We have already seen something of Theophilus' allusive use of scriptural words and phrases, but the extent to which New Testament language permeates his writings is not always recognized. Here we consider some of the mosaics derived from the New Testament and underlying what he says.

a. Sinners Who Cannot See God (1:2)

In this passage Theophilus lists sixteen kinds of sinners who cannot see God (cf. Matt. 5:8) or, in Paul's phrase, "will not inherit the kingdom of God" (I Cor. 6:9-10; cf. Matt. 5:3, 10). All his materials are derived from similar New Testament lists. The first six and the eighth come from I Corinthians 6:8-10; then Theophilus begins to weave together Romans 1:30 (Nos, 7, 10 [φθονερός for φθόνος, Rom. 1: 29], 11, 12 [ὑπερόπτης for ὑπερήφανος], and 15), Titus 1:7 (Nos. 9 and 13), and II Timothy 3:2 (Nos. 11, 12 [ὑπερόπτης for ὑπερήφανος], 14, and 15). The sixteenth, selling of children, is presumably a specific expression of *astorgoi* (Rom. 1:31; II Tim. 3:3) and *prodotai* (II Tim. 3:4).

b. The Emperor (1:11)

Theophilus ends his discussion of the Christian's duty toward the emperor by giving a mosaic of New Testament expressions. "Honor the emperor [I Pet. 2:17] by loving him [Rom. 13:8?], by obeying him [Rom. 13:1, 5; Titus 3:1; I Pet. 2:13], by praying for him [I Tim. 2:1-2]. For by doing this you do the will of God [I Pet. 2:15]." Then follows a quotation from Proverbs 24:21-22, to which I Peter alludes.

c. "Two Ways" (1:14)

Here the "eternal punishments" (singular in Matt. 25:46) are contrasted with the eternal good things resulting from good works. Theophilus relies almost exclusively on a combination of Romans 2:6-9 with I Corinthians 6:9-10 (cf. *Ad Autol.* 1:2) and a partial quotation from I Corinthians 2:9. His mentions of "joy" and "peace" come from Galatians 5:22, "rest" probably from Matthew 11:29, and "illicit idolatries" from I Peter 4:3 (as in 2:34).

d. A List of Vices (2:34)

In this passage we read that the prophets taught men to abstain from illicit idolatry and other things. Here the relationship to the New Testament is not so close, and while some phrases can be paralleled in it, the list seems to be based on the second table of the Decalogue. It ends with the Golden Rule in the negative form found in the "western" text of Acts 15:20 and 29 (and in *Didache* 1:2; but there seems to be no evidence to show that Theophilus used the *Didache*).

e. God's Plan of Redemption (2:27)

One more passage may perhaps show how Theophilus used the New Testament. Here he seems to be elaborating the meaning of Romans 5:17 in a manner quite un-Pauline. "As by disobeying man procured death for himself, so by obeying the will of God he who wills to do so can obtain eternal life for himself. For God gave us a law and holy commandments; everyone who does them [cf. I John 5:2] can be saved [Matt. 19:25; Mark 10:26; Luke 18:26] and, attaining to the resurrection [Heb. 11:35], can inherit imperishability [I Cor. 15:50]." By providing such mosaics Theophilus creates a New Testament theology which reinforces his Jewish-Christian ideas. We may note that when this passage was handed down in the *Sacra Parallela* its emphasis on works was diminished by the omission of "who wills to do so" and "a law and."[27]

[27] K. Holl, *TU* 20/2, 57 (No. 134). The author expresses his thanks for assistance given at various times and in various ways by Professors A. S. Pease, A. D. Nock, and W. C. van Unnik.

6

THE BOOK OF WISDOM AT ALEXANDRIA

Reflections on the History of the Canon and Theology

THE HISTORY of the canon and the history of theology are closely related, especially as regards the use of books viewed as theologically significant. Such a book is the Wisdom of Solomon, which often played an important role in the theological thought of those who accepted it as scripture. Our purpose is to determine what this role was.

First of all it should be stated that while Wisdom was regarded as a part of the Solomonic corpus, and therefore was treated as belonging to the Old Testament rather than to the New, it was not used by Palestinian or Hellenistic Jewish writers; its transmission was a matter only for Christian concern.

A. EARLY USE OF THE BOOK OF WISDOM

Within the New Testament there are no clearly demonstrable allusions to Wisdom except in the Epistle to the Hebrews. Grafe tried to prove that Paul definitely used Wisdom, but as Windisch pointed out his proof is not absolutely conclusive.[1] It is more likely that Paul, like John,[2] knew ideas related to Wisdom but not the book itself. In Hebrews 1:3, however, there is clearly literary dependence on the book of Wisdom. In Wisdom 7:

[1] H. Windisch, "Die göttliche Weisheit der Juden und die paulinische Christologie," *Neutestamentliche Studien G. Heinrici* (Leipzig, 1914), pp. 222-23.

[2] G. Ziener, "Weisheitsbuch und Johannesevangelium," *Biblica,* 38 (1957), 396-418; 39 (1958), 37-60.

25-26 Wisdom is described as "a vapor of the power of God, and an emanation from the pure glory of the Almighty"; she is "radiance from eternal Light and an unspotted mirror of the working of God and an image of his goodness." So in Hebrews the Son of God is called "the radiance of his glory and the express image of his nature."

In *I Clement*, where Hebrews is definitely used (36:2-5), there are also echoes of Wisdom. Death entered the world because of envy (3:4), as in Wisdom 2:24. In generation after generation the Master has given a place of repentance to those who will to turn to him (7:5; Wisdom 12:10). "Who will say to him, What hast thou done? Or who will resist the might of his strength?" (27:5; Wisdom 12:12; 11:21). Ignatius of Antioch, too, makes use of this book. Phrases from Wisdom 7:29-30 and 18:14-15 underlie his description of Christ's manifestation (*Eph.* 19)[3] and the latter passage is reflected in his mention of "the Word proceeding from silence" (*Magn.* 8:2).[4]

Among the second-century apologists there are few traces of Wisdom. Justin never alludes to it, although, as Windisch pointed out, he explicitly called Christ "Wisdom" and used Proverbs 8:22 ff.[5] Melito of Sardis reflects a measure of confusion when he lists Old Testament books read in the East, probably among Jews and mentions Solomon's "Proverbs, also called Wisdom" (Eusebius, *H. E.* 4:26:14). This statement suggests that he did not know the book of Wisdom. The situation in regard to Irenaeus is rather unclear. He definitely alludes once to Wisdom (6:19) in his work *Adversus haereses* (4:38:3, Harvey ed., p. 296), as Eusebius pointed out (*H. E.* 5:8:8). Eusebius also stated (5:26) that in a book now lost Irenaeus mentioned Hebrews and Wisdom, quoting passages from both. Since—according to Stephanus Gobarus (*PG* 103, 1104D)—Irenaeus did not regard Paul as the author of Hebrews, it may be that he supported his opinion by showing that Wisdom was used in Hebrews but not in the Pauline epistles.

[3] See A. Cabaniss in *Vigiliae Christianae,* 10 (1956), 97-102.

[4] Windisch, *op. cit.,* p. 234 n. 1.

[5] *Ibid,* p. 227 n. 1.

On the other hand, Wisdom is definitely mentioned in the Muratorian list as acceptable in the Catholic church and as having been written by Solomon's friends in his honor—though the statement about authorship may suggest that there was some question about the book. And Wisdom 7:25 is certainly in the mind of the apologist Athenagoras, writing about the year 177 perhaps at Alexandria, when he first quotes Proverbs 8:22 ("the Lord created me as the beginning of his ways for his works") and then states that the Holy Spirit which spoke in Proverbs is called by Christians "an emanation of God, flowing forth and borne along as a ray of the sun" (*Legatio ad Graecos* 10:4). The mention of the sun's ray may conceivably reflect a text of Wisdom which, like that underlying the Armenian and Ethiopic versions, read *aktis* instead of *atmis*. It is worth noting that, like his contemporary Theophilus of Antioch, Athenagoras refers Wisdom passages to the Spirit rather than to the Son. This stage of theological development was soon to pass away in Alexandrian thought. More significantly, we see in Athenagoras' semiphilosophical theology that the book of Wisdom was already being used to provide a context, and a correction, for more popular Wisdom passages which might be taken either mythologically or too literally. He uses "emanation" to correct the word "created."

Within the next generation at Alexandria Wisdom was clearly and definitely treated as scripture. Clement so refers to it (*Str.* 5:108:2; 6:92:3) and he says that it was written by Solomon (6:93:2; 110:1; 114:1; 120:3). In his major writings, however, he never alludes to the important christological passage—Wisdom 7:25-26—of which later Alexandrians made much use. It can be traced, however, in a fragment to which we shall presently turn.

Origen has to admit (*De principiis* 4:6:6) that "it does not have authority in all things," but he himself uses it without any hesitation; those who do not use the book may perhaps be Jews. In later works he sometimes calls it *ἡ ἐπιγεγραμμένη τοῦ Σολομῶντος Σοφία* (e. g., *In Iohannem commentarius* 20:4, Preuschen ed., p. 331, 32; *Contra Celsum* 5:29); but this is what he had already said in *De principiis* (Koetschau ed., p. 33, 9): *Sapientia quae dicitur Salomonis*. Since in the late *Contra Celsum* (3:72) he cites Wisdom 7:25-26 as from "the divine word," neither the omission of

Wisdom from a list of Old Testament books "according to the Hebrews" (Eusebius, *H. E.* 6:25:2) nor his discussion of Jewish usage in the preface to his commentary on the Song of Songs (Baehrens ed., pp. 87-88) proves anything about his own attitude.[6]

B. CLEMENT'S THEOLOGICAL INTERPRETATION

We have already indicated that Clement did not entirely neglect Wisdom 7:25-26. In his lost *Hypotyposes* as described by Photius there is a clear allusion to these verses, and it occurs in a passage which Photius explicitly quotes (*PG* 103, 348B)[7]:

> The Son is also called Logos, with the same name as the paternal Logos, but he is a certain power of God such as an emanation of his Logos.

According to Photius, Clement tried to demonstrate the truth of his statement by using "some expressions of scripture." As he did so he could have found "emanation" (*aporroia*) only in Wisdom 7:25. We may add that if he regarded the Son as a power of God and because of (*aporroia*) also as the Wisdom of God, he doubtless had I Corinthians 1:24 in mind – as well as the *logos endiathetos* and *logos prophorikos* which R. P. Casey mentioned in his discussion of this passage.[8]

It is conceivable that this fragment of the *Hypotyposes* deals with what Clement on other occasions regarded as belonging to his secret tradition, for this tradition included ideas about "the Uncreated and his powers" (*Str.* 5:80:3). Perhaps, then, Clement refrained from quoting Wisdom 7:25-26 in his other works because exegesis of these verses was not to be divulged to the uninitiate.[9]

[6] See also R. P. C. Hanson, *Origen's Doctrine of Tradition* (London, 1954), pp. 45-46.

[7] Clement, Stählin ed., Vol. 3, p. 202 (fragment 23).

[8] "Clement and the Two Divine Logoi," *Journal of Theological Studies,* 25 (1923-24), 43-56; see also H. A. Wolfson, *The Philosophy of the Church Fathers,* 1 (Cambridge, Mass., 1956), 204-17.

[9] On this matter see Hanson, *op. cit.,* pp. 53-72.

C. ORIGEN'S THEOLOGICAL INTERPRETATION

Close to the beginning of the treatise *De principiis* (1:2:9 ff.) Origen provides an elaborate explanation of the christological meaning of Wisdom 7:25-26; unlike Clement he does not keep traditions secret. The term "vapor of the power of God" means that God's Wisdom, i. e., his Son, is the "strength" of God's power as exercised in creation and in providential care; like Clement (if our interpretation is correct) Origen then relates this exegesis to I Corinthians 1:24. The expression "emanation from the glory of the Almighty" means that Christ was the agent of Omnipotence in creation and in dominion over all; here Origen quotes John 1:3 ("all things came into existence through him") and 17:10 ("thine are mine, and I have been glorified in them"). Wisdom is radiance from God who is Light (cf. I John 1:5) and is analogous to the rays of the sun. As a mirror of the working of God, Wisdom perfectly portrays the Father, for the Son does what he sees the Father doing (John 5:19). Finally, since the Son is the "image of the Father's goodness," we understand how Jesus can say, "No one is good but God" (Mark 10:18; Luke 18:19). The Father alone is perfectly God; the Son proceeds from the Father; and in a Greek fragment from Justinian Origen explicitly denies that the Son is *autoagathos*.[10]

Similar points are made in Origen's exegetical works. In his ninth homily on Jeremiah (Klostermann ed., p. 70) he explains rather simply that the expression "radiance of glory" (Heb. 1:3) should be understood by analogy to the sun and its radiance: as long as the light produces the radiance, so long the radiance of God's glory is being generated. "Our Savior is the Wisdom of God; and Wisdom is 'the radiance of eternal light' [Wisd. 7:26]." This inference proves the existence of the eternal generation, confirmed by the use of the present tense in another Wisdom text, Proverbs 8:25. Again, in the commentary on John he insists that the Son as Wisdom is the image of God's goodness (6:57, Preuschen ed., p. 166, 6; 13:36, p. 261, 27). In *In Iohannem*

[10] *De principiis* 1:2:13; see also H. Crouzel, *Théologie de l'image de Dieu chez Origène* (Paris, 1956), pp. 95-98.

commentarius 13:25 (pp. 249, 29–250, 3) Origen provides the following exegesis for John 14:28, "The Father is greater than I":

> He is the "image of his goodness" and "radiance" not of God but of his glory and of his "eternal light," and "vapor" not of the Father but of his "power" and pure "emanation" of his omnipotent "glory" and "unspotted mirror of his working"—the mirror through which Paul and Peter and those like them see God, since he says, "He who has seen me has seen the Father [John 14:9] who sent me [12:45]."

Finally, in the late *In Matthaeum commentarius* (Klostermann ed., pp. 375-76) Origen discusses the same texts and reaches similar conclusions. He admits that the Son is called the image of God (Col. 1:15) but interprets this text in relation to Mark 10:18 (Luke 18:19) and John 14:28; the Savior is the image of God's goodness (Wisd. 7:26).

Nothing new occurs in the late apologetic work *Contra Celsum.* Here Origen contrasts the Stoic definition of wisdom with the picture provided in "the divine word" (3:62); he uses the phrase "radiance of eternal light" to prove that neither Jews nor Christians worship the sun, moon, and stars (5:10); and in describing the Son of God he uses both Hebrews 1:3 and Wisdom 7:25-26 (8:14). The subordinationist motif is maintained when he says that the *autologos*, the *autoalētheia*, the *autosophia* is "the image of his goodness" (6:63).

Obviously Origen believes that his christological synthesis is biblical in nature. It is a question whether or not it is entirely biblical in origin. The philosophical framework of his ideas seems to be derived from Middle Platonism, perhaps especially as set forth in the writings of Numenius – to which he refers in the treatise *Contra Celsum.* Numenius had stated, as we learn from Eusebius, that

> the first god is good-in-himself [*autoagathon*], while his imitator, the demiurge, is good [*agathos*]; the *ousia* of the first is one, while that of the second is another; the beautiful cosmos is a copy of the latter, made beautiful by participation [*metousia*] in the beautiful.[11]

[11] Leemans ed., p. 141, 3-6 (fragment 25) [Eusebius, *Praeparatio evangelica* 11:22].

In Numenius' view Plato (*Timaeus* 28c) had taught that only the demiurge is known among men, whereas the first mind, who is called the self-existent, is absolutely unknown among them.[12] It seems fairly clear that Origen developed his views in a context of this kind. For him the Father (a term also used of the first god by Numenius) is unknown to men except through the Son. The Father is good-in-himself, while the goodness of the Son is derived from that of the Father. Given such a starting point, it was inevitable that the verses from Wisdom should be pressed into service – the service of Christian Platonism.

The extent of his philosophical interpretation of Wisdom can be seen from his statement that Proverbs 8:22 ff., with its reference to Wisdom as "the beginning of God's ways," shows that she "contained within herself the beginnings or ideas or forms of the whole creation" (*De principiis* 1:2:2, Koetschau ed., p. 30, 7-8; cf. *In Iohannem commentarius* 1:19, Preuschen ed., p. 24, 2.). Wisdom is the bridge, so to speak, between the Bible and the Platonic "intelligible cosmos." [13]

Now, given all this philosophical background, and its tendency (like that of much biblical language) toward a subordinationist Christology, we encounter a difficult problem when we find Pamphilus (*PG* 14, 1308CD) quoting a fragment of Origen's exegesis of Hebrews in which the word *homoousios* occurs. As usual, Origen turns from Hebrews to the Wisdom of Solomon (7:25).

> Both of these comparisons ["vapor," "emanation"] most clearly prove that there is a sharing of substance by the Son with the Father. For "emanation" seems to be one substance *homoousios* with that body from which it is either an "emanation" or a "vapor."

Obviously this statement disagrees with what Numenius had said about the different *ousiai* of the first god and the demiurge; but there is no reason to suppose that Origen, who regarded revelation as superior to philosophical reason, could not have contradicted a philosopher, even one who was often right. More-

[12] Leemans ed., p. 141, 9-12 (fragment 26) [Eusebius, *Praeparatio evangelica* 11:18].

[13] On Origen's intelligible cosmos, see Wolfson, *op. cit.*, pp. 27-80.

over, subordinationism is only one aspect of Origen's Christology; the eternal generation of the Son plainly implies that the Son is consubstantial with the Father. And Origen's exegetical works as a whole demonstrate that he could, and did, look at his texts from various aspects, extracting every possible shade of meaning from them. We therefore regard this passage as genuine.[14]

From what we have already said it is clear that Wisdom 7:25-26 is a key passage in Origen's theology. It was important not only in itself but because it provided clear testimony to the revelation of the Son in the Old Testament.

D. DIONYSIUS' THEOLOGICAL INTERPRETATION

It is well known that Dionysius of Rome, and others, found the Alexandrians' theology rather difficult to understand. In his reply to his Roman namesake, Dionysius of Alexandria followed the lines already laid down by Origen. God was always Father, since Christ was always his Logos and Sophia and Power. Dionysius proved his point by appealing to Wisdom 7:26 (Feltoe ed., pp. 186, 11–187, 3).

> Since he is "radiance of eternal light," he is absolutely eternal. For since the light always exists, obviously there is always radiance. The existence of light is known by its casting radiance, and there cannot be non-illuminating light. Again, let us come to the examples: if there is a sun, there is a ray and there is daylight . . . .

Dionysius concludes by appealing to a Wisdom passage in Proverbs 8:30. A little later he returns to the book of Wisdom (Feltoe ed., p. 187, 17-21).

> Since God is light [I John 1:5], Christ is "radiance." Since he is spirit—for God, it says, is spirit [John 4:24] — analogously Christ is also called "vapor"; for, it says, he "is a vapor of the power of God" [Wisd. 7, 25].

Finally, Dionysius also argues that as God is the source of all

[14] Crouzel (*op. cit.,* p. 99) argues first for the authenticity of the fragment, then for its place in Origen's thought; our arguments converge.

good things the "river" that flows from him is designated as the Son (Feltoe ed., pp. 190, 15–191, 1).

> For logos [reason-word] is an "emanation" [Wisd. 7:25] from the mind. . . .

It is obvious that Dionysius is a fairly faithful adherent of Origen's teaching, specifically in regard to the christological application of Wisdom. He clearly differentiates two stages in the expression of the Logos (Feltoe ed., p. 191, 1-7; p. 197, 1-19). He does not appeal to Origen as the originator or transmitter of his teaching, however. As Bouma points out, Dionysius, like Origen, based his theology on scripture—even though in both cases the appeal to scripture is not altogether transparent.[15]

E. WISDOM IN THEOGNOSTUS

It has long been recognized that Wisdom is utilized in the fragment of Theognostus which Diekamp first published.[16] Theognostus lays considerable emphasis on the scriptural title "Wisdom." Logos, he says, refers to the outward expression of the thoughts contained in the mind of the Father, while Sophia "is better able to indicate the multitude of conceptions contained in him." At the end of the fragment he explicitly states that "he is also called radiance of the glory of God [Heb. 1:3] and unspotted mirror [Wisd. 7:26], terms which in a variety of ways preserve the idea of the Image." Since he is obviously making use of the Wisdom passage it may well be that when he says that "there is one Logos and one Sophia" he has in mind the mention of one Sophia in Wisdom 7:27.

More significant, but perhaps not usually noticed, is Theognostus' use of Wisdom in a fragment (Harnack ed., fragment 2) preserved by Athanasius (*PG* 25, 460c). Here he reiterates what

[15] S. J. Bouma, *Dionysius van Alexandrië,* (Purmerend, 1943), p. 137. The comparison of the Logos to a river flowing from the fountain which must be God's Wisdom is to be found in Philo, *De somniis* 2:42 (cf. *De fuga* 97, *Quod deterius* 115; H. Leisegang in *RE* 3A,1033).

[16] *Theologische Quartalschrift,* 84 (1902), 483-84; Harnack, *TU* 24/3, 77-78 (No. 4).

Origen had said about the *ousia* of the Son and develops his thought by using one of Origen's favorite proof-texts.

> The *ousia* of the Son originated from the *ousia* of the Father like radiance [Wisd. 7: 26] from light, like vapor [7:25] from water. The radiance is not the sun nor is the vapor the water, nor is it something foreign. The [*ousia* of the Son] is not the Father himself nor is it something foreign, but it is an emanation [7:25] from the *ousia* of the Father, without the *ousia* of the Father undergoing division. As the sun remains the same and is not diminished by the rays which poured forth from it, so the *ousia* of the Father underwent no alteration by having the Son as its image [7:26].

The outline of Theognostus' analysis is clearly provided by Wisdom 7:25-26.

Theognostus may also have relied on these verses when he argued, as Photius states (*PG* 103, 376), that the Son was limited by time and space, unlimited only in his activity (*energeia*). Presumably Theognostus shared Origen's view that only God could not be limited by time and space (*In Iohannem commentarius* 10: 4, Preuschen ed., pp. 174, 29—175, 3), but that the Son imitates the activity of the Father. Certainly he held that the Son was an "imprint of the *ousia* of the Father" [17] (cf. Heb. 1:3); one might suppose that he regarded the Son as the mirror of God's activity (Wisd. 7:26).

This Alexandrian teacher is especially interesting because he seems to make use of ideas derived from most of his predecessors. The title *Hypotyposes* may be derived from Clement, and his treatment of Sophia and Logos as equivalent to the *logos endiathetos* and *logos prophorikos* reminds us of both Clement and Philo.[18] The word he uses for "imprint," *ekmageion*, occurs in Philo (*Heres* 230). And when he says that "when God willed to fashion this universe he first hypostatized the Son as a kind of standard [*kanōn*] of the creative work," [19] we are reminded of Philo, who calls the ideas *kanones* (*De sacrificiis Abelis et Caini* 59) and says that when God willed to fashion this visible universe

[17] Harnack ed., p. 78 (fragment 4).

[18] *Ibid.*, p. 77 (fragment 3). Theognostus uses the definitions, not the terms.

[19] *Ibid.*, p. 77; Gregory of Nyssa, *Contra Eunomium,* Lib. 3, Tom. 2 (Jaeger ed., Vol. 2, p. 86, 24-26; *PG* 45, 661D).

he first prefigured the intelligible one as a model (*De opificio mundi* 16). Harnack was largely, but not entirely, right when he called Theognostus a rigorously traditionalist disciple of Origen.[20]

What is reflected without any question is the common Alexandrian use of Wisdom 7:25-26 for a semiphilosophical Christology.

F. OTHER INTERPRETATIONS OF WISDOM

Thus far we have seen that at Alexandria the biblical personification of Wisdom was kept relatively free of mythology because it was interpreted in relation to the Son and to a Platonic-Philonic conception of the intelligible world. The key passage in the book of Wisdom, 7:25-26, was viewed as an expression of philosophical theology.

Such was not always the case, even at Alexandria. Philo himself occasionally used mythological expressions, notably in his treatise *De ebrietate* 30-31, where he spoke of God as Father and Sophia as Mother, with "this world" as their "only and beloved son perceptible to the senses." He quoted Proverbs 8:22 and stated that it referred to "the mother and nurse of all." The quotation and the exegesis are important. First, this is Philo's only quotation of this verse from Proverbs; he never uses the other literature (Ecclesiastes, Song of Songs, Wisdom) ascribed to Solomon.[21] Second, H. A. Wolfson has explained Philo's exegesis of Proverbs in relation to its Hebrew text. By altering the vocalization of אמון in Proverbs 8:30 one could read אָמָּן or "fashioner" (*τεχνῖτις* in Wisd. 7:22); one could read אֹמֵן, "nurse"; or even אִמָּן, "their mother" (*γενέτις* in Wisd. 7:11-12).[22]

Wolfson points out that this exegesis is rabbinic in form and content. It is also Gnostic. Among the Valentinians, the fallen Sophia was called Achamoth. This mysterious name, with its

[20] *Op. cit.*, p. 92.

[21] H. E. Ryle, *Philo and Holy Scripture* (London, 1895), pp. xxviii-xxix; xxxiii-iv.

[22] *Philo*, 1 (Cambridge, Mass., 1947), 266-69.

plural ending, is certainly derived from Proverbs 9:1, where the Hebrew word for "wisdom" appears in the plural and is used with a singular verb.[23] We know that the Valentinians used this verse because it is quoted in Clement, *Excerpta ex Theodoto* 47:1, and referred to "the second Sophia." Gnostic speculation about this Hebrew word also occurs in the *Gospel of Philip* (p. 108, 11-12): there is not only *Echamoth* (interpreted as σοφία ἁπλῶς) but also *Echmoth*, the "wisdom of death," presumably because in Hebrew מות means "death."

The kind of speculation reflected in Philo and made explicit among the Valentinians recurs in the book *Baruch* by the Gnostic Justin (Hippolytus, *Ref.* 5:26:3). Here we learn that there are twenty-four angels, twelve of Elohim and twelve of Eden. The second angel of Elohim is called Amen; the second of Eden, Achamoth. This notion presumably reflects the references to Wisdom as אָמָן and as חָכְמוֹת in the book of Proverbs.

More venturesomely, we may suggest that a strange picture of the fall provided by the semi-Gnostic apologist Tatian (*Or.* 7, Schwartz ed., pp. 7, 25–8, 1) is based on Gnostic speculation about the Wisdom literature. Tatian says that men followed the "first-born" demon, who was "wiser" (Gen. 3:1) than others. Why is he called "first-born" (*prōtogonos*)? Maran thought that Tatian was alluding to the creature which according to Job (40:14, LXX; 40:19, Heb.) was formed as an *archē* or a ראשית and was called Behemoth (40:15, Heb.). One might even imagine that as the good Wisdom could be called Achamoth so the bad wisdom could be Behemoth–but this is probably going too far.

In opposition to mythological speculations of this kind, and of other kinds, Tertullian (*Adversus Valentinianos* 2) contrasts the Sophia of the Valentinians with the true Sophia of Solomon in the book of Wisdom.

G. CONCLUSION

The passages with which we have just been dealing show conclusively that some Gnostics, at least, were very fond of the

[23] See also Prov. 1:20; 14:1; 24:7.

Wisdom literature, but not of the Wisdom of Solomon. Indeed, there seem to be no traces of its use in their extant writings. On the other hand, the philosophical leaders of the school of Alexandria incessantly used the book of Wisdom in support of their christological views. This is to say that by including Wisdom in their canon of scripture they were able to interpret the other Wisdom literature in its light and to avoid the mythological speculations of the Gnostics. It was an indispensable resource for philosophical theology. We may doubt that this situation necessarily sheds any light on the origin of the book, but it does explain why, from the late second century onward, Alexandrian theologians regarded the book as an indispensable portion of the Old Testament.

III
EARLY CHRISTIANITY AND GRECO-ROMAN CULTURE

7

EARLY CHRISTIANITY AND PRE-SOCRATIC PHILOSOPHY

In Greco-Roman schools the study of philosophy often included use of collections of philosophical opinions arranged according to subjects, historical sketches of the rise and development of various schools, and—more as a branch of rhetoric than as a branch of philosophy—collections of piquant anecdotes about the philosophers' lives and deaths. For the early centuries of our era the collections of opinions are exemplified by the works edited by Hermann Diels in his *Doxographi Graeci*, while historical materials and anecdotes characterize the "lives of the philosophers" by Diogenes Laertius. In addition, there were in circulation various books, more or less ancient, which purported to contain the teachings of some of the more important wise men and philosophers of the remote past. Especially in the second century there was a remarkable rise of enthusiasm for the study of ancient thinkers, both Greek and oriental. This enthusiasm is reflected in the works of Plutarch, Numenius, Celsus, Maximus of Tyre, Sextus Empiricus, and Diogenes Laertius; in later times it was prominent among the Neo-Platonists.

Writing in the early first century, Philo of Alexandria had paid little attention to any of these primitive writers, though he sometimes used Heraclitus and Pythagoras; in his writings even the name of Thales, the first of the pre-Socratics, never occurs.[1] The situation was different by the time when Greek Christians were ready to come to terms with Greco-Roman culture, and therefore, as we shall see, Christian writers were much more concerned with the oldest writers.

[1] See H. A. Wolfson, *Philo* (see above, p. 80 n. 22), Vol. 1, pp. 85-86. Fragments of the pre-Socratics are cited from *Vorsokr.*

We shall begin our consideration of Christian use of pre-Socratic thought by examining the traces of early cosmological poetry that are ascribed to Orpheus, Musaeus, Epimenides, and Pherecydes of Syros.[2]

A. COSMOLOGICAL POETRY

a. Orphica

Apart from a possible, if unlikely, allusion to Orphic teaching in James 3:6, with its reference to "the wheel of birth," [3] there are no traces of Christian acquaintance with Orphic literature before the time of Athenagoras, rather late in the second century. When Athenagoras and other contemporary Christian apologists used the writings of Orpheus, they were participating in the literary discussion which flourished in their time. First, there was widespread interest in the writings of very ancient sages and seers; second, there was concern for the way in which such writings had originated and had been transmitted. Athenagoras says nothing about the second question. He is concerned only with what Orpheus taught and with pointing out how much inferior it is to Christian doctrine.[4] On the other hand, Tatian—more rhetorician than philosopher—quotes only one line from the Orphic poems, "Close the gates against the profane!" [5] but tells us more about Orpheus and "history." Orpheus taught the Greeks poetry and song and introduced them to the mysteries (*Or.* 1); he lived in the time of Heracles, before the Trojan war, and had Musaeus as a disciple (*Or.* 39, 41). In addition, Tatian knows the current theory that "all the works attributed to him were composed by Onomacritus the Athenian, who lived during the reign of the Pisistratids, about the fiftieth Olympiad" (*Or.* 41). This theory, which seems to be based on the statement of Herodotus

[2] Christian use of Homer and Hesiod deserves a separate analysis. On Homer see J. Daniélou, *Message évangélique et culture hellénistique* (Tournai, 1961), pp. 73-101.

[3] On this verse cf. J. H. Ropes, *The Epistle of St. James* (New York, 1916), pp. 235-39.

[4] *Legatio ad Graecos* 18:3-6; 20:1-5; 22:4; 32:1.

[5] *Or.* 8 (Schwartz ed., p. 9, 10); see fragments 59, 245-47, 334 in O. Kern, *Orphicorum fragmenta* (Berlin, 1922).

(7:6) that Onomacritus collected and edited the oracles of Musaeus, was widespread in the late second century, and was advocated by writers as diverse in outlook as Pausanias, Sextus Empiricus, and Clement of Alexandria.[6]

Theophilus of Antioch refers to the Orphic cosmogony indirectly when he quotes Aristophanes, *Aves* 695 (*Ad Autol.* 2:7), but since he does not regard the cosmogony as Orphic we need not discuss it at this point. The only explicit references to Orpheus occur in the third book, written fairly soon after the death of Marcus Aurelius (the other two books cannot be dated). Here he tells us that, like Homer and Hesiod, Orpheus claimed to have been "instructed by divine providence" (3:17, perhaps a reference to fragment 62 in Kern, but not necessarily so). More important, he knows that while Orpheus earlier believed in the existence of 365 gods, at the end of his life he rejected them, "maintaining in his Testaments that there is one God" (3:2). This statement is significant because it reflects the existence of the Jewish or Christian forgery also used in the writings of Clement of Alexandria, Pseudo-Justin (*Cohortatio*, *De monarchia*), and in the work ascribed to Aristobulus by Eusebius.[7] Orpheus has been recognized as a theological authority notable enough to have monotheism ascribed to him.

It is thus no surprise to find that about half the citations from the "theologian," "poet," and "hierophant" Orpheus which Clement provides come from the *Testaments*. Clement also knows the theories about the authorship of Orphic literature; he tells us that it is said to come from Onomacritus and that some oracles are referred to Musaeus (*Str.* 1:131); he himself ascribes four fragments to Musaeus (*Vorsokr.* B4-7).

Orthodox Christians were not the only ones to use Orphic materials, for in the *Refutatio* by Hippolytus we find Orphic verses being quoted both by the Naassenes and the Sethians.[8]

But while this literature continued to be employed by Christian apologists,[9] it is probably significant that none of the twelve

[6] Cf. I. M. Linforth, *The Arts of Orpheus* (Berkeley, 1941), pp. 330-52.

[7] Cf. O. Kern, *op cit.*, pp. 255-56.

[8] *Ref.* 5:8:43; 5:9:8; 5:19:11; 5:20:4-8.

[9] Pseudo-Justin, Arnobius, Lactantius; also the Clementine *Homilies/Recognitions*.

quotations in the *Praeparatio Evangelica* of Eusebius was made directly; all occur in quotations from quoters. After his time interest in Orphic literature was largely confined to Neo-Platonist writers.

b. Epimenides

Another shadowy sixth-century writer on cosmology was Epimenides of Crete, who may have provided the line "in him we live and move and are" which we find in Acts 17:28. The reasons for such an ascription of the line are discussed by K. Lake, but any conclusion is most uncertain.[10] There is better evidence for giving Epimenides the famous words assigned to a Cretan "prophet" in Titus 1:12: "Cretans are always liars, evil beasts, lazy gluttons." Clement of Alexandria (*Str.* 1:59:1) is the first to identify this quotation as coming from Epimenides.[11]

But early Christian writers made little use of Epimenides. Tatian (*Or.* 41) identified him only as a pre-Homeric writer who came to Sparta (cf. Clement, *Str.* 1:133:2). Clement knew nothing significant about him and contributed only the identification which we have mentioned. The rest is silence.

c. Pherecydes

Among the sixth-century wise men whose memory was revered in Hellenistic and Roman times was Pherecydes of Syros, but early Christian writers made little use of the writings ascribed to him. He appears in Tatian (*Or.* 3) only as the teacher of Pythagoras, though Clement refers to his "theology" (*Str.* 5: 50:3) and quotes a fragment (*Str.* 6:9:4). The anti-Christian writer Celsus quoted from him.[12] He seems to have been more popular among Gnostics, since he was mentioned by Isidore, son of the famous Basilides of Alexandria;[13] and there is probably an allusion to his "marriage of Zeus" in the book *Baruch* by the Gnostic Justin.[14]

[10] F.J.F. Jackson-K. Lake, *The Beginnings of Christianity,* 5 (London, 1933), pp. 247-51.

[11] Cf. C. Spicq, *Les épîtres pastorales* (Paris, 1947), pp. 242-44.

[12] Origen, *Contra Celsum* 6:42; see H.O. Schröder in *Hermes,* 74 (1939), 108-10.

[13] Clement, *Str.* 6:53:5.

[14] See chap. 13 below.

d. The Seven Wise Men

The only early apologist who alludes to the seven wise men of Greece is Tatian, and at the point where he does so something seems to have gone wrong with the text (*Or.* 41). He tells us first about "the men who are esteemed wise"–Minos, Lycurgus, Draco, Solon, and Pythagoras; then he indicates that all of them lived after Moses. (Minos lived eleven generations after Inachus, Moses' contemporary; Lycurgus, after the capture of Troy; the others, after the Olympiads began.)

> We have shown [*Or.* 31] that the Olympiads began 407 years after the capture of Troy. Since these facts have been demonstrated, we shall make brief remarks about the age of the seven wise men. The oldest of these, Thales, lived about the fiftieth Olympiad; and I have already spoken briefly of those who came after him.

But Tatian has mentioned only one wise man, Pythagoras, who conceivably could be dated later than Thales. Therefore we must assume that "the men who are esteemed wise" must be different from the seven wise men, and that the names of the latter group have dropped out of the text.

Thus we do not know whom Tatian regarded as the seven wise men. Generally, Greco-Roman writers agreed in including the names of Thales, Bias, Pittacus, and Solon; the other three varied.[15] Two lists from the late second century are in agreement as to the seven names, though not as to their order. They include the four already mentioned and, in addition, Chilon, Cleobulus, and Periander.[16]

Clement of Alexandria used a source about the seven wise men which divided them into geographical groups, pointed out the differences in the traditions, and set forth the sayings traditionally ascribed to them (*Str.* 1:59:1–61:4). This source presumably gave him the materials with which he continued to discuss the early history of philosophy and the successions in various schools

[15] Note that Tatian treats Solon not as one of the seven but as a lawgiver (cf. Theophilus, *Ad Autol.* 3:6, and the list published by H. Diels in *Abhandlungen der preussischen Akademie zu Berlin, Philos.-hist. Kl.* (1904), No. 2, p. 6, col 6).

[16] Diogenes Laertius 1:13 (cf. 41-42); Hyginus, *Fabulae* 221 (Rose ed., pp. 144-45).

(1:62 ff.). He assigned dates to only two of the wise men (Thales, Olympiad 50; Solon, Olympiad 46), in both instances deriving the dates from Tatian.[17] At another point, probably once more making use of Tatian, he refers to "Lycurgus and Solon and the seven wise men" (1:107:5).

For Clement the only correlation between Christianity and the wise men seems to be through Epimenides, who as we have seen was quoted by Paul. Clement says that Epimenides was sometimes regarded as the seventh of the wise men (*Str.* 1:59:2).

Some of Clement's materials about the seven are clearly derived —ultimately—from Aristotle's treatise *On Philosophy*, as Festugière and Daniélou have pointed out.[18]

B. THE HISTORY OF GREEK PHILOSOPHY

Before dealing directly with the use of pre-Socratic (or, more accurately, pre-Platonic) philosophy among early Christian writers we should say something about the ideas of the early history of philosophy which are to be found among them.

Wolfson has shown (*Philo* [see above, p. 80 n. 22], Vol. 1, pp. 141-42) that in Philo there seem to be three views of the origin of true statements among early Greek philosophers. (1) Sometimes philosophers are regarded as having derived some of their ideas from the Old Testament. (2) Sometimes they seem to have used "their native reason." (3) Sometimes philosophy is regarded as a divine gift to the Greeks—a conception intimated in the *Timaeus* of Plato (47b). It should be stated, however, that these views are not highly developed in Philo. We cannot say that he was deeply concerned with the question, partly because in his view the revelation given through Moses was chronologically prior to the rise of Greek philosophy. He did not have to be concerned with a revelation later in date than the philosophers.

[17] *Str.* 1:65:1-3. Tatian's date for Thales seems to be unique.

[18] A.-J. Festugière, *La Révélation d'Hermès Trismégiste,* 2 (Paris, 1949), 224; Daniélou, *op. cit.,* p. 127.

The question about the history of Greek philosophy had to be considered more fully by early Christian writers, the most important of whom were Justin and Clement. Before turning to them we should briefly discuss the less significant contributions made by Tatian, Theophilus, and Irenaeus.

Tatian wrote a violent attack upon Greek culture in general, and few of his criticisms of philosophy give any indications that he understood it. Toward the beginning of his *Oration* there is an attack upon the "arrogance" of Greek philosophers (*Or.* 2-3), based on gossip like that related by Diogenes Laertius. The philosophers "dogmatize," but their views are really based on "probable conjectures and sophistical reasoning" (*Or.* 12); they contradict one another (*Or.* 25). Of their views Tatian knows little more than could be found in doxographical collections. He adds that since Thales, oldest of the seven wise men, lived about the fiftieth Olympiad he was obviously later than Moses (*Or.* 41).

Theophilus agrees with Tatian's skeptical view that Greek philosophy and theology is based on nothing but conjecture. Homer and Hesiod made use of "hypothesis" (*Ad Autol.* 2:5-6), and indeed all the theological poets taught "by conjecture and human understanding"—though sometimes they came to be free from demons, became sober, and agreed with the prophets (2:8). What he says of the poets obviously applies to the philosophers, for he devotes considerable space to arguing that Plato, "who seems to have been the wisest of the Greeks," actually spoke by "conjecture"; he proves this point by quoting *Republic* 683 b-c (3:16). Like Tatian, but more elaborately, he uses doxographical materials to show that the philosophers contradicted one another (2:4; 3:7). Their doctrines were not only contradictory but futile (3:2). Once more, there is no intelligent understanding of Greek philosophy, and therefore there is no need to analyze its history.

Irenaeus too is most unsympathetic. He has a certain enthusiasm for Plato, since he said (*Timaeus* 29e) that the Demiurge is good; therefore he was better than the Gnostic Marcion (*Adv. haer.* 3:25:3-5, Harvey ed., pp. 135-36).[19] This is not to say that

[19] Irenaeus also quotes *Leges* 715e-716a.

Plato was very good. Indeed, his doctrine about reincarnation and the cup of oblivion is positively bad; Plato provided no proof for it but simply made a dogmatic statement (2:33:1-2, p. 377). This statement may reflect, at some remove, the Academic and Skeptical discussions of whether or not Plato was a dogmatist (Cicero, *Academica* 1:46; *Lucullus* 74; Sextus Empiricus, *Pyrroneioi hypotyposeis* 1:221-25).

As for pre-Platonic philosophy, what Irenaeus knows of it is derived primarily from doxographical sources. In *Adv. haer.* 2:14:2-6 (Harvey ed., pp. 289-96) he explains that the ancient philosophers were atheists, since they provided materialistic or, at any rate, nontheological explanations of the origins of things. Thales and Homer mentioned water. Anaximander spoke of "the boundless"—which, Irenaeus adds, contained in itself "seminally" the origin of all; his addition may be derived from Stoic sources or, more probably, his own effort to relate early philosophy to Gnosticism. Anaxagoras, "who was called atheus" (Irenaeus seems to be substituting *atheus* for *physicus*), taught that animate beings were made from seeds which fell from heaven. Diels (*Dox.* 94, 172) has shown that Anaxagoras is probably confused with Euripides; we may add that the confusion may have been intentional, since Irenaeus is comparing this view with Gnostic ideas about descents. A similar observation can be made about what Irenaeus says of Democritus, who "first said that many and various forms [i.e., *eidōla*] descended from the whole into this world." The rest of what Irenaeus relates is either simply doxographical or derived from current criticisms, especially of the Cynics and of the *minutiloquium* of Aristotelians (compare Justin).

Irenaeus' sole purpose in discussing early Greek philosophy is to show that Gnostic ideas are derived from it. The water of Thales is the Bythos of Gnostic schemes; the Boundless and its seeds are Bythos and the Aeons; the seeds which Irenaeus ascribes to Anaxagoras are those which come from the Mother in Valentinian thought; and the Void and atoms of Democritus are equivalent to the Valentinian Pleroma—so he claims.

It cannot be said, therefore, that Irenaeus is really acquainted with the history of Greek philosophy; indeed, he distorts it for polemical reasons. Only when he does not recognize an idea as philosophical can he accept it (see below).

The situation is quite different when we turn to the more philosophical Christianity represented by Justin and Clement.

Justin's ideas about the history of philosophy are like his philosophical ideas generally, which C. Andresen and W. Schmid have conclusively demonstrated to have come from Middle Platonism.[20] Philosophy, he says as a Platonist, is a divine gift which "was sent down to men" (*Dial.* 2:6). Here, like Philo, he echoes the statement of Plato in *Timaeus* 47b (compare also Cicero [Posidonius?] in *Tusculanae disputationes* 1:64 and Clement, *Str.* 1:36:1). The statement is made more precise by the Middle Platonist Atticus: Plato was "so to speak truly sent down from the gods" (Eusebius, *Praeparatio evangelica* 11:2:4). But we shall presently see that Justin usually has Socrates rather than Plato in mind, or at least the Socratic Plato. Therefore he (or his teacher) may have had in view the idea of Antiochus of Ascolon —highly influential in Middle Platonism—that Socrates "first called philosophy down from heaven" (Cicero, *Tusculanae disputationes* 5:10). By this statement Antiochus meant that Socrates turned from the obscurities of physics to the study of ethics (*Academica* 1:15).

Originally this heaven-sent philosophy was one, at a time when there were no Platonists, Stoics, Peripatetics, Theoretics, or Pythagoreans (*Dial.* 2:1). Only later did followers of the first philosophers stop investigating the truth (Socrates investigated, Plato, *Apologia* 28e, 38a). These followers simply admired the perseverance, self-control, and remarkable language of their predecessors, and regarded whatever they said as true. The epigoni were content to transmit what their teachers taught, though with some additions to it. For this reason they were known by the name of "the source of the teaching" (a Platonic expression, *Symposium* 177d, *Phaedrus* 257b).

Such an idea was characteristic of eclecticism in the Hellenistic age, especially as represented by Antiochus. In his view the true

[20] C. Andresen in *Zeitschrift für die neutestamentliche Wissenschaft,* 44 (1952-53), 157-95; also *Logos und Nomos* (Berlin, 1955); W. Schmid in *Hermeneia Regenbogen* (Heidelberg, 1952), pp. 163-82.

philosophy, chiefly ethical (Socrates!), was maintained both by the Academy and by Peripatetics as late as the time of Polemo, and even by Polemo's pupils Arcesilas and Zeno (Cicero, *De finibus* 4:3; *Academica* 1:34-35). The original unity was broken when Stoicism came into existence as a sect. (It was fairly easy for Antiochus to maintain this view because in his time the esoteric writings of Aristotle were lost.) Later on, this picture was modified. Numenius of Apamea, for example, maintained that the true Platonic doctrine had been abandoned in the early Academy, by Speusippus, Xenocrates, and Polemo themselves (Eusebius, *Praeparatio evangelica* 14:5:1). Justin's view is close to that of Numenius, for he laments the existence even of "Platonists."

The idea of the original unity of philosophy was, of course, dear to eclectic philosophers—like Justin. "Whatever is said well by anyone belongs to us Christians" (*Apol.* 2:13:4). This eclectic slogan was used by the Stoic Seneca in speaking of Epicurean teaching: "whatever is said well by anyone is mine" (*Epistulae* 16:7; cf. 12:11). It recurs, with an explicit reference to "the eclectic philosophy," in Clement of Alexandria (*Str.* 1:37:6). Justin also stated that "the teachings of Plato are not alien to those of Christ, but they are not absolutely similar—just as is the case of the others, Stoics and poets and prose writers" (*Apol.* 2:13:2). Among all there are "seeds of truth" (*Apol.* 1:44:10); and Andresen has shown that this expression, used in regard to ethics, is well paralleled in Antiochus and Middle Platonists.[21]

But what is the true philosophy, according to Justin? Obviously we must here differentiate what he thought before his conversion from what he thought later. Before his conversion he "rejoiced in the teachings of Plato" (*Apol.* 2:12:1) and rejected, in general, those of Stoics, Peripatetics and Pythagoreans. Stoics were weak in theology; Peripatetics were subtle and mercenary; Pythagoreans required too much preliminary study (*Dial.* 2:3-5). It is likely that as a Platonist Justin could have benefited from a little study of Aristotle, for the "old man" who overturned his Platonism used arguments essentially Peripatetic.[22]

[21] *Zeitschrift für die neutestamentliche Wissenschaft*, 44 (1952-53), 170-77. On the eclecticism of Antiochus cf. R.E. Witt, *Albinus and the History of Middle Platonism* (Cambridge, 1937), pp. 24-26.

[22] See chap. 8 below.

In any event, Justin had not encountered them. We may assume that before his conversion Justin was what he says he was, a Platonist. And in the Platonic school he presumably learned about Socrates, who taught with a *logos alēthēs*, and *exetastikōs* (*Apol.* 1:5:3). The first expression seems to refer to the true, ancient doctrine of Greek philosophy, as Wifstrand has shown with references to Celsus; he cites especially *Meno* 81a.[23] The second expression refers to Socrates' insistence upon examining questions fully, upon investigating them, as we have already seen. "No man is to be honored before the truth" (*Republic* 595c, quoted in Justin, *Apol.* 2:8[3]:6).

But after his conversion Justin came to find that there were some flaws in Plato's reasoning, especially in regard to his doctrine of the soul, and he therefore reinterpreted some of his Platonic views. The *logos alēthēs* came to be not the true ancient doctrine but the Logos; and Justin thus says that Greeks were instructed *through* Socrates *by* Logos, while barbarians (Christians) have now been instructed *by* the Logos himself, directly (*Apol.* 1:5:4).

This is to say that the doctrine of the incarnation of the Logos involved a shift in the meaning of the word *logos* as Justin understood it.

Yet even as a Christian Justin continued to revere, or perhaps revered more, the memory of Socrates, whose martyrdom he found analogous to that of Christ (*Apol.* 1:46:3; 2:7[8]:1). Socrates—for Justin was a true eclectic—was not alone, however. Like him, Heraclitus was really a Christian (1:46:3); because of "the implanted Logos" some Stoics were hated and put to death, and as examples Justin mentions Heraclitus and Musonius "in our times" (2:7:1). Presumably Justin mentions Heraclitus not simply because Stoics regarded him as a pre-Stoic Stoic but because at the beginning of his philosophical treatise he spoke of the Logos. The fact was well known in Justin's time.[24] Justin needed a pre-Socratic witness to Christian teaching. The notion

[23] *Die Wahre Lehre des Kelsos* (Lund, 1942), pp. 9-10.

[24] References in R. Walzer, *Eraclito: raccolta dei frammenti* (Florence, 1939), pp. 41-42.

that the true ancient theology was represented by Heraclitus (among others) is fairly common in Greco-Roman writers.[25]

Even as a Christian, then, Justin still adhered to a schematic picture of the history of philosophy which was not Christian in origin. It can be set forth very briefly. Heraclitus was a Christian because he represented old, true revelation and spoke of the Logos. Socrates was obviously a Christian because he searched for the truth and, like Heraclitus, was martyred. Xenophon (summarized in *Apol.* 2:11:2-7) reflected the teaching of Socrates. And Musonius Rufus was presumably right because he was, in effect, "the Roman Socrates." [26]

This is to emphasize the fact that as Justin became a Christian the center of gravity in his history of philosophy shifted from Plato to Socrates. He retained considerable enthusiasm for Plato, but he now regarded what was true in Plato's writings as derived from Moses (*Apol.* 1:44:8; 59:1; 60:1)—and, it should be added, from Socrates.

Part of the "preparation for the gospel" in Justin's philosophical career lay in this historical analysis. In Middle Platonism he had already learned about the original unity of philosophy, and this made it possible for him to attempt a historical correlation between philosophy and Christianity. Negatively, that is to say for antiheretical purposes, the historical theory was also valuable. Originally the Christian faith was one, but at a later time it came to be corrupted by heretics who, like philosophers, are called by the name of "the source of the teaching"—Marcionites, Valentinians, Basilidians, and Satornilians (*Dial.* 35:6). It may well be the case that Justin's idea about the rise of heresy is historically true. But the framework of his thought about the subject, a framework later extremely influential, seems to have been derived from his previous study of the development of Greek philosophy. Just as Socrates was followed by inferior philosophers who corrupted the true doctrine, so Christ was followed by Simon, Menander, and Marcion. Such an idea of uniform truth followed by complex error is characteristic of Justin's time.[27]

[25] See R. M. Grant, *The Letter and the Spirit* (London, 1957), pp. 10, 23, 28.
[26] See C. E. Lutz, *Musonius Rufus* ("Yale Classical Studies," 10 [New Haven, 1947]).
[27] Grant, *op. cit.*, pp. 18-30.

If our analysis is correct, we have shown that much of Justin's thought is derived not from Philo but from Middle Platonic sources. Indirectly, as we shall see, we have also shown that Justin's ideas are more striking and perhaps more significant than those of Clement of Alexandria, to whom we now turn.

We are fortunate enough to possess a thorough study of Clement of Alexandria on the origin of Greek philosophy, made by Einar Molland[28]. His brilliant analysis does not need to be repeated here. It is enough to summarize his conclusions. He points out that while Clement sometimes makes use of the traditional Jewish and Christian view that Greek philosophers borrowed from Moses and the prophets, his most complete analysis is provided in *Str.* 1:94:1-7, where he gives four explanations of the origin of philosophy. (1) The philosophers' true statements came to them by accident or by good fortune; this means that they were given to them by divine providence. (2) The true ideas were derived from a natural conception or a common intellect; but this too comes from God. (3) If the truths come from "a previous proclamation or a pronouncement of statements coincident with ours," the philosophers are like the prophets of the Old Testament. (4) The philosophers actually had the vision of God, though imperfectly. As Molland shows, the fourth view is that of Clement himself—though the others are not rejected.

This is to say that Clement assigns a very high value to Greek philosophy, especially that of Plato and Pythagoras. But what of the history of philosophy? Here Clement's thought is even less consistent than usual. In *Protrepticus* 64:2-3 he gives a list of godless philosophers who regarded the elements as primary principles; the list is different from that of Irenaeus, though the notion of godlessness is the same. The list recurs, in summary form, in *Str.* 1:52:4.[29] In *Str.* 1:59 there is a conventional catalogue of successions. More interesting, however, is the view (to which Molland refers) tracing philosophy back to Pythagoras, Pherecydes, and Thales, and behind them to oriental peoples such

[28] *Symbolae Osloenses,* 15-16 (1936), 57-85; see also *The Conception of the Gospel in the Alexandrian Theology* (Oslo, 1938), pp. 40-69.

[29] First list: Thales, Anaximenes, Diogenes of Apollonia, Parmenides, Hippasos, Heraclitus, Empedocles; second: Diogenes, Thales, Hippasos, atomists.

as the Egyptians, the Indians, the Babylonians, and the Magi. When we get back to the first generation of men, we find them instructed by the Son. The Son (Logos) was the first teacher, but in the course of tradition his teachings were corrupted by human additions. This theory recalls what we have already found in Justin.[30]

It may be added that in the first book of his *Refutatio* Hippolytus provides a collection of doxographical sources to set the stage for his view that Gnostic heresy comes from philosophy. As an example, we need quote only *Ref.* 5:20:4: "the whole teaching of the Sethians is from the ancient theologians Musaeus and Linus and Orpheus."

In our investigation we have now seen that the history of Greek philosophy was used by early Christian writers for two purposes. Negatively, it was used to trace the history of error. The philosophers provided either a model or a source for the activities of Gnostic heretics. Positively, it was used to show the priority of true philosophical teaching to the teaching of falsehood. In this way it provided a model for the history of Christianity and Christian heresy.

Relying on the customary second-century view that the old was the true, Christians felt fairly free to make use of the insights of those pre-Socratic philosophers who, like Socrates himself, were not "naturalists," that is to say "atheists."

We now turn to the use which was made of various pre-Socratic thinkers.

C. THE PHILOSOPHERS

a. The Milesians

Thales we have already mentioned as one of the seven wise men; but in Greco-Roman sketches of the history of philosophy he was also regarded as the earliest of the pre-Socratics. Thus Irenaeus, making use of a doxographical list, mentions him first and says that he said that the origin and beginning of everything

[30] On Clement's ideas see also Grant, *op. cit.*, pp. 85-87.

is water.[31] A similar doxographical statement occurs in the *Plea* of Athenagoras (23:4).[32] These statements are quoted only to illustrate the errors of philosophers who did not possess the benefits of revelation.

When making use of doxographical materials, Clement treats Thales more highly. He was acquainted with ancient oriental wisdom, since he was a Phoenician who encountered Egyptian prophets (*Str.* 1:66:2); as one of the seven wise men (see above) he uttered wise sayings such as "know thyself," and he was the founder of the Ionian school of philosophy (1:59-62). He held the true doctrine that God has neither beginning nor end (5: 96:4). And he correctly predicted an eclipse (1:65:1).

Of the other Milesians the early Christian writers know little. We have already discussed Irenaeus' statement about Anaximander. Clement mentions both him and Anaximenes, once listing their opinions about first principles (*Protrepticus* 66:1; 64:2), once providing a list of successions (*Str.* 1:63:2).

b. Pythagoras and the Pythagorean Tradition

In the writings of Philo, according to Leisegang's index, there are a dozen allusions to Pythagorean teaching, especially in regard to the symbolic meaning of the number seven, but there is only one quotation from the Pythagorean slogans (*Quod omn. prob.* 2 = Symb. 14). Actually Pythagorean doctrine did not constitute a major source of Philo's philosophical teaching, as a glance at Wolfson's *Philo* will make clear.

One must therefore suppose that when Clement of Alexandria calls Philo a Pythagorean (*Str.* 1:72:4; 100:3) he has in mind chiefly Philo's love of symbolism, which he shares with him. (Clement calls Numenius a Pythagorean too, *Str.* 1:150:4.)

The descriptions of the early Christians in Acts as "having everything in common" (2:44) and constituting "one heart and one soul" (4:32) may owe something ultimately to Pythagorean

[31] Irenaeus, *Adv. haer.* 2:14:1 (Harvey ed., p. 289); cf. *Dox.* 171.

[32] *Dox.* 301, 21; 307 a 9-14; discussion, pp. 88-91. Tatian (*Or.* 26) says, "while you are staring up to heaven, you fall into a pit"; according to Diogenes Laertius (1:34) such an accident happened to Thales.

models, but it is unlikely that Luke knew much about Pythagoras.[33]

Among the apologists, the first reference to Pythagoras occurs in Justin's first apology (18:5), where there is a mention of his writings along with those of Empedocles, Plato, and Socrates (?).[34] When Justin was beginning his study of philosophy he had a brief encounter with a Pythagorean teacher, but the prerequisites for elementary Pythagoreanism were too much for him (*Dial.* 2). He knew, however, that Pythagoras was a significant figure in the history of philosophy (*Dial.* 5-6).

Tatian said that Pythagoras' doctrine, derived from Pherecydes, was ridiculous (*Or.* 3); the doctrine he has in mind is that of the (innate) immortality of the soul (*Or.* 25), and its transmigration–for Pythagoras said that he was once Euphorbus, a Trojan hero. In *Or.* 41 Tatian dated Pythagoras in the sixty-second Olympiad.[35]

Theophilus knows rather less about Pythagoras than Tatian does. He speaks of the futility of Pythagoras' visits to the grottoes of Egyptian priests[36] and to the pillars of Hercules (*Ad Autol.* 3:2). He also accuses Pythagoras of "defining Nature" and speaking of the spontaneous operation of everything while denying the concern of the gods for men (3:7; cf. 26); but here he seems to have confused Pythagoras with Epicurus.[37]

Irenaeus knows that the Carpocratian Gnostics have images of Christ, Pythagoras, Plato, and Aristotle, but he gives no indication as to the meaning of these images to the sect.[38] He himself uses Pythagoras only as a stick with which to beat the Valentinians, especially the Marcosian group; their tetrads and other numbers come from the Pythagoreans.[39]

It is in the writings of Clement of Alexandria that Pythagorean teaching is most highly regarded. Clement found the collection

[33] See H. J. Cadbury in *The Beginnings of Christianity,* 5 (London, 1933), 399 n. 2.

[34] See p. 107 n. 51.

[35] According to Diogenes Laertius 8:45 he flourished in the sixtieth Olympiad.

[36] See Diogenes Laertius 8:3; Clement, *Str.* 1:66:2.

[37] More correctly in *Dox.* 589, 9.

[38] *Adv. haer.* 1:25:5 (Harvey ed., p. 210).

[39] *Adv. haer.* 1:1:1 (p. 9); 2:14:5-6 (pp. 297, 299).

of Pythagorean symbols made by Androcydes very useful as a parallel to Philonic and Christian allegorization (*Str.* 5:27:1–31:2).[40] In his writings there are three quotations from the *Golden Verses* ascribed to Pythagoras, five from the *Gnomai*, and twelve from the *Symbola;* in addition there are ten expressions which parallel those used by Pythagoreans. Nine of the *Symbola* occur in the section from Androcydes, where one of them is said to come from *hoi mystai* (5:30:5).

As for the later Pythagorean teachers, Philolaus (cited as an authority by Philo, *De opificio mundi* 100) is quoted by Athenagoras for his teaching about God as superior to matter. Athenagoras also knows, evidently from a doxographical source, the doctrines of the obscure Pythagoreans Lysis and Opsimus. The former taught that God is the ineffable number; the latter, that he is the difference between the greatest number and the one just before it (*Legatio ad Graecos* 6:1). Clement too quotes from Philolaus (*Vorsokr.* B14; *Str.* 3:17:1) and—without a reference to its author—from a letter ascribed to Lysis (*Str.* 5:57:2).

c. Heraclitus

In Diels' collection there are 130 probably genuine fragments of Heraclitus. Only twenty of these were provided by authors who wrote before the second century of our era. In that century, as we have already seen, there was a real revival of concern for Heraclitus as for other "ancient" writers. Thus Plutarch provides us with nineteen fragments of Heraclitus, Diogenes Laertius with eleven, Marcus Aurelius with five, Celsus with four, Sextus Empiricus with three, Maximus of Tyre with two, and Numenius with one. Christian writers were also enthusiastic about Heraclitus. We have seen that Justin highly valued his life and probably, his thought, though he does not quote from his book. Tatian, as we should expect, does not regard him so highly, speaking of him as self-taught and arrogant and interpreting his saying "I explored myself" to mean "I taught myself."[41] It is in the writings of Clement and Hippolytus that,

[40] Grant, *op. cit.,* p. 8.

[41] *Or.* 3 (Schwartz ed., p. 3, 11) [*Vorsokr.* B101; Plutarch, *Adversus Coleten* 20:1118c].

for different reasons, most of the Christian quotations from Heraclitus occur.

It is a question whether or not these quotations were doxographical in origin. Here it is worth noting that Sextus Empiricus knows something about the sequence of Heraclitus' sayings (*Adversus mathematicos* 7:132-33) and that Diogenes Laertius (9:5) describes a "current book" as derived from Heraclitus' treatise *On Nature* and divided into three parts, "on the all," "political," and "theological." We may suggest that Heraclitus' book, certainly known to Aristotle,[42] was available in the second century, either in its original form or in a revised edition.

Clement quotes or alludes to no fewer than thirty-nine fragments of Heraclitus, sixteen of which have been transmitted only through him; and we should agree with P. Valentin that he knew Heraclitus' work.[43] Valentin suggests that Clement admires Heraclitus because of his "rational–not rationalistic–thought."

On the other hand, the twenty fragments quoted by Hippolytus are chiefly intended to show the origin of the heresy of Noetus; seventeen of them occur in *Ref.* 9:9-10, which deals with this subject. One quotation (*Vorsokr.* B25) and one allusion (B92) are derived by Hippolytus from the Gnostic Naassenes (*Ref.* 5:8:42, 44; 5:8:6), and another quotation comes from the Peratae (*Vorsokr.* B36; *Ref.* 5:16:4). Hippolytus is no admirer of Heraclitus.

Similarly Tertullian quotes or refers to Heraclitus chiefly in order to criticize him, especially in the treatise *De anima,* in which the references come primarily from a Skeptical source.[44] *Eadem via sursum et deorsum* (*Vorsokr.* B60; *Adversus Marc.* 2:28:1) is shared with Hippolytus (*Ref.* 9:10:4) but probably comes from a doxographical source. Gossip about the philosopher's death, probably derived from Tatian, occurs in the treatise *Ad martyras* (4:5).

In Origen's writings there are only four quotations from Hera-

[42] *Rhetorica* 3:5 (*Vorsokr.* A4).

[43] *Recherches de science religieuse,* 46 (1958), 27-59.

[44] See J. H. Waszink, *Tertulliani de Anima* (Amsterdam, 1947), pp. 174, 217, 227, 241.

clitus, all of which occur in the apology *Contra Celsum*—and all four come not from Origen but from Celsus.[45]

In other words, the enthusiasm of Justin and Clement for Heraclitus was not widely shared by other Christian writers, though Neo-Platonists and antiquarians continued to quote from him.

One mysterious fragment (*Vorsokr.* B62) deserves special attention because of the variety in its transmission. This can best be seen in a tabular arrangement.

(1) *ἀθάνατοι θνητοί, θνητοὶ ἀθάνατοι* (Hippolytus, *Ref.* 9:10:6);

(2) *θεοὶ θνητοί, ἄνθρωποι ἀθάνατοι* (Pseudo-Heraclitus, *Quaestiones homericae* 24; Maximus of Tyre 10:4);

(3) *ἄνθρωποι θεοὶ θνητοί, θεοὶ ἄνθρωποι ἀθάνατοι* (Lucian, *Vitarum auctio* 14; a parody);

(4) *θεοὶ ἄνθρωποι, ἄνθρωποι θεοί* (Clement, *Paedagogus* 3:2:1).

This table suggests that Clement's quotation has not (as is sometimes supposed) necessarily been "Christianized"; on the other hand, his version is not likely to be the original one. Unfortunately Philo, who could have helped us trace the transmission of the text, does not do so; he quotes only the last part of the saying: "We live their death, we die their life" (*Legum allegoriarum* 1: 108; cf. *De fuga* 55).

d. Xenophanes

Diels edited forty-two fragments from the *Elegies*, *Silloi*, and *On Nature* by Xenophanes. The writers from whom the largest numbers of these fragments come are as follows: Athenaeus six (five from the *Elegies*), Sextus Empiricus five, Diogenes Laertius four, Clement of Alexandria four, Herodian four, and Simplicius three. Thus most of the fragments come to us from second- or third-century writers, though the quotations from the *Silloi* and *On Nature*—the more theological works—seem to be exclusively doxographical in origin. The description of Xenophanes' works by Diogenes Laertius (9:18) does not prove that Diogenes had firsthand acquaintance with them.

[45] *Contra Celsum* 1:5 (7:62); 5:14; 6:12; 6:42; cf. C. Andresen, *Logos und Nomos* (see above, p. 93 n. 20), p. 126.

The oldest Christian use of anything ascribed to Xenophanes may perhaps be found in the eighth chapter of the *Plea* of Athenagoras, where the arguments against the existence of more than one god appear to be derived from those ascribed to the pre-Socratic philosopher in the pseudo-Aristotelian treatise *De Melisso Xenophane Gorgia* (977 a 23-39; *Vorsokr.* A28).[46] Athenagoras does not mention Xenophanes but he may have him in mind.

What is probably the most important early Christian use of Xenophanes occurs in the treatise *Adversus haereses* by Irenaeus, although Irenaeus does not name, and perhaps did not know, his source.

The twenty-fourth fragment in Diels is to be found (anonymously) in Sextus Empiricus, *Adversus mathematicos* 9:144: God οὖλος ὁρᾷ, οὖλος δὲ νοεῖ, οὖλος δὲ τ' ἀκούει. It can be identified as belonging to Xenophanes because of verbal parallels in Plutarch (*Dox.* 580, 16 = *Vorsokr.* A32) and Diogenes Laertius (9:19 = *Vorsokr.* A1). The saying was also handed down, and used by Greek and Latin philosophers, in nominal form; thus in the *Natural History* of Pliny (2:14) we read that *Deus totus est sensus, totus visus, totus auditus, totus animae, totus animi, totus sui.* There is no reference to Xenophanes, any more than in Seneca (*Quaestiones naturales,* praef. 14; *totus est ratio*) or in Clement of Alexandria:

> (the Logos) ὅλος νοῦς, ὅλος φῶς πατρῷον, ὅλος ὀφθαλμός (*Str.* 7:5:5); (God) ὅλος ἀκοὴ καὶ ὅλος ὀφθαλμός (*Str.* 7:37:6).

This is to say that the saying circulated anonymously and was subject to modification.

Irenaeus makes use of it no fewer than five times. God is wholly *cogitatus, sensus, oculus, auditus—et totus fons omnium bonorum* (1:12:2, Harvey ed., p. 111)

sensus spiritus sensuabilitas ennoea ratio auditus oculus lumen—et totus fons omnium bonorum (2:13:3, p. 282)

visio auditus (2:13:8, p. 285)

[46] On this passage see W. Jaeger, *The Theology of the Early Greek Philosophers* (Oxford, 1947), pp. 51-54 and 212 n. 34. Athenagoras' argument is discussed more fully in my *The Early Christian Doctrine of God* (see above, p. xxi n. 9) pp. 105-10.

mens ratio spiritus-operans lux ...mens logos (2:28:4, p. 354)
lumen mens substantis—et fons omnium bonorum (4:11:1, p. 175).[47]

The expression *fons omnium bonorum* is Platonic in origin; compare *Timaeus* 29e (which Irenaeus quotes, *Adv. haer.* 3:25:5, Harvey ed., p. 136) and Platonists like Philo (in Eusebius, *Praeparatio evangelica* 8:12:12)[48] and Numenius (in Chalcidius 296; Leemans ed., pp. 93, 1-2).

It will be noticed that what Irenaeus does is to take the saying—found in its purest form in the third and first examples—and add to it other attributes of God which were characteristic of second-century Platonism. In some instances Platonic and Johannine terminology overlap, for in John 4:24 God is Spirit, while in I John 1:5 he is Light.

In three instances (the second, fourth, and fifth) additional statements also seem to reflect the views traditionally ascribed to Xenophanes. God is

simplex et non compositus et similimembrius [ὁμοιομερής, the term of Anaxagoras, cf. Lucretius, *De rerum natura* 1:830]
et totus ipse sibimetipsi similis;
semper idem et similiter exsistens;
perfectus in omnibus, ipse sibi aequalis et similis.

As one example out of many from the doxographical tradition we cite Hippolytus (*Dox.* 565, 25-26 = *Vorsokr.* A33, 2): God as *hena kai homoion pantē.*

In Irenaeus' opinion this statement is a universally valid axiom of theology. The second quotation is introduced by the words *quemadmodum adest religiosis ac piis dicere de deo.* The third is stated thus: *qui dicit eum totum visionem et totum auditum... non peccat.* And the fourth correlates it with biblical doctrine: *sicut ex scripturis dicimus.*[49] This is to say that the teaching of Xenophanes is one of the pillars of the theology of Irenaeus.

In addition to this fragment of Xenophanes, Clement of

[47] For the first passage see Epiphanius, *Pan.* 33:2:4-5 (Holl ed., Vol. 1, p. 450, 3-6).

[48] In *De opificio mundi* 21 Philo alludes to *Timaeus* 29e.

[49] Cf. T. B. Allworthy in *Journal of Theological Studies,* 39 (1938), 248; also C. C. J. Webb, *ibid.,* 40 (1939), 36-37, and B. Hemmerdinger, *ibid.,* 17 (1966), 308-09.

Alexandria quotes four others, none of which are found in other writers independent of Clement. Fragment 14 occurs in *Str.* 5:109:2: "But mortals suppose that gods are begotten and have clothing, voice, and form like theirs." Since the basic idea of this fragment is attested by two other excerpts (fragments 11 and 12), both found in Sextus Empiricus, it may be accepted as genuine. Fragment 15 (*Str.* 5:109:3) reads thus: "But if oxen [horses] and lions had hands or could write with their hands and make things as men do, horses and oxen would describe the forms of the gods as like theirs and would give them bodies with forms like their own." This is simply a more striking expression of the idea found in the preceding fragments. Fragment 16 has been restored to metrical form by Diels, relying on the paraphrase given by Clement (*Str.* 7:22:1): "Various peoples portray the gods' forms as like their own..., the Ethiopians black and simian, the Thracians ruddy and blue-eyed." This is the same anti-anthropomorphic view, expressed in much the same way as in the other fragments. Fragment 23 is open to more suspicion (*Str.* 5:109:1).

> There is one God, greatest among gods and men,
> Neither in form nor in thought similar to mortals.

The primary reason for suspecting the authenticity of the fragment lies not in what it says, for the doxographical tradition tells us that Xenophanes regarded God as one, or according to Aristotle [50] said that the One was god, but in the form of expression. In Clement's time many Jewish and Christian forgeries, intended to demonstrate the monotheism of the ancients, were in circulation; Clement himself used some of the fictitious quotations. It is therefore not certain that Xenophanes was a monotheist in the way Clement would like him to be, although—as we have already seen when discussing Athenagoras—he was so regarded in Clement's time.

Three quotations from Xenophanes in the *Refutatio* of Hippolytus need not detain us, for one of them (*Vorsokr.* B34) occurs in his doxographical section (*Ref.* 1:14:1) and two more

[50] *Metaphysica* A5 = *Vorsokr.* A30.

(*Vorsokr.* B27, 33) are found (*Ref.* 10:6:4; 7:2) in a section directly derived from Sextus Empiricus.

The importance of Xenophanes, then, for early Christian writers lies partly in what he actually wrote and partly in what he was supposed to have taught. The most significant example of his influence is to be found in the writings of a Christian theologian who almost certainly did not know what his source was.

e. Parmenides

Parmenides is mentioned only by Clement, who says that he introduced fire and earth as gods (*Protrepticus* 64:2). This statement is merely doxographical, as Pseudo-Galen shows (*Dox.* 564), but Clement also knows fragments from Parmenides' poems (*Vorsokr.* B1, 2, 5, 8, 10) and cites them in support of his own views.

f. Zeno of Elis

This Zeno, not the Stoic, is also mentioned only by Clement, who uses a succession list to show that he was the successor of Parmenides (*Str.* 1:64:3). Like Plutarch (*Vorsokr.* 19, A7) and Diogenes Laertius (9:27), Clement says that he spat at the tyrant who was putting him to death; Clement derives this information from Eratosthenes (*Str.* 4:56:1). Tertullian too treats Zeno as a martyr (*Apologia* 50:9).

g. Empedocles

The first Christian to mention Empedocles is Justin, who lists him among philosophers who wrote books in which the consciousness of souls after death was mentioned (*Apol.* 1:18:5).[51] Tatian criticizes him: "the eruptions of fire in Sicily demonstrated the imposture of Empedocles, because though not a god he nearly persuaded men that he was" (*Or.* 3). The story that Empedocles committed suicide on Etna is told from earlier sources by Diogenes Laertius (8:69-70), though, as Diogenes indicates, its truth was open to question.

[51] Oddly enough the list includes Socrates; W. Schmid (*Zeitschrift für die neutestamentliche Wissenschaft,* 40 [1941], 119-20) emends to "Xenocrates," with a reference to Plutarch, *De Iside* 360 d.

Theophilus claims that Empedocles "taught atheism" (*Ad Autol.* 3:2); Irenaeus treats him as a materialist along with Anaxagoras and Plato (*Adv. haer.* 2:14:4, Harvey ed., p. 294); and Clement lists him among godless philosophers who regarded the origins of things as material (*Protrepticus* 64:3; *Str.* 1:52:4). Yet Clement also lists him among ancient seers (*Str.* 1:133:2) and relates that he was called "wind-stopper" because he stilled a storm (*Str.* 6:30:1-3; Diogenes Laertius 8:60, from Timaeus).

Fragments of Empedocles (fairly common in Plutarch, Sextus Empiricus, and Diogenes Laertius) first appear among Christians in the *Plea* of Athenagoras, who quotes several lines from him (22:1-2). These come from *Vorsokr.* B6 and B17.

Vorsokr. B6 consists of three lines, attested by Sextus Empiricus (*Adversus mathematicos* 9:362; 10:315), Hippolytus (*Ref.* 7:29:4), and the doxography of Aëtius (*Dox.* 287 a 8-11). A strange corruption in Athenagoras' text introduces the name of Epicurus into a line of Empedocles and clearly shows that he is following a doxographical source; for Epicurus is mentioned, in the context of *Vorsokr.* B6, both by Sextus Empiricus (both times) and Aëtius.[52] (Athenagoras quotes only the first line of the fragment.)

Vorsokr. B17, a long fragment, occurs in full only in the Neo-Platonist Simplicius, but the two lines (18 and 20) quoted by Athenagoras were common property. Lines 18-20 occur in Sextus Empiricus (*Adversus mathematicos* 9:10), while lines 18 and 20 are found separately in two works of Plutarch (*Quomodo adulescens poetas audire debeat* 22:63 d; *Amatorius* 13:756 d).

Line 18 of *Vorsokr.* B17 leads us toward the writings of Clement of Alexandria, where (*Str.* 6:17:4) a fascinating composite quotation includes it. This quotation consists of *Vorsokr.* B6, 1, B17, 18, and B21, 9. We need not assume, as we might be tempted to assume, that Clement or a doxographer before him constructed this composition. The text of Empedocles must have been rather corrupt, as we can see by noting that B17, 7-8 is identical with B26, 5-6.

Whatever the state of the text may have been, Clement valued

[52] See R. M. Grant, "Notes on Gnosis," *Vigiliae Christianae,* 12 (1958), 145-46.

Empedocles highly, presumably because he was a miracle-working seer. He gives twenty fragments from the poems, eleven of them unique. Some of the quotations, like the mixture to which we have just referred, are intended merely to show that Empedocles borrowed from Pythagorean doctrines; more of them show that he was acquainted with philosophical-theological truth.

Hippolytus, too, often quotes Empedocles (10 fragments), but he uses his works chiefly to illustrate the origin of Simonian and Marcionite heresy.

h. Anaxagoras

The memory of Anaxagoras was preserved among the early Christians with no more favor than one would expect. His scientific interests presumably accounted for Irenaeus' statement that he was called an atheist (*Adv. haer.* 2:14:2, Harvey ed., pp. 290-91), and his trial for impiety (on the ground that he taught that the sun was a hot stone and the moon was earth) is evidently at the base of Tatian's remark that he "courted death from an insane love of fame among men" (*Or.* 19; cf. 27). Clement was content to transmit traditions about Anaxagoras without criticism. As a follower of Anaximenes, he brought philosophy to Athens (*Str.* 1:63:2; cf. Diogenes Laertius 2:16). His "first principles" were the Boundless and Mind (*Protrepticus* 66:1; *Str.* 2:14:2). He taught that the goal of life was contemplation (*Str.* 2:130:2). And he was the first editor of a book (*Str.* 1:78:4).[53]

Hippolytus provided a lengthy doxographical discussion of his views (*Ref.* 1:8).

Anaxagoras' disciple Metrodorus of Lampsacus was criticized by Tatian (*Or.* 21) for transferring everything to allegory in his work *On Homer*, in which he treated Hera, Athena, and Zeus as "substances of nature and arrangements of elements"; in the same context Tatian mentions Hector, Achilles, Agamemnon, Helen, and Paris. With these remarks we may compare two testimonia given by Diels (*Vorsokr.* 48, A4 and 6); Metrodorus taught that Agamemnon symbolized the aether, Achilles the Sun, Helen the

[53] On this obscure statement see Stählin's note *ad loc.* in *GCS*.

earth, Alexander (Paris) the air, and Hector the moon, while followers of Anaxagoras held that Zeus was mind, Athena art.[54]

i. Democritus

Since Democritus was well known as an atomist—and therefore, like Epicurus, as "godless"—it is not surprising that some Christians were rather hostile toward his memory. Tatian ridicules his treatise *On Sympathies and Antipathies* (*Or.* 17), evidently unaware that it is a late forgery.[55] He knows that followers of Democritus are opposed to Aristotle (*Or.* 25). Irenaeus too criticizes Democritus, but on the ground that he founded atomism and "first said that many and various forms descended from the whole into this world" (see above, p. 92). Tertullian faintly praises him (*Apologia* 46:11).[56]

Athenagoras, on the other hand, is better disposed toward him, mentioning him in a group of "martyrs" for philosophy which consists of Pythagoras, Heraclitus, Democritus, and Socrates (*Legatio ad Graecos* 31:1). He says Democritus was exiled from Abdera—a statement for which there is no other evidence.

Clement quotes eight fragments from Democritus' writings, regarding them all as expressions of the truth. This favorable judgment can be explained on two grounds. (1) Democritus, in Clement's view, used old oriental sources (*Str.* 1:69, 4-6). (2) Because of his observation of the heavens he was even called Wisdom (*Str.* 6:32:2).

In other words, the tradition about the sage Democritus has led both Athenagoras and Clement, not to mention Tertullian, to forget his atomism. Clement even speaks, in his sermon *Quis dives* (11:4), of "Democriti" as examples of voluntary poverty.[57]

j. Protagoras and Critias

Two pre-Socratic critics of popular religion deserve mention. These are Protagoras and Critias, mentioned together by The-

[54] On the work of Metrodorus see W. Nestle in *Philologus,* 66 (1907), 503-10.

[55] See M. Wellmann, *Die Φυσικά des Bolos Demokritos, Abhandlungen der preussischen Akademie der Wissenschaften zu Berlin* (1928), No. 7.

[56] See A. Gellius, *Atticae noctae* 10:17:1 (*Vorsokr.* 55, A23).

[57] For parallels see Stählin's note *ad loc.* in *GCS.*

ophilus (*Ad Autol.* 3:7). Protagoras was famous for his suggestion that theological problems were too difficult for him (*Vorsokr.* 74, B4); the form in which Theophilus reports this saying is close to that provided by Sextus Empiricus (*Adversus mathematicos* 9:56),[58] and presumably reflects doxographical information. Theophilus gives no quotation from Critias, but there is a long one in Sextus Empiricus (9:54), just before the quotation from Protagoras.

Of Protagoras Clement says only that he heard Democritus and invented "eristic" (*Str.* 1:64:4; 6:65:1). Presumably Clement finds the philosopher insufficiently favorable toward religion: his attitude was doubtless shaped by Plato. As for Critias, Clement quotes from him only once, to illustrate his use of Euripides (*Str.* 6:9:1-2). Elsewhere, like many ancient writers, Clement ascribes his play *Peirithys* to Euripides (*Str.* 5:36:1; 114:2).

Presumably Christian writers were unenthusiastic about these two writers because they went too far in attacking religions and attacked religion as well.

D. CONCLUSION

Generally speaking, Christian writers were unenthusiastic about early Greek cosmological poetry except insofar as they could relate it to the theory of a primal revelation commonly held in the second century or could make use of monotheistic forgeries ascribed to the old poets. Only Clement admires the seven wise men, and he does so because of their gnomic ethical teaching.

As for the history of philosophy, the two Christian writers who were much concerned with it regarded philosophy as originally one and divine but later distorted by human corruptions. Hippolytus knew more about the details of this history than either Justin or Clement did, but he viewed philosophy simply as the source of heresy. His method is like that of Irenaeus, his teacher.

[58] For Theophilus' text see U.V. Wilamowitz-Moellendorff in *Sitzungsberichte der preussischen Akademie der Wissenschaften zu Berlin* (1911), No. 763; he reads εἴπερ with Epiphanius, *Ancoratus* 104:2.

Pre-Socratic philosophers are favored by Christian writers because of their search for philosophical theology and their criticism of pagan religion, as well as for their ethical insights. Because of the Platonic sympathies of many early Christians, there was little liking for the naturalists either early or late. Democritus provides an odd exception, chiefly because a new "image" of him had been created in the Hellenistic age. The criticisms of religion by Protagoras and Critias were largely neglected because they went too far.

Perhaps the most interesting use of pre-Socratic thought was made by Irenaeus, who did not know that Xenophanes was responsible for a doctrine of God which the church writer regarded as fundamental.

8

CAUSATION AND GENERATION IN EARLY CHRISTIAN LITERATURE

A. PREPOSITIONAL AND PROPOSITIONAL THEOLOGY

One of the most important ways in which early Christians set forth their understandings of the relation of God and Christ to the created world was by the use of various prepositions which are often identical with those used in hellenistic philosophy to indicate causal relationships. In philosophy the most important causal systems were those of the Platonists and the Aristotelians. A collection of philosophers' opinions current in the first century of our era describes Plato as using a threefold analysis of causes: ὑφ' οὗ, ἐξ οὗ, πρὸς ὅ; the primary one among them was the efficient cause (ὑφ' οὗ), "which is mind." Aristotle, on the other hand, used a fourfold classification: material (ἐξ οὗ), efficient (ὑφ' οὗ), formal (καθ' ὅ), and final (δι' ὅ).[1] A theological analysis based on the fourfold scheme is provided by Philo in his treatise *On the Cherubim* 125-27. The primary cause, ὑφ' οὗ, is God; the material cause, ἐξ οὗ, consists of the four elements; the instrumental cause, δι' οὗ, is the Logos; and the final cause, δι' ὅ, is God's goodness.[2] Obviously the terminology was variable, but what remained constant was (1) the notion that cause existed, (2) the notion that cause could be classified in a logically consistent way, and (3) the notion that there were either three or four causes. Systems with either more or fewer were not popular, for those with more seemed too complex and those with two were often regarded as implying the existence of

[1] Compare the threefold classification by the Middle Platonist Albinus, *Eisagōgē* (Hermann ed., p. 163, 35-37); fourfold in Clement, *Str.* 8:18:1 and Origen, *In Iohannem commentarius* 1:17-19 (Preuschen ed., pp. 22-23); fivefold according to some Platonists in Seneca, *Epistulae* 65:7-8. The doxographical materials are in *Dox.* 309-10.

[2] See H. A. Wolfson, *Philo* (see above, p. 80 n. 22), Vol. 1, pp. 265-66.

three or four. The latter situation seems to be reflected in I Corinthians 1:30, where God is the one ἐξ οὗ and Christ is the one ἐν ᾧ (=δι' οὗ; cf. I Cor. 8:6); in Athenagoras, *Legatio ad Graecos* 10:1, where God is the one ὑφ' οὗ and the Logos is the one δι' οὗ (compare Philo); and in *Legatio ad Graecos* 22:8, where Isis-*physis* is described as both the one ἐξ ἧς and the one δι' ἧς. The more common threefold classification occurs in I Corinthians 8:6, where we find God ἐξ οὗ, Christ δι' οὗ, and God εἰς ὅν. In a doxology, on the other hand (Rom. 11:36), Paul can speak without making any distinctions of God as the one ἐξ οὗ, δι' οὗ, and εἰς ὅν. In form his statement resembles what Marcus Aurelius says to *physis* (*Meditationes* 4:23): ἐκ σοῦ, ἐν σοί, εἰς σέ; but the Stoic emperor, it would appear, means "in" by ἐν. In Colossians 1:16 we read that "in" Christ everything was created—and here too ἐν apparently means "in," as the next verse suggests—and everything was created δι' αὐτοῦ καὶ εἰς αὐτόν. If this verse reflects a causal system, as seems to be implied by the parallel in I Corinthians 8:6 and by the way in which Colossians 1:15-20 is constructed, the primary cause is implied by the mention of "the invisible God," and the scheme is a fourfold one.

In Hebrews God is the primary cause (ἐποίησεν, 1:2) while the Son-Sophia is the instrumental cause (δι' οὗ); but both final and instrumental causation can be ascribed to God himself (δι' ὃν τὰ πάντα καὶ δι' οὗ τὰ πάντα, 2:10). Finally, in John 1:1-3 we find that the Logos was both θεός and πρὸς τὸν θεόν (related to God as to the final cause?); in addition, πάντα δι' αὐτοῦ ἐγένετο. The creative work of the Son is the creative work of the Father, but the Father is the primary cause while the Son-Logos is the instrumental cause. Compare Athenagoras, *Legatio ad Graecos* 10:2 (surely based on John): πρὸς [from] αὐτοῦ καὶ δι' αὐτοῦ πάντα ἐγένετο, ἑνὸς ὄντος τοῦ πατρὸς καὶ τοῦ υἱοῦ.[3] The prepositions are transferable, not so much because of the ambiguities in hellenistic Greek as because of the theological view that the functions of the Father and the Son were both inseparable and separable. Thus Barnabas (12:7) can say of Jesus that ἐν αὐτῷ πάντα καὶ εἰς αὐτόν.

[3] For contemporary hellenistic parallels see E. Norden, *Agnostos Theos* (Leipzig, 1913), pp. 240-50, 347.

The Father is thus the efficient cause of all (Philo; I Cor. 8:6; Rom. 11:36), the instrumental cause (Rom. 11:36; Heb. 2:10), and the final cause (Rom. 11:36; Heb. 2:10; probably Col. 1:20). (He is also "over all, through all, in all," Eph. 4:6, and human beings, at least, are "in" him, Acts 17:28.) The Son is never described as the efficient cause in the New Testament; he is the instrumental cause (I Cor. 8:6; Col. 1:16; John 1:3) and the final cause (Col. 1:16). The function of the Holy Spirit in this kind of scheme is much less clear. An interpolation in I Corinthians 8:6 attested by Gregory Nazianzen would remedy the deficiency by stating that "in" the Holy Spirit are all things, and we are in him; but this is certainly not part of the original text.

Whether or not any New Testament writer had a clearly defined causal system of a philosophical type, it is obvious that causal relations played a significant part in the thought of some of them. This point can be reinforced by considering some passages in I Corinthians in which hierarchical relationships are expressed in various ways. (1) In I Corinthians 3:22-23 we read that *(a)* everything belongs to you; *(b)* you belong to Christ; *(c)* Christ belongs to God. (2) In I Corinthians 11:3 we read that *(a)* the "head" of the wife is the husband; *(b)* the "head" of the husband is Christ; *(c)* the "head" of Christ is God. And (3) in I Corinthians 11:8-9 and 12 we read that *(a)* woman is "from" man (Adam's rib) and "because of" man; *(b)* man (now) comes into existence "through" woman; and *(c)* everything is "from" God. The hierarchical relations are expressed in causal terms.

Naturally the idea of causation, especially in relation to final causes, is not always expressed with prepositions. The idea of God's purposive activity is inevitably related to world views in which eschatology is prominent; the idea of purposive activity, both human and divine, is reflected in Paul's fondness for the word ἵνα; and the idea that divine and human activity cannot be meaningless or purposeless is expressed when he uses such word as *kenos*, *mataios*, and *eikē*. Nothing could be farther from New Testament thought than the world-weariness of Ecclesiastes.

It is just at this point that modern world views often diverge from the view which seemed self-evident to most ancient writers both Christian and non-Christian. Modern ideas of causation and of the analysis of causation are quite different from those reflected in early Christianity, and in any attempt to "demythologize" the New Testament these ideas have to be taken into account.

B. THE ORIGIN OF JESUS

Another New Testament theme in which prepositions and causality have an important part is the origin of Jesus. In some expressions related to origins, cause and origin are almost indistinguishable. "I came from the Father and I came into the world" (John 16:28) is a statement in which two kinds of "spheres" are contrasted; but the spheres are evidently related to questions of origin. In John 3:6 is the clear contrast, "That which is born of the flesh is flesh, and that which is born of the Spirit is spirit." In another passage (1:13) a triple negative statement shows what is *not* the true origin of believers (blood, will of the flesh, will of man) as contrasted with what it really is: ἐκ θεοῦ. Such statements about origins we may expect to shed some light on the theological purpose of statements about Jesus' conception and/or birth. Thus we read in Matthew 1:20 that what has been generated *in* Mary is ἐκ πνεύματος ἁγίου; the same meaning is conveyed by Luke 1:35: Holy Spirit will come upon thee, and power from the Most High will overshadow thee; *therefore* the holy product will be called the Son of God. The origin of Jesus is to be sought in the work of the Holy Spirit. It is therefore rather surprising to read in Galatians 4:4 that the Son of God came into (human) existence ἐκ γυναικός and in Romans 1:3 that he did so ἐκ σπέρματος Δαυίδ, though in the latter passage the phrase ἐκ σπέρματος is qualified by the phrase κατὰ σάρκα (cf. Rom. 9:5). It can be argued, of course, that in each passage Paul is laying emphasis on the humanity of Jesus, and this argument is valid. But why did he use the preposition ἐκ when in I Corinthians 11:8-12 his statements imply that it is not correct? We must probably conclude that the argument in I Corinthians 11 is rather forced (as, indeed, much of it seems to be) and that Paul would ordinarily have spoken of human parentage as he does in Philippians 3:5, where he calls himself "a Hebrew, of [ἐξ] Hebrew parents."

The agency of Mary in the conception is emphasized by Ignatius when he speaks of Jesus Christ as conceived by (ὑπό) Mary "of [ἐκ] the seed of David and of [ἐκ] the Holy Spirit" (*Eph.* 18:2).[4] These passages all make it clear enough that the causal origin of Jesus' humanity lies in his having been conceived by a human mother.

In the writings of Justin, however, there is a certain confusion about Jesus' origin. In semi-credal passages he invariably speaks of Jesus' origin διὰ [τῆς] παρθένου (*Apol.* 1:31:7; 46:5; *Dial.* 63:1; 85:2); elsewhere he uses the preposition διά twelve times, ἐκ only twice, ἀπό once, and the phrase "son of a virgin" once. We might suppose that this usage meant nothing significant were it not that he twice states that "the blood of Christ was not from human seed [or, the human race] but from divine power [or, the power of God]."[5] The mode of Christ's conception was different from ours. We are begotten from moist sperm (*Apol.* 1:61:10) or from a tiny seed, and from this come bones, sinews, and flesh (1:19:1). But Christ, born not of human seed but of divine power, had blood which was different from ours. In the view of many ancient writers human blood is contributed by the mother. Therefore we may conclude that Justin used the word διά in relation to Christ's generation through Mary because she actually did not contribute his blood—or, for that matter, his bones, sinews, and flesh. Intentionally or unintentionally, Justin came very close to Gnostic views of Christ's origin.

Certainly his view was the Gnostic one. Various passages in the writings of Irenaeus show that it was characteristic of Ptolemaean-Valentinian thought to hold that Christ came *per Mariam;* Irenaeus insists against them that the only correct expression is ἐκ Μαρίας.[6] Some Gnostics avoided this kind of dis-

[4] The formulas which Ignatius uses elsewhere convey the same meaning: *Eph.* 7:2; 20:2 (he was Son of Man because of his Davidic descent); *Trall.* 9:1; *Smyrn.* 1:1.

[5] *Apol.* 1:32:9 (cf. 11); *Dial.* 54:2.

[6] E. g., *Adv. haer.* 1:7:2; 3:16:1; 22:1-2. See H. J. Schoeps, *Vom himmlischen Fleisch Christi* (Tübingen, 1951), pp. 6-7.

cussion by maintaining that the Savior was (1) γεννητὸς καὶ παθητός (i. e., human) but also (2) ἐξ ἁγίου πνεύματος καὶ παρθένου (Clement, *Excerpta ex Theodoto* 23:3). But this statement presumably reflects an accommodation to church doctrine—at least in part; Ignatius more reasonably relates generation and passibility to the human nature derived from Mary, nongeneration and impassibility to the divine nature derived from God (*Eph.* 7:2).

It is obvious that in discussions of this kind biological considerations are extremely important, and that in trying to determine what the modern significance of them may be we have to examine not only the general ideas about causation which are involved but also the question as to what ancient writers did or did not know about the process of conception.[7] It would appear that before we can classify the theological statements about virginal conception as derived from (1) historical tradition, (2) myth, or (3) poetry we must first try to determine exactly what those who made these statements had in mind.

C. ORIGIN AND CONCEPTION

Finally—a topic to which consideration of the origin of Jesus has led us—we may say something about the notions of causality and of biology involved in the early Christian ideas of conception in general. Quite a few years ago, H. J. Cadbury pointed out that there seems to be a certain measure of confusion in the language which New Testament writers use when they speak of this subject.[8] Whatever the sources of this confusion may be, it exists, and it continues in the writings of the earlier patristic writers. We may add that there is something quite different from confusion in what both Jesus and Paul say about marriage;

[7] See W. Dettloff, "Virgo-Mater. Kirchenväter und moderne Biologie zur jungfräulichen Mutterschaft Mariens," *Wissenschaft und Weisheit,* 20 (1957), 221-26, with the literature there cited.

[8] "The Ancient Physiological Notions underlying John I. 13 and Hebrews XI. 1," *Expositor,* 9 (1924), 430-36; more emphasis on Jewish sources in C. Spicq, *L'épître aux Hébreux,* 2 (Paris, 1953), 349.

neither of them ever explicitly relates it to the production of offspring. Just as neither says that marriage is intended for this purpose, so neither says anything about children as he discusses either marriage or divorce. Nowhere in the New Testament is there even an allusion to Genesis 1:28: "Increase and multiply."

We shall not, therefore, expect to find conception discussed in the New Testament at all, and the writers among whom it is discussed are the apologists of the late second and early third centuries. (1) Outside the church the most common view, which goes back to Aristotle, was that semen (the formal cause) provided soul for the embryo, while the catamenia (the material cause) provided its body. (2) The Stoics, on the other hand, held that semen consisted of two elements, corporeal moisture and psychic *pneuma*, the latter evidenced by heat and foam. The body of the embryo was derived from the *pneuma* of the semen, combined with the female's *pneuma* (part of her soul). Thus according to Aristotle the embryo was the product of both father and mother, while in the Stoic view it was derived almost exclusively from the father. (All ancient writers were completely unaware of the existence of the ovum.) In either case the semen was obviously animate, even if only potentially. (3) A minority view, ascribed to Pythagoras and others, was that both males and females emitted semen; this was too hypothetical to seem credible.

The statements of hellenistic Jews and Christians on this subject are not altogether consistent. The common view (1) is reflected in the book of Wisdom (7:2) and in Philo (*De opificio mundi* 132); but Philo also sets forth the Stoic view as his own (*De opificio mundi* 67). The least we can say is that he was not concerned with the subject. What looks like the Stoic view (2) is expressed by Justin in the passages quoted above and by Theophilus of Antioch (*Ad Autol.* 1:8): "God fashioned you out of a moist substance and [epexegetical *kai*] a tiny drop." Athenagoras (*Legatio ad Graecos* 35:6) condemns abortion on the ground that the embryo is animate; and it is probably animate because it owes its life to semen, as his comparison of intercourse to planting seeds suggests (33:2). Clement of Alexandria usually holds that the *pneuma* of the semen produces the soul of the embryo, even though in *Excerpta ex Theodoto* 17:2 he states that the embryo is produced from the mixture of two seeds. Finally, Tertullian reflects the same Stoic opinion. In his treatise *De carne Christi* (19:21-23) he holds that the "matter" of the semen, which is the heat of blood, is nourished by the mother's blood (cf. *De anima* 27); and when he is explicitly attacking contraception he says that "the whole fruit is already present in the semen" (*Apologia* 9:8).

Generally speaking, medical writers were aware that there was a difference between contraception and abortion (e.g., Soranus, *Gynaeciorum* 1:61), although hellenistic Jews and Christians either unintentionally or intentionally confuse the two.[9] It is fairly clear that when early Christian writers condemned contraception they did so largely on grounds derived from the scientific philosophy of their day. Unfortunately this scientific philosophy was based on inadequate scientific knowledge.[10]

We might perhaps suppose that when Paul speaks of *hē phusikē chrēsis* in Romans 1:26-27 he is implying that he agrees with the whole Stoic context in which such an expression is often found. But neither in this passage nor in I Corinthians 7:2-5 does he say anything about procreation as the goal, or even a goal, of sexual intercourse. Whereas his Stoic contemporary Musonius (fragment 13A, Hense ed., p. 67) stated that "the purpose of marriage is a common life and sharing in the production of children," and the great Galen (*De usu partium* 14:9, Helmreich ed., p. 313) was to say that the final cause of intercourse was the perpetuation of the race, Paul says nothing of the sort. His silence—eschatologically conditioned or not—must be respected as much as what he does say, especially at a point like this. He agrees with the Stoic moralists when he discusses mutuality in marriage; he does not necessarily agree with them at other points.

[9] E. g., Philo (in Eusebius, *Praeparatio Evangelica* 8:7:7); Athenagoras, *Legatio ad Graecos* 35:6; Clement, *Paedagogus* 2:96:1; Tertullian, *De exhortatione castitatis* 12. Hippolytus (*Ref.* 9:12:25) makes a distinction but condemns both.

[10] For Greek thought on this subject see J. Ilberg, "Zur gynäkologische Ethik der Griechen," *Archiv für Religionswissenschaft,* 13 (1910), 1-19. On conception see J. H. Waszink, *Tertulliani de Anima* (see above, p. 102 n. 44), pp. 342-46.

D. PREPOSITIONS AND DEMYTHOLOGIZING

We have now discussed three subjects related to causation and have tried to suggest that in each case the early Christian writers should be allowed to say what they do say, whether or not their statements raise problems in our own times. In the first case, we have suggested that a causal pattern of thought underlies many important New Testament statements and that in New Testament exegesis this pattern needs to be considered as fundamental. In the second case, we have seen how difficulties arose when some later Christian writers did not pay adequate attention to what the New Testament says. In the third case, we have argued that the silence of the New Testament also deserves respect and that some of the statements of later Christian writers are based on an inadequate grasp of biological phenomena. Obviously such cases raise considerable difficulties either for those who wish to maintain an unaltered tradition or for those who wish to "demythologize" only a few parts of it. All alike must constantly pay close attention to the earliest representations of the Christian faith.

9

ARISTOTLE AND THE CONVERSION OF JUSTIN

AT THE end of his article on "Justin and Middle Platonism" (*Zeitschrift für die neutestamentliche Wissenschaft*, 44 [1952-53], 157-95), C. Andresen points out that before his conversion Justin was "a religious philosopher" of "orthodox" Middle Platonism,[1] and that his conversion brought him to the Christian theology of history proved out of scripture. This picture of his conversion needs to be supplemented by an analysis of the strictly philosophical factors in it.

Among the Middle Platonists there were those, as Andresen notes (*ibid.*, p. 162 n. 19), who taught that the soul was not immortal (cf. Hippolytus, *Ref.* 1:19:13; Atticus in Eusebius, *Praeparatio evangelica* 15:9:2). Atticus, writing in the second half of the second century, denounced those who thus combined Aristotelian with Platonic doctrines. "Since all the doctrines of Plato are really attached to and dependent upon the divinity and immortality of the soul, he who does not accept this overturns the whole philosophy of Plato" (*ibid.* 15:9:5). But as a beginner in Platonism Justin had not been forewarned on this matter; indeed, he knew nothing of Aristotelianism except that it was "subtle" (*Dial.* 2:3).[2] He was therefore completely unprepared to deal with an "old man" who proceeded—in Atticus' terms, *Praeparatio evangelica* 15:9:6—"to deprive the soul of immortality and every other power," following the lines laid down by Aristotle, Dicaearchus, and other Peripatetics.

The "old man" had as his chief aim the proof that knowledge

[1] Cf. W. Schmid in *Hermeneia Regenbogen* (see above, p. 93 n. 20), pp. 163-82; also Andresen, *Logos und Nomos* (see above, p. 93 n. 20), pp. 308-72, for a comparison with Celsus.

[2] Aristotle's second-century critics called him obscure; cf. Atticus in Eusebius, *Praeparatio evangelica* 15:9:13; Irenaeus, *Adv. hear.* 2:14:4 (Harvey ed., p. 296).

comes only from sense-perception or from the Holy Spirit, and that the Platonic vision of God by the soul is impossible (*Dial.* 4:1). He therefore brought two sets of arguments against "the divine and immortal soul" (4:2), first showing that it has no special affinity with God and, second, that it is not immortal.

The first group of arguments shows that the soul's vision of God must depend on virtue, not on some innate quality, since (1) the souls of animals do not have the vision, (2) the human soul does not remember the vision if it has had it, and (3) it is wrongly said to transmigrate into the bodies of animals. Plato is wrong on all these points.

The second group of arguments shows that the soul is not immortal. Two arguments are used. (1) The soul is not immortal because *(a)* it is a part of the cosmos, which had a beginning; *(b)* what is immortal has no beginning; *(c)* therefore the soul, which had a beginning, is not immortal. (2) The soul is not immortal because *(a)* it is not life, since life would move something else, not itself; *(b)* it has life; *(c)* therefore it participates in something (life) of which it can be deprived.

These arguments deprived the soul of immortality and the powers of vision and transmigration. They produced Justin's conversion. Since the foundation of his Platonism had been removed and he could no longer "rejoice in the doctrines of Plato" (*Apol.* 2:12:1), he could only ask the "old man" for a new source of religious truth; this he found in the prophets of the Old Testament, who described what they had actually heard and seen under the inspiration of a Holy Spirit (*Dial.* 7:1).

The source of these arguments is significant. Such Peripatetics as Strato (fragment 123, Wehrli ed.) attacked the innate immortality of the soul by asking about the immortality of irrational animals and plants.[3] Strato also argued (fragment 127) that if souls had knowledge derived from reminiscence they could not have lost it.[4] And among Platonists themselves there was some

[3] Albinus (Hermann ed., p. 178, 21-26) avoids this difficulty by stating that irrational souls are probably mortal, and that the (human) soul has life innate with it (p. 178, 18).

[4] Justin should have said that according to *Phaedrus* 249c-d the soul does not forget the vision of God (cf. Maximus of Tyre, *Orationes* 11:9-10). For the whole argument on reminiscence cf. J. H. Waszink, *Tertulliani de Anima* (see above, p. 102 n. 44), pp. 303-7.

doubt about the transmigration of souls; some favored it, relying on *Timaeus* 41d, while others denied it, citing *Phaedrus* 250b (Hippolytus, *Ref.* 1:19:13).[5]

As for the immortality of the soul as such, Panaetius also used the argument that *quicquid natum sit interire; nasci autem animos* (Cicero, *Tusculanae disputationes* 1:79); at this point as at others (Cicero, *De finibus* 4:79) he may have followed Dicaearchus. To be sure, Atticus (Eusebius, *Praeparatio evangelica* 15:6:11) meets this objection by holding that coming into existence does not lead to passing away if God, the "best cause," so wills; but Justin was unaware of his argument.

The Peripatetics also pointed out that the soul is not life (Alexander of Aphrodisias, *Quaestiones* 2:8, Bruns ed., p. 54, 15) and, following Aristotle (*De anima* 1:3, 406 a3), argued that life produces movement in something other than itself (Alexander, *Quaestiones* 2:2, Bruns ed., p. 47, 3; cf. Sextus Empiricus, *Adversus mathematicos* 10:8; *Pyrroneioi hypotyposeis* 3:65-69). When the "old man" states that the soul lives by participating in life, he is reiterating the Aristotelian doctrine as set forth in doxographical teaching (*Dox.* 416, 3): "the soul is not immortal but participates in something divine."[6]

The positive doctrine of the "old man" is not Peripatetic but Christian, though its affinities to Plutarch have been pointed out by G. Verbeke.[7] We are here concerned only with his attack on Justin's Platonism. Justin did not recognize the source of the attack, though his pupil Tatian was aware that "Aristotle discredits the immortality of the soul" (*Or.* 25).[8] We thus answer the implicit question in the statement of Professor J. H. Waszink: "In the Christian Platonism of Justin nothing Aristotelian has been found as yet."[9] It was there, though Justin did not recognize it as such.

It is, of course, possible that there never was an "old man" and

[5] Cf. F. Cumont, *Lux perpetua* (Paris, 1949), p. 203 n. 6.

[6] Cf. Irenaeus, *Adv. haer.* 2:34:4 (Harvey ed., p. 383).

[7] *L'évolution de la doctrine du Pneuma* (Louvain, 1945), pp. 421-22.

[8] On Aristotle in Tatian and later Christian writers cf. A. J. Festugière, *L'idéal religieux des grecs et l'évangile* (2nd ed.; Paris, 1932), pp. 221-63.

[9] "Aristoteles," *Reallexikon für Antike und Christentum,* ed. T. Klauser, 1 (Stuttgart, 1950), 658.

that Justin's conversion took place in some less objective way. He may have been influenced by debates within Middle Platonism itself, debates in which Peripatetic arguments were employed. But from his account it seems fairly clear that before and after his conversion he was looking not so much for a theology of history as for a source of ultimate truth.[10]

[10] It is a pleasure to note that N. Hyldahl, *Philosophie und Christentum: eine Interpretation der Einleitung zum Dialog Justins* (Copenhagen, 1966), p. 169, states that "R. M. Grant is to be credited with . . . having perceived that the argumentation of the stranger is anti-Platonic," although he suggests that the documentation given above is one-sided and too limited. In regard to *Dialogue* 6:1-2 Hyldahl is willing to speak of "a kind of Aristotelianism twice removed" (p. 224), but prefers to treat the passage as Stoic in origin (p. 226).

10

THEOPHILUS OF ANTIOCH TO AUTOLYCUS

A. USAGE AND COMPOSITION

The three books to Autolycus of Theophilus of Antioch enjoyed a considerable measure of popularity among later Christian writers. His work was used not only by Greek but also by Latin writers. Eusebius found it in one of the libraries he used, probably at Caesarea;[1] it was also employed by Methodius, Epiphanius, Procopius of Gaza, and John of Damascus.[2] Novatian, Lactantius, and Jerome certainly knew his writings; probably Minucius Felix should be added to the list.[3] Three manuscripts of the *Ad Autolycum* survive; two are copies (one incomplete) of a third, an eleventh- or twelfth-century manuscript now in Venice.[4]

In recent years the microscopic investigations of Loofs[5] have raised a new problem: the relation of Theophilus to Irenaeus. Most students[6] have rejected his arguments without explaining the striking resemblances between the two authors. Let us first examine the dates of Irenaeus' work and of Theophilus'. As for

[1] Eusebius, *H.E.* 4:24 (cf. 6:20:1; 32:3).

[2] N. Bonwetsch, *Die Theologie des Methodius von Olympus* (Göttingen, 1903), pp. 163-64; U. v. Wilamowitz-Moellendorff, "Ein Stück aus dem Ancoratus des Epiphanios," *Sitzungsberichte der preussischen Akademie der Wissenschaften zu Berlin* (1911), pp. 759-72 (cf. also *Panarion,* Holl ed., Vol. 1, pp. 169, 14; 171, 3; 217, 6; 378, 19); Procopius, *Commentarius in Genesin* 2 (*PG* 87¹, 157B, 164B; cf. M. Richard, "Les fragments exégétiques de Théophile d'Alexandrie et de Théophile d'Antioche," *Revue biblique,* 47 [1938], 387 ff.); K. Holl, "Fragmente vornicänischer Kirchenväter aus dem Sacra Parallela" (*TU* 20/2, 56-57.

[3] Novatian, *De trinitate* 2; Lactantius, *Divinae institutiones* 1:23:2; Jerome, *De viris inlustribus* 23; Minucius Felix, *Octavius* 18:10.

[4] Werner Jaeger suggests a date later than the eleventh century.

[5] F. Loofs, *Theophilus von Antiochien adversus Marcionem* (*TU* 46/1).

[6] In most detail, F. R. M. Hitchcock, "Loofs' Theory of Theophilus of Antioch as a Source of Irenaeus," *Journal of Theological Studies,* 38 (1937), 130 ff., 255 ff.

Irenaeus, the five books *Adversus haereses* were apparently written in their present order, and Book 3 was written in the time of Eleutherus (3:3:3); but this date is too vague to help us. In *Adv. haer.* 2:22:2 he refers to a persecution and presumably has in mind the deaths of the martyrs of Lyons about 177. We can say no more than that he wrote between 178 and 189.[7]

Compared with Irenaeus' orderly work, the apology of Theophilus is somewhat unsystematic. The first book is an apology complete in itself; he calls it a *homilia* (2:1); it is close to the diatribe. The second book he calls a treatise *(syngramma)*; it also could stand alone. The third book is a *hypomnēma*, a collection of materials or memoranda.[8] It is a composite book; the first fifteen chapters deal with Christian morality, while chapters 16-29 are concerned with proving Christianity older and truer than all the poets and other writers. The only precise notice for dating these books is found in 3:27, where the chronography of Chryseros the Nomenclator ends with the death of Marcus Aurelius (March 17, 180). This part of Book 3 was therefore not finished before that date. About the same time there was a persecution of the Christians (3:30). Here Theophilus may be referring to the martyrdoms at Scilli on July 17, 180, or to later events. But what of the other books? The self-sufficiency of Book 1 makes it likely to have been composed first. It may have been Theophilus' first effort. And it is noteworthy that its "rationalistic" tone is considerably diminished in the other two books. Unfortunately the first book provides no clear evidence for its date.

The second book develops themes touched upon in the first, and after an attack on pagan gods leads up to an interpretation of the beginning chapters of Genesis. This is reinforced by quotations from the Sibylline Oracles and an anthology of Greek poetry. There is no way of dating the book. (The same observation applies to the first half of Book 3.)

We may conclude that Irenaeus might well have known the first two books *Ad Autolycum*, but that they are not likely to

[7] On these dates see F. Vernet, "St. Irénée," *Dictionnaire de théologie catholique,* eds. A. Vacant-E. Mangenot (Paris, 1899-1950), Vol. 8, pp. 2400 ff.

[8] Archytas in Diogenes Laertius 8:80; H. J. Cadbury in F. J. F. Jackson-K. Lake, *The Beginnings of Christianity,* 2 (London, 1922), 9 ff.

have formed the core of his own work. In the first place, a detailed analysis of the principal passages claimed by Loofs reveals striking differences. In the second place, why would Irenaeus have wanted to use Theophilus' work? The theological outlooks of the two writers are dissimilar. Irenaeus has the peace and certitude of a born Christian;[9] Theophilus is a convert who has read himself into the church (1:14). Irenaeus stands for what he knows as Christian tradition;[10] Theophilus seems to be working out his own theology. At the most important point where Theophilus shows theological originality—his application of the Stoic-Philonic distinction between the *logos endiathetos* and *logos prophorikos* to Christ (2:22)—Irenaeus explicitly rejects his idea.[11]

In briefly examining the composition and usage of Theophilus' three books we have come to the problem of his work as a theologian and apologist. First we shall examine his purely apologetic work, the first book to Autolycus, which was probably his earliest composition along these lines.

B. THE FIRST BOOK TO AUTOLYCUS

The first book has been called an example of confused rationalism.[12] Theophilus begins with a broad discussion of the love of truth which he assumes animates Autolycus, and then, turning to his opponent's ironic demand, "Show me your god," impugns his morality. Only the pure in soul (heart, Matt. 5:8) can see God. Your sins prevent the eyes of your soul from seeing (1:2). Here Theophilus is reinterpreting the vision of God in terms of the Philonic "eyes of the soul."[13] Autolycus

[9] T.-A. Audet, "Orientations théologiques chez Saint Irénée," *Traditio,* 1 (1943), 15 ff.

[10] *Ibid.,* pp. 22-23. Note the frequency with which Irenaeus refers to his teachers.

[11] *Adv. haer.* 2:13:2 (Harvey ed., p. 282), 28:4-5 (pp. 354-55); Audet, *op. cit.,* pp. 49-50.

[12] Cf. O. Clausen, "Die Theologie des Theophilus von Antiochien," *Zeitschrift für wissenschaftliche Theologie,* 46 (1903), 99; J. Lortz, *Tertullian als Apologet,* 2 (Münster, 1928), 5.

[13] *De confusione linguarum* 92, *De mutatione nominum* 3; K. E. Kirk, *The Vision of God* (New York, 1932), p. 38. Theophilus seems to be replying to something like the attack of Celsus in Origen, *Contra Celsum* 6:66.

cannot see, for he is disobedient to the law of God as set forth in the Decalogue. But he makes another request: "Show me the visible form of your god, since you see." Theophilus replies that the form of God is unspeakable and inexpressible. This idea is a commonplace of Judaism and early Christianity; it is found frequently in Philo, and according to John 5:37 Jesus tells the Jews that they have never seen the "form" of God. Then follows a series of appellations of God with the corresponding attribute to which each refers. These appellations and attributes were common in Hellenistic Judaism and among early Christian apologists (see chap. 5 below). At the end of the series Theophilus happens to mention the wrath of God. "Then you will say to me, Is God angry? Very much so" (1:3). This surprising statement, contradictory to the philosophical definitions he is about to give, shows not only his boldness in countering unanimous philosophical opinion,[14] but also his incomplete synthesis of philosophical and religious ideas.

The next few lines (1:4) sound a great deal like a section from some manual of Stoic theology. But since the Stoic elements and the Jewish elements which follow are so closely connected, he probably found them already fused in Hellenistic Judaism where the ideas had been taken over and interpreted by Philo.

In this section Theophilus says that God has no beginning, for he is uncreated; he is unchangeable, for he is immortal. He is called God because he placed *(tetheikenai)* all things in his steadfastness, and because he runs *(theein); theein* is to run and to move and to be active and to nourish and to foresee and to govern and to make all things live. But he is Lord, because he rules over the universe; Father, because he is before all things; Fashioner and Maker, because he is creator and maker of the universe; Highest, because he is above all; Almighty, because he himself rules and embraces all things.

According to Athenagoras the Stoics considered God *athanatos, akinētos, anaalloiōtos,* as well as *agenētos* and *aidios.* Zeno, Cleanthes, and Chrysippus called God *aidios,* while Chrysippus applied the same epithet to Zeus and called him *aphthartos.*

[14] Cicero, *De officiis* 3:102; M. Pohlenz, *Vom Zorne Gottes* (Göttingen, 1909).

These attributes were taken from the Stoics by Philo, who calls God *aidios*, *aphthartos*, and *atreptos*. Similarly Justin calls God *agenētos* and *aphthartos*. The word *anarchos* is apparently not applied to God by Philo, though Leisegang's index in the Cohn-Wendland edition is not complete, but it is so applied by Tatian and Clement of Alexandria. Like the other words here used to describe God, it probably comes to Theophilus from Stoicism. One of the etymological meanings of *theos* perhaps comes to him from a Jewish source: the derivation from *tithēmi*, found as early as Herodotus, was taken over by Philo. But the other meaning, though found in Plato, was exploited by Stoics: "They [Posidonius and Cleanthes] say that stars and constellations are called gods [*theous*] from *theein*, i.e., *trechein*, because they are always in motion."[15] Then in the last sentence of this quotation Theophilus gives a list of five Hellenistic Jewish names of God: *kyrios*, *patēr*, *dēmiourgos*, *hypsistos*, *pantokratōr*, with fairly obvious explanations of each one.

With these observations Theophilus touches briefly on creation. First, he believes, his argument can be still further improved by five parallels from the world of nature, four of which come from the Stoics probably through Philo.[16] He himself supplies a fifth. God is invisible; so is the soul, the helmsman, the sun, the king. Theophilus' own contribution is the parallel of the seed in the pomegranate (1:5) which reminds us of the Stoic comparison of God to honey in a honeycomb.[17] The comparison as he gives it is not quite right, for originally it must have been $\frac{\text{seed}}{\text{pomegranate}} = \frac{\text{man}}{\text{God}}$. Theophilus has to alter it to avoid identification of God with the world, and it now reads, "thus the whole creation is surrounded by the spirit of God, and the surrounding spirit with the creation is surrounded by the hand of God." But Logos and Sophia are the hands of God in 2:18; and in 2:10 Logos, spirit, and Sophia are identified. Let

[15] For the Stoics, M. Adler's index to *SVF*; for Philo, H. Leisegang's index to Cohn and Wendland's edition of Philo; for the earlier apologists E. J. Goodspeed, *Index apologeticus* (Leipzig, 1912). θεός from τίθημι : Herodotus 2:52, Philo, *De confusione linguarum* 137; from θέειν: Plato, *Cratylus* 397 c-d, Macrobius, *Saturnalia* 1:23:3.

[16] These four comparisons are to be found in *De Abrahamo* 74-76.

[17] Zeno, *SVF* 1:155.

us conclude that Theophilus' idea of the Spirit of God is somewhat unclear, especially in his first book.

In 1:6 Theophilus' style abruptly changes. His writing takes on a liturgical tone. And his description of the wonders of creation is much like that found in the old Jewish prayers Christianized in *Constitutiones Apostolicae* 8:12:9-15.[18] The floridity of this liturgy is not "primitive"; but the church of Antioch in 180 was not primitive either. An anaphora including a fairly lengthy preface seems to have been known to Justin.[19] Theophilus undoubtedly rewrites the preface which he would employ in the Eucharist; but it must have been much like what we find in *Ad Autol.* 1:6, containing passing allusions to the cosmological chapters of Job and to the Psalms.

The next chapter combines thoughts of God as creator and of God as physician, who will "raise your flesh immortal with your soul." At that time "made immortal, you will see the Immortal." This is perhaps an interpretation of I John 3:2, "We shall be like him, for we shall see him as he is," in the light of I Corinthians 15:53-54, according to which we shall "put on immortality."

In 1:8 Theophilus insists on the necessity of faith. Here he is not far from the New Testament. At this point faith to him does not mean rational inference from analogies, but confidence. Faith in the latter sense is needed by farmers, sailors, sick men, and students, who trust respectively the earth, the boat and captain, the doctor, and the teacher.[20] Theophilus claims that one ought to trust God, for he made each man out of nothing (a man has no existence before that of his father and mother) and formed him out of a tiny seed, which itself once did not exist. Since the seed was not really created out of nothing, the oddness of this argument is obvious. Theophilus endeavors to prop it up by mentioning his opponent's belief in miracles worked by gods who

[18] W. Bousset, "Eine jüdische Gebetssammlung im siebenten Buch der apostolischen Konstitutionen," *Nachrichten der Gesellschaft der Wissenschaften zu Göttingen*, phil.-hist. Kl. (1915), pp. 435 ff.; E. R. Goodenough, *By Light, Light* (New Haven, 1935), pp. 306 ff. If my hypothesis is correct, the similarity between *Constitutiones Apostolicae* 8:12:19 and *Ad Autol.* 2:27 noted by A. D. Nock and F. E. Brightman (*Journal of Theological Studies*, 30 [1928-29], 395) would be due to borrowing by Theophilus.

[19] *Dial.* 41; cf. *I Clem.* 19-20 and G. Bardy, "Expressions stoiciennes dans la Ia Clementis," *Recherches de science religieuse*, 13 (1922), 73 ff.

[20] Otto (*ad loc.*) observes that this is a common patristic argument.

are merely statues. But his conclusion—belief in resurrection—is hardly convincing.

Perhaps for this reason Theophilus turns aside to attack the gods as deified dead men. A resounding list of false gods, false because vulnerable, was becoming a tradition of Christian apologetic. It could lead to the conclusion (1:10) that these are not gods, but "images, the works of men's hands" (Ps. 103:4; 134:15) and "unclean demons" (Ps. 96:5). The perennial question of emperor-worship is briefly discussed, and the usual answer, that he deserves "legitimate honor," is given (1:11).

A brief transitional chapter (1:12) seems awkwardly placed. The subject looks back to the beginning of the apology, and might well have been discussed there. The name "Christian" is not absurd, but very suitable because of six parallels. (Theophilus does not mention the name of Christ.) The improvement resulting from the use of chrism is evident in the case of ships, towers, houses, human beings, and statues. It is perhaps less evident that air and earth are "anointed" by light and spirit. And Theophilus concludes with an invitation to Autolycus to become anointed with the oil of God encountered at baptism.

Finally we are able, thus prepared, to discuss the question of resurrection (1:13). "Show me even one man raised from the dead, so that seeing I may believe," says Autolycus. Unlike Quadratus, the earliest apologist, or even Irenaeus,[21] Theophilus is unable to bring forth any examples. He contents himself with three somewhat inconsistent preliminary rebuttals. Faith is of no value where there is evidence;[22] moreover you accept the "resurrections" of Heracles and Asclepius; finally you would probably not accept the evidence if I did provide it. Nevertheless—and here we come to the apologetic argument—God has provided many analogous examples. Theophilus, following the apologetic tradition,[23] sets forth four of them. There are "resurrections" of seasons, days and nights; of seeds and fruits; of the moon

[21] Quadratus in Eusebius, *H.E.* 4:3:2; Irenaeus, *Adv. haer.* 2:32:4.

[22] Probably Theophilus is working over John 20:29; in 1:14 he paraphrases John 20:27.

[23] I Cor. 15, *I Clem.* 24-25, Justin, *Apol.* 1:19, etc. See P. Nautin, *Je crois à l'Esprit Saint dans la Sainte Église pour la Résurrection de la chair* (Paris, 1947), pp. 30-32.

(monthly); and of the invalid who first loses weight and then regains it. Theophilus sees that the last example may be almost too natural, for the regained weight is due to foods; but he expresses belief that the work of restoration is God's.

An example of his rationalistic tendency may be seen in the discussion of seeds. They sometimes are swallowed by a sparrow or some other bird, then eliminated in deserted places, where they grow into trees. In *I Clement* 24-25 seasons and seeds are followed by the example of the phoenix, from the corruption of whose flesh "there springs a worm" which turns into another phoenix. Does Theophilus, skeptical of the existence of the phoenix, alter the content of the story?

His concluding chapter (1:14) combines personal testimony to his conversion by reading the prophets and finding their predictions fulfilled in order *(taxei)* with a warning about the future punishment they foretold.

The lack of intellectual rigor in this brief apology is evident. Theophilus' stress on arguments for the excellence of the name "Christian" reveals his wounded self-esteem, but hardly impresses the reader favorably. Where he adds his own contributions to the apologetic tradition we find them unconvincing (pomegranate seed, sparrow, sick man). He cannot finally distinguish between Christian and philosophical "faith"; he would agree with Aristotle that "faith is a sort of demonstration."[24] Unfortunately Theophilus' demonstrations do not demonstrate. Perhaps aware of his unconvincingness as a philosopher, in his later works he lays greater stress on revelation.

C. COMMENTARY ON GENESIS AND CHRISTIAN ETHICS

Most of the second book to Autolycus is concerned with the book of Genesis and its proper interpretation. In imperial times an interest in cosmogony was widespread,[25] and the book of

[24] *Rhetorica* 1:1:11; cf. R. E. Witt, *Albinus and the History of Middle Platonism* (see above, p. 94 n. 21), pp. 33-34; *SVF* 3, 147, 10 (No. 548); E. Aleith, *Paulusverständnis in der alten Kirche* (Berlin, 1937), p. 39.

[25] A. D. Nock, "The Genius of Mithraism," *Journal of Roman Studies,* 27 (1937), 111; A. Heidel, *The Babylonian Genesis* (Chicago, 1942), pp. 65-66.

Genesis was much admired and criticized.[26] Christians wrote commentaries on the hexaemeron,[27] sometimes highly speculative.[28] One of the most rationalistic, that of Hermogenes, was attacked not only by Tertullian[29] but even by Theophilus himself. According to Eusebius[30] the three books to Autolycus were different from the one against the heresy of Hermogenes, in which testimonies from the Apocalypse of John were used. But the commentary in Book 2 to Autolycus may well have provided Theophilus with material for later use against Hermogenes; it may be a first draft, since in 2:28 the serpent is called demon and dragon (cf. Rev. 12:9). In any event, the relation between *Ad Autol.* 2 and *Adversus Hermogenem* must have been close.[31]

The chapters (9-33) of exegesis of Genesis contain the passages of Theophilus most frequently cited by later writers, and they reveal him as the forerunner of the later Antiochene school of scriptural interpretation.[32] In them, as in the work of the later Antiochenes, there is a strong note of literalism and a clear reliance on Jewish exegesis.

Man begins from a foundation when he starts to build, but God's greater power is shown in his beginning not only *ex nihilo* but from above; for the heaven was made first in place of the roof.[33] Then came earth (the soil and foundation), abyss (the multitude of waters), darkness (caused by the heaven which God made, severing the waters and the earth like a lid), spirit

[26] *De sublimitate* 9:9 (Jahn-Vahlen ed., p. 19); Numenius, in Clement, *Str.* 1:150; *Corpus Hermeticum* 1:3; Galen, *De usu partium* 11:14 (Helmreich ed., Vol. 2, p. 158).

[27] For example, Rhodo (Eusebius, *H.E.* 5:13:8), Apion, and Candidus (*H.E.* 5:27); F. E. Robbins, *The Hexaemeral Literature* (Chicago, 1912).

[28] E. g., Simon Magus (Hippolytus, *Ref.* 6:15), Satornilus (Irenaeus, *Adv. haer.* 1:24:1, Harvey ed., p. 196), Marcus (1:18:1, p. 169).

[29] *Adversus Hermogenem.*

[30] *H.E.* 4:24.

[31] In *Vigiliae Christianae,* 3 (1949), 228-29, I showed that Tertullian, evidently following Theophilus against Hermogenes, uses the same text of Genesis.

[32] On Jewish influence see C. H. Kraeling, "The Jewish Community of Antioch," *Journal of Biblical Literature,* 51 (1932), 130 ff.

[33] Reading (Otto ed., p. 94) *τόπον ἐπέχοντος ὀροφῆς*, against L. Paul in *Neue Jahrbücher für Philologie und Pädagogik,* 113 (1876), 115, and E. Bruhn in *Commentationes philologae quibus O. Ribbeckio . . . congratulantur discipuli Lipsienses* (1888), p. 496.

borne above the waters (animating the creation, like the soul in man). This spirit is subtle and the water is subtle, so that the spirit nourishes the water and both of them, penetrating everywhere, nourish creation. The spirit had held the place[34] of light between the water and the heaven so that the darkness might not touch the heaven, which was nearer God. The heaven was like a dome-shaped covering over lump-like matter. Then the command (Logos) of God shone like a lamp and illuminated this roomlike region under heaven. (Moreover it was God who gave the names to created things, not man.) This heaven is invisible to us; the heaven we see is called "firmament," and half the water was taken up into it for rains, showers, and dews. The remaining half was left on earth for rivers, fountains, and seas. At first it covered the whole earth, especially hollow places, but then God through his Logos collected it in one place, and the previously dry land became visible, yet without form. Then God formed it and adorned it with herbs, seeds, and plants (2:13). On the fourth day the luminaries were made, after plants and seeds. This order was intended to refute the opinions of philosophers, who say that things growing on the earth are produced from the heavenly bodies. What is posterior cannot produce what is prior. These luminaries also contain the pattern and type of a great mystery: the sun is a type of God (surpassing moon in power and glory, remaining ever full and perfect) while the moon is a type of man (waning monthly, "dying," rising again). So the three days before the luminaries are types of the triad God, Logos, Sophia. The fourth day is the type of man, who needs light. Moreover the arrangement of the stars is typical: the bright fixed stars are in imitation of the prophets; the less bright are righteous men; and wandering planets are a type of the men who have wandered from God and abandoned his law and commandments (2:15). The fifth day saw the production of the creatures which came out of the waters. God blessed them in order to show the future blessing of baptism. Carnivorous animals are types of robbers and murderers and godless persons, but in general the fish and reptiles "received no specially distinctive

[34] Reading τόπον with Maranus and Otto against manuscripts' τύπον.

property" (2:16). On the sixth day God did not bless the animals he made but reserved his blessing for man. Quadrupeds are a type of men who mind earthly things, while birds are a type of those who fly upward in spirit. There are also birds which do not fly; these are sinful men. Wild beasts *(thēria)* are so called from their being hunted *(thēreuesthai)*—for everything was originally good, but when man, the master of the house, sinned, the slaves naturally, sinned too. Therefore when man comes back to his original, natural condition, the animals will once more be gentle (2:17). Finally, man, the only work created by God's hands, Logos and Sophia, came into existence (2:18). "Man became a living soul"; therefore by most persons the soul is called immortal. And God placed him in the eastern regions, "excellent for light, brilliant with a very bright atmosphere, possessing the finest plants" (2:19).

For his exegesis Theophilus generally turns back to his Jewish or Jewish-Christian teachers. Almost everything in his exegesis can be paralleled in Jewish haggadic literature. His two heavens, the one invisible, the other visible, are found in the Septuagint reading of Genesis 1:1, especially as interpreted by Philo, or in Deuteronomy 10:14 ("the heaven, and the heaven of heavens"), as interpreted by some of the Tannaite rabbis of the second century. The idea that God unlike man begins building from above is somewhat like the story in *Bereshith Rabbah* 1:13: "The rabbis said, Mortal man builds an edifice, and if he succeeds according to his intentions he can widen it as the building rises; but if not, he must broaden it below and narrow it at the top. The Holy One, blessed be he, is not so, however." Indeed, one of the many points on which the first-century schools of Shammai and Hillel disagreed was that of the order of creation; the school of Shammai, like Theophilus, maintained that heaven came first.[35] It is "parallel to the case of a king who first made his throne and then his footstool, for it is written, 'The heaven is my throne, and the earth is my footstool' (Isa. 66:1)." The division of the

[35] *Bereshith Rabbah* 1:15 (quotations from *Bereshith Rabbah* are taken from *Midrash Rabbah,* ed. H. Freedman and M. Simon, Vol. 1 [London: Soncino Press, 1939]); cf. L. Ginzberg, *Die Haggada bei den Kirchenvätern* (Berlin, 1900).

waters into equal parts is also rabbinic.[36] And the idea that the waters were put half in the firmament and half on earth is paralleled in *Bereshith Rabbah* 4:4: "R. Johanan said, The Holy One, blessed be he, took all the primeval water and poured half in the firmament and half into the ocean." The collection of the waters was made by the Logos; in *Bereshith Rabbah* 5:4 we read, "R. Levi said, Some interpreters, e.g. the Son of 'Azzai and the son of Zoma, interpret: The voice of the Lord became a guide to the waters, as it is written, 'The voice of the Lord is over the waters' (Ps. 29:3)." Theophilus' idea that the creation of the sun and the moon on the fourth day refutes philosophers is not quite paralleled by a Jewish view.[37] "R. 'Azariah said in R. Manian's name, The orb of the sun alone was created to give light; yet if so, why was the moon created? Because the Holy One, blessed be he, foresaw that the peoples of the world would treat them as divinities. Said the Lord, If they are two, opposed to each other, and yet the peoples of the world treat them as divinities, how much more would they do so if there were but one!" The restoration to gentleness of wild animals is to be found in the prophetic writings (Isa. 65:25). Finally, man as the only work of both God's hands is found in the later than second-century *Abot de-R. Nathan*:[38] "How do we know that Adam was made by the two hands of God? Because it says, 'Thy hands have formed me' (Ps. 119:73)." The "most persons" who considered the soul immortal are doubtless chiefly Greeks, but some Jews were included among them who so interpreted "Man became a living soul."[39]

Man, who was made by God's Logos and Sophia, was placed in a region to the east, after his formation. For he was made on the sixth day but formed only after paradise was made, after the seventh day (2:23). There were two trees in paradise which were unlike any others on earth—and paradise was on earth (not in one of the heavens). Three of the four rivers flowing out of Eden can be identified; Gihon is the Nile, and certainly we know

[36] *Bereshith Rabbah* 4:5.
[37] *Ibid.* 6:1.
[38] *Abot de-R. Nathan* 1:18; Ginzberg, *op. cit.,* p. 22.
[39] Compare Wisdom 8:19-20; 9:15.

the Tigris and Euphrates, which lie at our borders (2:24). Man's duties in the garden were to keep the divine commandments. But Adam disobeyed. Though the tree of knowledge and its fruit were good, not deadly as some think,[40] his transgression brought death. Adam was still an infant, unable to receive knowledge rightly. God was not grudging to him, as some think;[41] God wanted to test him, to see if he would obey his commandment. Moreover he wanted man to remain simple and sincere, in infancy; and it is right for children to obey their parents, and not to know too much for their age. We grow in knowledge as in years. And when a law requires abstinence from something, the law is not the cause of punishment, but disobedience and transgression. For this cause Adam was ejected from paradise (2:25). But God was a great benefactor to man in his keeping him from being forever in sin. Therefore he punished him so that at some future time he might return to paradise. This is why in Genesis the story seems to show man placed twice in paradise: the first time was when he was placed there; the second will be fulfilled after the resurrection and judgment. Just as a defective potter's vessel is remolded and made new and whole, so it happens to man in death. He is broken up so that at the resurrection he may be found healthy, i.e., spotless and just and immortal. God's question, "Where art thou, Adam?" (Gen. 3:9) is not really a question but a call to repentance and confession (2:26). Is man naturally mortal? Immortal? Nothing at all? No, he was made neither mortal nor immortal by nature. For if God had made him immortal from the beginning, he would have made him God; and if mortal, God would seem to be the cause of his death. God made him capable of either death or immortality; had he kept the commandment he would have been immortal. For God made him free and self-controlled. Though man acquired death for himself by his neglect and disobedience, God in his philanthropy and mercy gives him eternal life if he will obey the law and holy commandments which God gave us. He who keeps them can be saved and at the resurrection can inherit incorruption (2:27). After Adam was driven out of paradise he knew his wife Eve

[40] Doubtless Marcionites; cf. Apelles in Ambrose, *De paradiso* 7:35.
[41] Probably Marcionites.

(Gen. 4:1). God made her from his rib, not because he could not form her separately, but because he knew that a multitude of gods were going to be introduced by men through the deceit of the serpent. For though God is one, even at that time deceit was undertaking to spread secretly a multitude of gods and to say, "Ye shall be as gods" (Gen. 3:5). In order to refute this idea God did not make man and woman separately. In fact the creation of the two of them, in order that there might be greater benevolence between them, demonstrates the mystery of the sole rule of God. Adam prophesied that man would leave his father and mother and cleave to his wife, which is actually the case. Eve was so called because she was deceived by the serpent and became the origin of sin; the evil demon who spoke through the serpent, and still works in men possessed by him, is also called Satan, demon, and (from *apodedrakenai,* he fled from God) dragon; he was originally an angel (2:28).

These six chapters describing the fall of man, like those interpreting the story of creation, are largely derived from Jewish sources. The tree of knowledge puzzled the rabbis; some said its fruit was wheat, others grapes. "R. 'Azariah and R. Judah b. R. Simon in the name of R. Joshua b. Levi said, Heaven forfend (that we should conjecture what the tree was): The Holy One, blessed be he, did not and will not reveal to man what that tree was."[42] Philo, on the contrary, takes the tree as an occasion for allegorization: "This description is, I think, intended symbolically rather than literally, for never yet have trees of life or of understanding appeared on earth, nor is it likely that they will appear hereafter."[43] Man's duty in the garden was to study and keep the Law.[44] The idea of Adam as an infant is implied in *Bereshith Rabbah* 22:2: "R. Huna and R. Jacob in R. Abba's name said, No creature ever copulated before Adam; it is not written, man knew, but And the man; Knew intimates that he made known sexual functions to all." So Clement of Alexandria explains that before the fall Adam and Eve had no intercourse because they

[42] *Bereshith Rabbah* 15:7.
[43] *De opificio mundi* 154.
[44] *Bereshith Rabbah* 16:5; cf. Ginzberg, *op. cit.,* p. 38.

were children; their sin consisted in their premature marriage.[45] This view, which to some extent was shared by Irenaeus and other fathers, was rejected by Augustine.[46] Not all the third-century rabbis agreed that Adam was an infant: "R. Judah b. R. Simeon said, Eve too was created fully developed. R. Johanan said, Adam and Eve were created as at the age of twenty."[47] Adam's return to paradise and God's goodness toward him were matters for discussion in the late second century: "R. Judah and R. Nehemiah differ. R. Judah said, He was sent forth from the garden of Eden in this world and in the next. R. Nehemiah maintained, He was sent forth from the garden of Eden in this world, but not in the next. In R. Judah's view he laid a severe punishment upon him, while in that of R. Nehemiah he was lenient toward him. . . . R. Joshua b. Levi said, When he created him, he created him by his attributes of justice and mercy, and when he banished him, he likewise banished him in accordance with his attributes of justice and mercy."[48] The closest parallel to Theophilus' idea of God as potter is to be found in Sirach 38:29-30, but it was common.[49] God knew where Adam was, but he wanted him to consider what he was. According to Philo, God uttered not a question but "rather a threat and a conviction."[50] "Neither mortal nor immortal" is a Hebrew idea, according to Nemesius, bishop of Emesa in Syria in the fourth century, though some Jews thought of Adam as created immortal.[51] Man's free will is stressed in a fourth-century interpretation: "R. Tifdai said in R. Aha's name, The Lord reasoned: If I create him of the celestial elements he will live [forever] and not die; while if I create him of the terrestrial elements, he will die and not live

[45] *Protrepticus* 3, *Str.* 3:94 and 103.

[46] Irenaeus, *Adv. haer.* 3:22:4 (Harvey ed., p. 124); Augustine, *De peccatorum meritis et remissione* 1:37 (*PL* 44, 149); X. Le Bachelet in *Dictionnaire de théologie catholique,* Vol. 1, p. 370.

[47] *Bereshith Rabbah* 14:7.

[48] *Ibid.* 21:7.

[49] Isa. 14:9; 64:8; Jer. 18:1 ff.; *Testaments of the Twelve Patriarchs, Naphthali* 2:2-5 (Charles ed., pp. 45-46); Rom. 9:21.

[50] *Quaestiones in Genesin* 1:45 (Aucher ed., p. 30); see *Questions and Answers on Genesis,* trans. Ralph Marcus (Cambridge, Mass., 1953), pp. 25-26.

[51] Nemesius, *De natura hominis* 1 (Matthaei ed., p. 45); Wisdom 2:23-24; C. H. Dodd, *The Bible and the Greeks* (London, 1935), p. 160.

[in a future life]."[52] The idea that Eve was created from Adam to demonstrate that God is one is found in the Mishnah.[53] The picture of Adam as a prophet is derived from the deep sleep, like prophetic ecstasy, into which he fell.[54] The confusing sentence qualifying the "evil demon who spoke through the serpent" (2:28), partly based on Apoc. 12:9, is clarified by Clement: εὖα is the cry of Dionysiac enthusiasts.[55] The impossible etymology for δράκων is perhaps Theophilus' own.

Not all Theophilus' information about the past comes from the "prophets" of the Old Testament. Some of it is confirmed by the *Sibylline Oracles*, from which he gives three quotations (2:3, 31, 36).[56] The Sibyl herself, unlike Greek poets and philosophers, was inspired by God in the same way as the prophets (2:9). Theophilus can even speak of "the Sibyl and the rest of the prophets" (2:38).

Presumably Theophilus writes his interpretation of Genesis in opposition to more speculative interpreters, even though he does not mention them. His preliminary refutation of the schools (2:4; see chap. 11 below) includes an attack on Stoicism and Platonism which might well be aimed also at Hermogenes.[57] Perhaps relying on Hermas[58] he declares that the primary teaching of the inspired prophets is creation out of nothing, for there is not anything contemporaneous with God (2:10). Hermogenes denied this.[59] But in the exegesis proper Theophilus refrains from debate. His interpretation is addressed primarily to outsiders, who need not know anything about heresies except that they are like rock-bound islands (2:14). The teachers of truth and the lovers of truth (2:14; cf. 1:1) are to be found in churches.

Theophilus often tries to give a systematic, orderly picture of

[52] *Bereshith Rabbah* 14:3.

[53] *Sanhedrin* 4:5 (Danby ed., p. 338); Ginzberg, *op. cit.*, p. 25.

[54] So the LXX renders Gen. 2:21; a prophet in Clement, *Str.* 1:135; Tertullian, *De anima* 21; Ginzberg, *op. cit.*, p. 35.

[55] *Protrepticus* 12.

[56] See J. Geffcken, *Die Oracula Sibyllina* (Leipzig, 1902), pp. 227 ff.

[57] E. Heintzel, *Hermogenes der Hauptvertreter des philosophischen Dualismus in der alten Kirche* (Berlin, 1902), p. 5.

[58] *Mandates* 1:1; a favorite text of the ancient church.

[59] Tertullian, *Adversus Hermogenem* 2.

Christian thought. He collects "testimonies" about the Old Testament teaching concerning the "monarchy of God," the origin of the world, and the creation of man (2:35). In a later chapter (2:38) he presents passages of the Old Testament bearing on the destruction of the world by fire and on providence. This collection of quotations leads directly to further poetical verses which are derived from an anthology used constantly by Theophilus.[60] From this anthology he borrowed the idea of arranging verses topically, although Justin had already done the same thing.[61]

The second book to Autolycus is Theophilus' most sustained effort at writing theology. Like his apology (Book 1), it is not altogether successful. Compared with the writings of Justin, of Melito of Sardis, even of Athenagoras, of Irenaeus, we feel that something is lacking. That something seems to be a firm grasp on the apostolic tradition. Apologetic convention is probably responsible for his failure even to mention the name of Jesus, for Tatian is similarly reticent. But just here we might have expected a successor of Ignatius to escape from convention into religious reality.

D. ETHICS AND CHRONOLOGY

Some characteristic writing of Theophilus is to be found in his last book to Autolycus. Here he combines apologetic arguments with not too intelligent use of a few sources, but produces results which on his own grounds are fairly satisfactory. Three topics are discussed: the folly of Greek philosophy and religion (1-8), the ethical quality of Christian teaching (9-15), and the antiquity of the biblical revelation (16-30).

His principal source for the opinions of philosophers is a doxographical work, a list of philosophers' opinions arranged by subjects. Unfortunately Theophilus is not content to copy this source; he feels that he must improve it. For example, to a list of

[60] H. Diels in *Rheinisches Museum,* N. F. 30 (1875), 177; A. Elter, *De gnomologicorum graecorum historia atque origine* (Bonn, 1893), p. 136.

[61] Justin, *Apol.* 1:15-17.

those who recommend incestuous marriages he adds the name of Epicurus: "And Epicurus himself, along with his teaching atheism, advised intercourse with mothers and sisters, even in spite of the laws which forbid this" (3:6). As Diogenes Laertius 10:118 makes clear, Epicurus' view was precisely the opposite. In discussing atheists (3:7), Theophilus asserts that Plato regards the gods as material, that Pythagoras rejected providence, that Euhemerus said there were no gods and everything was governed automatically. This analysis is hardly correct. And Theophilus' denunciation of Greek religion is only slightly more interesting.

His discussion of Christian morality is more intelligent. In addition to his analysis of the Decalogue[62] he makes an effort to systematize Christian ethics. His model is the poetic anthology he so often employs. In chapters 11-14 he provides a discussion of four main headings of the law, thus anticipating the later Christian theory of the cardinal virtues.[63]

Heading	Biblical verse
metanoia	–Isaiah 55:6-7
	Ezekiel 18:21-23
	Isaiah 31:6 and 45:22
	Jeremiah 6:9
dikaiosynē	–Isaiah 1:16-17
	Isaiah 58:6-8
	Jeremiah 6:16 (also Ps.-Jerem.?)
	Hosea 12:6; 13:4
	Joel 2:16
	Zechariah 7:9
semnotēs	–Solomon: Proverbs 4:25-26
	Matthew 5:28, 32
	Solomon: Proverbs 6:27-29
(philanthrōpia)	–Isaiah 66:5
	Matthew 5:44, 46; 6:3
	Titus 3:1; I Tim. 2:1-2
	Rom. 13:7-8

[62] See my article, "The Decalogue in Early Christianity," *Harvard Theological Review,* 40 (1947), 1 ff.

[63] K. E. Kirk, *Some Principles of Moral Theology* (London, 1920), pp. 33 ff.

Such a fourfold division of virtues is originally Stoic,[64] but soon passed into Hellenistic Judaism where we find it in IV Maccabees 1:2-4 *(phronēsis, sophrosynē, dikaiosynē, andreia)* and Wisdom 7:7. Philo, who found these four virtues in the four rivers flowing out of Eden,[65] also tells us[66] that it was customary to divide synagogue lectures into two parts, one on the *eusebeia* and *hosiotēs* due to God and the other on the *philanthrōpia* and *dikaiosynē* due to men. Doubtless from such lectures Theophilus acquired not only his fourfold division of virtues but most of the texts to illustrate them. It is interesting to observe, however, that the last two virtues are illustrated by texts from both testaments. Such "syntheses" were produced in opposition to the Antitheses of Marcion in the latter half of the second century; they are intended to show the agreement of the Old Testament with the New. Such a collection is to be found in the lectures of the anonymous presbyter written down from memory by Irenaeus.[67] The four virtues themselves are "apologetic" in character; *metanoia* is substituted for *phronēsis*, *semnotēs (mechris ennoias*) for *sophrosynē*, and *philanthrōpia* for *andreia.* Thus the *De virtutibus* of Philo is divided under the headings *peri andreias*, *peri philanthrōpias*, *peri metanoias*, and *peri eugeneias*, and may originally have included a section *peri eusebeias.*[68] *Dikaiosynē* had been included in the *De specialibus legibus* 136-238, as Philo himself says.[69]

I have discussed elsewhere the biblical and post-biblical chronology of Theophilus.[70] In it he makes use of three sources: the Bible, Josephus, and Chryseros the Nomenclator. To suspect him, as Werner does,[71] of the intention to provide an eschatological scheme is over-subtle. It is just because he was unaware

[64] Stobaeus, *Eclogae* 2:6:5, Diogenes Laertius 7:92.

[65] *Legum allegoriarum* 1:63.

[66] *De specialibus legibus* 2:63.

[67] Irenaeus, *Adv. haer.* 4:32:1 (Harvey ed., p. 254).

[68] E. R. Goodenough, *An Introduction to Philo Judaeus* (New Haven, 1940), p. 52.

[69] *De virtutibus* 1. For the possible use of a somewhat similar anthology in *I Clem.* see now my discussion in R. M. Grant and H. H. Graham, *First and Second Clement* (*The Apostolic Fathers: A New Translation and Commentary,* Vol. 2; New York, 1965), pp. 10-13.

[70] See *Vigiliae Christianae,* 12 (1958), 136-44.

[71] M. Werner, *Die Entstehung des christlichen Dogmas* (Bern, 1941), p. 86.

of the eschatological implications of a world-chronology that his work became useless for his successors. In conclusion, we may say that the third book to Autolycus is characterized by much of the same ineptness that we find in the other two. Why must Theophilus make mistakes in attacking philosophers? Why must he give the Decalogue without some of the commandments and with some "judgments" from Exodus 23? Why is Book 3 partly repetition of Book 1 and why does it discuss two very loosely related subjects, Christian morality and the antiquity of Israel? The answers to some of these questions probably lie in the environment at Antioch; others find their solution in the man himself. Brought to Christianity by reading the prophets under the guidance of Jewish teachers, interpreting Christianity apparently on his own, he developed a theological system which was purely individual and was not destined to remain Christian. Of his successor Maximus nothing is known. But the next bishop of Antioch, Serapion, had to write a book to Domnus, "who had fallen away from the faith of Christ at the time of the persecution to Jewish superstition."[72] It is tempting to find in Domnus a follower of Theophilus.

E. THEOLOGY

The theological outlook of Theophilus is strikingly like that of Paul of Samosata, whom Bardy describes thus: "A theologian only because of the circumstances, the Samosatan was much more concerned with reconciling Jewish and pagan beliefs with the Gospel, on a monotheist basis, than with penetrating into the richness of the Catholic faith."[73] We have already briefly considered Theophilus' discussion of the attributes of God and of God as creator; let us turn to his teaching concerning the "hands" of God–Logos and Sophia.

a. Logos

Though God himself is known through his works (1:4, 5;

[72] Eusebius, *H.E.* 6:12:1.

[73] G. Bardy, *Paul de Samosate* (Bruges, 1923), p. 33; cf. Epiphanius, *Pan.* 65:2.

2:10) and through the prophets inspired by him (2:9; 3:17), Theophilus regards these activities of revelation as performed not directly by God himself, the one without beginning, changeless, immortal (1:4), but by his "hands" or powers, Logos and Sophia.

The chief interest to us in Theophilus' doctrine of the Logos is his distinction between the Logos *endiathetos* and the Logos *prophorikos,* apparently first made in the third century B.C. by the Stoic Chrysippus. In Stoic and other philosophical thought after his time, Logos as a psychological term meant both reason and voice or word. Within man it was reason, and expressed reason became voice or word. Logicians made a distinction between courses of study intended to train the mind and those to train the voice. Sextus Empiricus, following Chrysippus, says that man does not differ in his *prophorikos logos* (voice) from the irrational animals—for crows and parrots and magpies utter distinct sounds—but in his *endiathetos* (reason). Also following Chrysippus, a scholion on the *Theogony* of Hesoid identifies Iris with the *prophorikos logos* since *eirō* is the same as *legō*. And Galen says that "the philosophers" distinguish between the two logoi. The distinction is also to be found in Plutarch, as well as in the allegorists Cornutus and Heraclitus[74] who identify Hermes with the power of speech. In Philo there are many references to this distinction: for example, in the *vita Mosis* 2:129 he states that there are two logoi for each of us, the *prophorikos* and the *endiathetos.* The former serves for explanation, the latter for truth. God too has a Logos, but Philo avoids dividing it as he does its human counterpart.[75]

In the early Christian apologists this distinction is transferred to the divine Logos. Justin[76] compares the generation of the Logos to our human experience. When we express some logos (thought) we beget a logos (word); but it is not diminished in the process. Tatian[77] draws a similar parallel. And Athenagoras[78] says that the Logos was the first-begotten of the Father,

[74] *SVF* 2, 223, 137, 135; Plutarch, *De Iside* 7; Cornutus, *Theologiae graecae compendium* 16; Heraclitus,*Quaestiones homericae* 72.

[75] *De specialibus legibus* 4:69 *De vita Mosis* 2:127-29; J. Drummond, *Philo Judaeus,* 2 (London, 1888), 172 ff.

[76] *Dial.* 61:2.

[77] *Or.* 5 (Schwartz ed., pp. 6, 4).

[78] *Legatio ad Graecos* 10; cf. G. Bardy, *Athénagore* (Paris, 1943), pp. 56 ff.

but not as a creature, for from the beginning God, being eternal Nous, had the Logos (reason) in himself, for he is eternally reasonable. Here the distinction between *endiathetos* and *prophorikos* is at least implicit, and as Geffcken[79] points out, the expression "first-begotten" is taken from Justin, while the general idea seems to be Philonic. Such speculation was current to such an extent that Irenaeus devotes considerable space to rejecting these anthropomorphisms.[80] God's thoughts are not like those of men. While his condemnation is directed against the Valentinians it probably includes the speculations of the apologists as well. Similarly Clement[81] remarks that "we maintain that the essential Logos is God in God, who is also said to be 'in the bosom of the Father,' continuous, undivided, one God." The expression "essential" is an attempt by Clement to avoid the term *endiathetos.*

This distinction is made by Theophilus in 2:10, "God having his own Logos *endiathetos* in his own bowels begot him with his own Sophia,[82] bringing him forth before everything," and in 2:22 where the voice which Adam heard in Eden was the Logos, God's son. Originally the Logos was always *endiathetos* in the heart of God; it was his counselor, mind, and understanding *(phronēsis)*. "When God desired to make what he wished, he begot this Logos *prophorikos,* the firstborn of all creation,[83] not emptying himself of Logos (reason), but begetting Logos (a word) and conversing with his Logos continually" (2:22). Then follows a quotation from the first chapter of the Fourth Gospel; but clearly the emphasis is laid on the phraseology of Stoic psychology. The ambiguity of the Logos Christology comes from the ambiguity of the Greek word, and the decline of the doctrine was due to this confusion.

Theophilus, in formulating his Logos doctrine, is primarily

[79] *Zwei griechische Apologeten* (Leipzig-Berlin, 1907), p. 181.

[80] See above, p. 128 n. 11.

[81] *Excerpta ex Theodoto* 8.

[82] On such triads see H. Usener, "Dreiheit," *Rheinisches Museum,* N.F. 58 (1903), 1 ff., 161 ff., 321 ff. Cf. also Athene, who according to Ps.-Heraclitus 20 and other Stoic writers is *phronēsis*; following Chrysippus, Diogenes of Babylon *in eo libro qui inscribitur de Minerva partum Iovis ortumque virginis ad physiologiam traducens diiungit a fabula* (Cicero, *De natura deorum* 1:41; cf. Cornutus, *Theologiae graecae compendium* 20, Lang ed., p. 35, 6).

[83] Col. 1:15.

interpreting the words of scripture, though in terms derived from Stoic-Philonic psychology. Few of the functions of the Logos are assigned to the Logos *endiathetos*. Like reason in man it is situated in God's bowels (2:10) or heart (2:22). This idea is derived from the primitive psychology of the Old Testament.[84] It is always with him (2:10, 22); it is his counselor, mind, understanding (*symboulos, nous, phronēsis* 2:22). It is the *archē* in which God made heaven and earth (2:13). This interpretation of Genesis 1:1 and Proverbs 8:22 apparently begins in Colossians 1:16-18,[85] and is very common in early Christianity; ordinarily the "beginning" is referred to the Logos as Son.[86] In Theophilus' exposition the Son is mentioned only once and then it is made clear that he is the "voice" (Logos *prophorikos*) of God, which Adam heard in the garden (2:22). Before its generation or utterance by the Father, the Logos was not a person distinct from him. It was essentially one of his attributes (1:3).

When God desired to create the world, however, he generated or uttered the Logos, which then became *prophorikos*. The process was not effected all at once, however, for God brought the Logos (and Sophia) into being before everything else (2:10). Through the Logos he created the world. At this point the fundamental ambiguity of the term Logos becomes evident, for the Logos is no longer merely God's reason—though it always remains to converse with him (2:22)—but also his command (*diataxis* 2:13) and voice (*phōnē* 2:22). Clearly here Theophilus is interpreting the prologue to the Fourth Gospel, where at the beginning was the Logos and the Logos was *pros ton theon* and the Logos was the true light. And this prologue itself is an interpretation of Genesis 1:1-3; the Logos, as Theophilus says, is the command of God, shining like a lamp in an enclosed room, lighting the regions under heaven (2:13). By his Logos God brought together the water into one place (2:13). The three timeless days before the luminaries were made are types of God and his

[84] As a Greek writer, Theophilus is not quite accurate in his exegesis, for the bowels should be the seat of emotion rather than of reason. I owe this observation to R. Lansing Hicks.

[85] C. F. Burney, "Christ as the APXH of Creation," *Journal of Theological Studies*, 27 (1925-26), 160 ff.

[86] Aristo of Pella (M. J. Routh, *Reliquiae sacrae* [2nd ed; Oxford, 1846], Vol. 1, p. 95); Tatian, *Or.* 5; Irenaeus, *Epideixis* 43; etc.

Logos and his Sophia (2:15). In fact God made everything by his Logos; but he considered everything as by-products; the only work of his own[87] hands was man. Yet he did not [88] say, "Let us make man according to image and according to likeness," as if he needed assistance; for he said "Let us make" to none other than his own Logos and his own Sophia (2:18). The stress on "his own" makes it likely that Theophilus did not regard Logos and Sophia as helpers but as instruments of God's own will. The idea that God used instruments in creation is taken over from Platonism—where the instruments are really collaborators—by Greek-speaking Jews who wanted to explain away the anthropomorphic "hands" of God in the Old Testament.[89] When this interpretation of Genesis 1:26 as referring to the Logos was taken over by Christians, as in Justin, conservative Jewish teachers rapidly rejected it. In Palestinian Judaism the doctrine of "two powers" was condemned by the rabbis,[90] and the teachers of Trypho interpreted this verse as addressed by God either to himself or to the elements from which man was to be made.[91] Other teachers explained it as God's giving an example to man by asking advice of the angels.[92]

The work of the Logos was not finished when it had played its part in the creation of man, for it was not God whom Adam heard or who walked in the garden of Eden, but the Logos in the person of God (*enprosōpōs*). "Since the Logos is divine [*theos*] and begotten of God, whenever the Father of All wishes he sends it to some place; when it arrives it is heard and seen—having been sent by him—and thus is found in one place" (2:22). Thus are explained the theophanies of the Old Testament; it was not the Father of All who appeared to men, but his Logos, in his form. Moreover the Logos inspired Moses, Solomon, and the

[87] See chap. 5 above, p. 64 n. 24.

[88] Supplying οὐχ with Loofs, *op. cit.* (see above, p. 126 n. 5), p. 68.

[89] *Timaeus* 41c, 42e; Aristobulus in Eusebius, *Praeparatio evangelica* 8:10:7; Philo, *De opificio mundi* 72 ff.

[90] G. F. Moore, *Judaism in the Age of the Tannaim,* 1 (Cambridge, Mass., 1927), 364.

[91] Justin, *Dial.* 62.

[92] Ginzberg, *op. cit.* (see above, p. 136 n. 35), pp. 19 ff.

prophets, by coming down on them[93] and through them speaking forth the details of creation and everything else (2:10).

The Logos *prophorikos* or *phōnē* is also the *euangelios phōnē* (3:13). And therefore we may conclude that in 2:22 among the appearances of the Logos is included that in Christ—whose name Theophilus never mentions. Such an appearance need not be an incarnation. As in the case of Moses (2:10) the Divine Logos could have spoken through Christ as through an instrument. But if it could appear in the person (*prosōpon*) of God, it could probably appear in the flesh; it could become flesh, as Justin[94] explicitly teaches. Though it is the Logos, not Christ, to whom Theophilus refers as the Son of God, his definitions are taken from the books of the New Testament, and he certainly knew the Fourth Gospel. Although he explains the Logos in Stoic terms, it comes to him from the Gospel of John.

b. Sophia

In the theology of Theophilus, Sophia is one of the two hands of God. Before the creation it was, like the Logos, within God (2:9-10); God begot it with the Logos before everything else. The function of Sophia was the ordering of the invisible heaven and the chaos which God had created by his Logos (1:7; 2:33), for "God by Sophia founded the earth."[95] This "manifold Sophia of God"[96] gave names to all the component parts of the world. It prepared the parables of nature as proofs of the resurrection (1:13). It inspired the prophets (2:9), and it now purifies men's hearts and heals the eyes of their spirits (1:7).

Here as elsewhere Theophilus is reworking and interpreting biblical materials. The idea of Sophia as a power separate from God is expressed in Proverbs 8:1-31, Sirach 24:1-22, and Wisdom of Solomon 7:22 ff. In the New Testament of Theophilus, Christ is represented as Sophia in Matthew 11:28-30, a passage apparently based on Sirach 51:33-34. In the Pauline epistles Christ is

[93] As the *rhēma* came down on John the Baptist (Luke 3:2); *rhēma* = *logos:* Jer. 1:1-2, 4, etc.

[94] *Apol.* 1:5:4; 1:66:2.

[95] Prov. 3:7, quoted in 1:7.

[96] Eph. 3:10, quoted in 1:6.

the Sophia of God (I Cor. 1:24; Col. 1:15-18). Leisegang[97] suggested that the middle term by which Christ is equated with Sophia is *pneuma*, for Christ is *pneuma* in II Corinthians 3:17; but this is highly uncertain. In Luke 11:49 Sophia is represented as speaking about the deaths of the prophets; it is not clear whether it is identified with Christ or not. In the Fourth Gospel, as Leisegang remarks,[98] the Logos takes over all the functions which Sophia and *pneuma* had in Paul.

Theophilus was compelled to synthesize these divergent elements. While Philo has similar difficulties in equating Sophia and Logos and in keeping them distinct, Theophilus is rewriting not Philo but the New Testament. He may be influenced by Wisdom 9:1-2, where God makes all things by his Logos and by (ἐν) his Sophia forms man. While this originally meant simply "with reason and in wisdom," a literal-minded theologian could interpret it more precisely.

According to Rendel Harris[99] Theophilus reached his theory of Logos and Sophia "by a bifurcation of the original Wisdom into Word and Wisdom, the *trias* being thus an evolution of a previous *duas*; if we prefer to put it so, we may say that Theophilus identified the Wisdom-Christ, now detached from the Logos-Christ, with the Holy Spirit." It might better be said that in reading the prophets of the Old Testament, especially Solomon, Theophilus found Sophia playing the role which, when he read the works of the inspired John, he found ascribed to Logos. In the two passages in which his logos-doctrine is most clearly presented (2:10, 22) he is careful to state that Logos and Sophia are the same.

c. Spirit

To Theophilus "Spirit" has two meanings. In the first place it is the breath of God, which we ourselves breathe (1:7); it sustains the world and surrounds everything (1:5), like the *anima mundi* of the Stoics.[100] But the idea is essentially derived

[97] H. Leisegang, "Sophia," *RE* 3^A, 1034.

[98] *Ibid.*, 1035.

[99] J. R. Harris, *The Origin of the Prologue to St. John's Gospel* (Cambridge, 1917), p. 22.

[100] Wisdom 1:7; Aetius, *Placita* $1{:}6{:}1^I$ = *Dox.* 292.

from the Bible; if God held his breath the world would perish.[101] This spirit is life-giving: at the creation it was borne over the waters so that it could nourish water and then with water nourish the whole creation; it could mingle with water because both water and spirit are fine subtle elements (2:13). Before light came into existence, spirit between heaven and water kept darkness from touching God (2:13). After light shone forth, spirit with it "anointed" the air and everything under the heaven (1:12).

In the second place it is a medium of revelation, though not quite a personal agent like Logos or Sophia, both of whom are identified with it (2:10; 1:7). "We Christians are taught by a holy spirit which spoke in the holy prophets and foretold everything" (2:33). This spirit gave the prophets the wisdom which is from God (2:9). The prophets are *pneumatophoroi.* They became musical instruments of God (2:9-10); this is a Stoic-Philonic idea.[102]

Spirit is not primarily a person or hypostasis; it is the life-giving breath of God (1:3), or, as the Stoics were accustomed to define it, a wind.[103] This idea is also characteristic of biblical thought, since *ruach* in Hebrew means both "wind" and "spirit." Theophilus' idea of the subtlety of spirit doubtless comes from Wisdom 7:22-23, where it is stressed as one of the attributes of the spirit that is, or is in, Sophia. He often identifies spirit with Sophia. In 1:7 he shows that God made everything through his Logos and Sophia, for by his Logos "the heavens were established and by his spirit all their might" (Ps. 32:6, LXX). In 1:13 he refers to I Corinthians 12:11, "All these worketh the one and the same spirit," in the words, "All these worketh the Sophia of God." But the identification is not systematic or thoroughgoing. As Puech suggests,[104] Theophilus may prefer to work with the concept of Sophia as the third member of his triad rather than with that of Spirit because of the confusion involved in the latter term. But the triad is so fluid that we cannot be

[101] Job 34:14, quoted in 1:7.

[102] 2:9, 22; 3:12, 17; cf. P. Lejay in *Bulletin d'archéologie chrétienne,* 2 (1912), 43 ff.

[103] Aetius, *Placita* 3:7:2 (*Dox.* 374).

[104] *Histoire de la littérature grecque chrétienne,* 2 (Paris, 1928), 211.

certain, since as Theophilus himself says (2:10) Logos is Spirit of God and Beginning and Sophia and Power of the Highest.

Behind all his definitions lie the Christologies of the New Testament. It is Christ who is the Logos,[105] who is the Spirit,[106] who is the Beginning,[107] or in the Beginning,[108] and who is the Sophia of God and the Power of God.[109] In his doctrine of God and of what was to be known as the Trinity, Theophilus is not guided by the tradition of the church as was, e.g., Irenaeus. He was an individual interpreter of the inspired writings.

d. Eschatology

Last of all we may consider Theophilus' interpretation of the final fate of man and the world. As in so many other instances, at this point Theophilus tries to combine Hebrew and Greek ideas. Following the Old Testament he says that man will be raised by God (1:7, 8). In the resurrection is included every man (1:13), even those who are dead (2:38). On the other hand, man can in his lifetime become a god: *genētai theos* (2:27, compare 2:24). This idea is Theophilus' expression of an idea which was becoming common in the Christian theology of his time.[110] The idea of immortality is rare in Christian literature until we reach the apologists; originally it was simply regarded as a gift from God to man. But in Hellenistic thought, as A. J. Festugière[111] remarks, "Immortality presupposes becoming divine, for to become immortal one must be a god; immortality in the fullest sense is strictly a divine privilege." He cites[112] the words of Hippolytus in *On the Theophany:* εἰ ἀθάνατος, ἔσται καὶ θεός. Even to Philo such a statement would have seemed difficult. "One must become God—which is impossible—in order to comprehend God."[113]

[105] John 1:1; Rev. 19:13.
[106] II Cor. 3:17.
[107] Gen. 1:1; Col. 1:15; Rev. 22:13.
[108] John 1:1.
[109] I Cor. 1:24.
[110] Cf. J. Gross, *La divinisation du chrétien d'après les pères grecs* (1938).
[111] *L'idéal religieux des grecs et l'évangile* (see above, p. 124 n. 8), p. 39; cf. R. Bultmann in *Theologisches Wörterbuch zum Neuen Testament,* ed. G. Kittel (Stuttgart, 1933-), Vol. 1, pp. 23 ff.
[112] Festugière, *op. cit.,* p. 40; Hippolytus, *On the Theophany* (Achelis ed., p. 262, 9).
[113] Fragment 2 (ed. T. Mangey [London, 1742]) = John of Damascus, *Sacra Parallela* (*PG* 96, 472A).

In regard to the fate of the world Theophilus stresses the ἐκπύρωσις, a phrase he takes from the Stoics along with much of its content. The destruction of the world by fire is not portrayed in the Old Testament. The fire in Malachi 3:19 and Isaiah 30:28, 30, which Theophilus quotes, works only the destruction of the wicked, as does the "lake of fire" in Revelation 19:20. But in the early second century II Peter 3:10 states that at the day of the Lord "the heavens shall pass away with a great noise, and the elements shall be dissolved with fervent heat, and the earth and the works that are herein shall be burned up." Apparently, however, Christians are to escape the "cosmic bonfire" in some way, and they "look for new heavens and a new earth" (II Peter 3:13). Very similar and perhaps derived from the epistle is the view of Theophilus, though he expresses it in Stoic terms as ἐκπύρωσις and ἀποκατάστασις. Justin had been aware of the similarity of Christian and Stoic teaching on this subject: according to him the Sibyl and Hystaspes had predicted the destruction by fire of all corruptible things, and the Stoics taught that God himself would be resolved into fire; yet Justin had rejected this view, for God is the creator, not the creation.[114] But while the Stoic *ekpurosis* and *apokatastasis* were to be recurrent phenomena,[115] in the opinion of Theophilus and other Christians they occur but once; there is to be one *ekpyrosis tou kosmou* (2:37-38) accompanied by one *apokatastasis,* when man will cease from sinning and the wild animals will become gentle again (2:17). For the wicked there waits an eternal fire (1:14). In Theophilus' mind, as in the Bible, it is not quite clear whether the renewal is to be on this earth, as paradise was (2:24), or in heaven.

F. CONCLUSION

In his theological system Theophilus depends almost entirely on the Greek Old Testament and on the books which were coming to be regarded as the New Testament. In his interpretation

[114] *Apol.* 1:20:1-2.
[115] *SVF* 2, 625.

of the Old Testament he relied on his Jewish teachers; Judaism was flourishing in Antioch at the end of the second century, and in several areas Christians and Jews were closely related. For the New Testament he relies on his own synthesis; while he knows the apology of Justin he makes almost no use of it. His doctrine of God, while essentially based on scripture, is so greatly influenced by Stoic and Hellenistic Jewish concepts that when he declares that God is angry at sinners the anthropomorphic expression is surprising. In his doctrine of the Logos he attempts to apply to the Logos of the Fourth Gospel the distinction of Stoic and Philonic psychology between the *logos endiathetos* and the *logos prophorikos*. In the Old Testament, especially the Wisdom of Solomon, and in some early Christian writings he found another hypostasis, the Sophia of God. He endeavors to explain Sophia as one of the two "hands" of God, the other being Logos; but since in Christianity the concept of Logos is fundamentally a development out of that of Sophia, and since in the New Testament they are both based on the person of Christ, this distinction was not destined to survive. Theophilus himself says that they are identical. His doctrine of Spirit is also based on the Old Testament, but since Sophia has taken its place in his *trias*, it becomes vague and contradictory.

The most important part of scripture to Theophilus was the cosmogony in Genesis. In his time a lively interest was taken in ancient oriental cosmogonies, and he sets forth the true one in his second book to Autolycus. His exegesis is sober and ordinarily literal, though he finds ethical meanings in the various kinds of animals which God made on the several days of creation. Almost every element in his exegesis can be paralleled in the haggadic interpretations of the rabbis. Concerning the fall of man and the early history of mankind Theophilus again follows Genesis as it was interpreted by the rabbis. His eschatology seems to be based on earlier Christian teachers, however, possibly, as for the coming ἐκπύρωσις, on II Peter. While he uses the Stoic terms, such as ἐκπύρωσις and ἀποκατάστασις, his teaching is grounded in a literal interpretation of the New Testament.

The few scholars who in recent decades have devoted special attention to Theophilus have received strikingly divergent impressions of his ability. H. Gelzer,[116] studying the chronographical work of Julius Africanus, mentions "the crude chronological efforts of Theophilus of Antioch." Independent analysis confirms this judgment. His theological views have occasioned more discussion. Writing on the presentation of Christianity as monotheism in the Greek apologists, J. Lortz[117] remarks: "In this respect Theophilus is the most radical among the Greek apologists." O. Clausen[118] had earlier gone so far as to compare Theophilus' rationalism with that of Aristotle and the Stoa, and had said: "One cannot describe Theophilus as a 'Christian' character." G. Bardy,[119] on the other hand, denies any originality to Theophilus.

> Instead of a personal system, we have rather more likelihood of finding the simple echo of traditional teaching in Theophilus. When he speaks of the Trinity—and he is the first author with whom we find the term *trias* used of God—or when he explains that when God wanted to make what he had planned he generated the Word by bringing him forth—and he is also the earliest Christian writer to apply this Stoicizing epithet (*prophorikos*) to the Word—he is doing nothing extraordinary. He is using words already in circulation in his environment, formulas which everyone, at least in the Christian schools, knew at Antioch. That fact should be taken into account by all who seek for innovations.

This view, based on Theophilus' treatise, seems partly justified, although we know little of Christian schools at Antioch.

Only one critic, F. Loofs,[120] who was attempting to prove the dependence of Irenaeus on Theophilus, has become extravagant in speaking of his ability. "Both as a writer and as a theologian he was greater than Irenaeus." To this statement W. Bauer[121] replies: "I find it impossible to identify this theologian, who towers above Irenaeus, with the insipid chatterer of the *Apologia ad Autolycum*." The severity of this condemnation is matched by

[116] *Sextus Julius Africanus und die byzantinische Chronographie*, 1 (Leipzig, 1880), 22.

[117] *Tertullian als Apologet*, 2 (see above, p. 128 n. 12), 5.

[118] "Die Theologie des Theophilus von Antiochien," *Zeitschrift für Wissenschaftliche Theologie*, 46 (1903), 99.

[119] *Paul de Samosate* (see above, p. 145 n. 73), pp. 148-49.

[120] *Op. cit.* (see above, p. 126 n. 5), p. 431.

[121] *Rechtgläubigkeit und Ketzerei im ältesten Christentum* (Tübingen, 1934), p. 23 n. 2.

a comment of V. Schultze,[122] to whom it "appears out of the question that an Antiochene bishop could have penned a writing so riddled with inanities and errors."

It is evident that most scholars have no very high opinion of Theophilus of Antioch. And the purpose of the present study has not been to present an apology for his work. But in the course of the analysis it has perhaps become clear that some of Theophilus' aberrations are due to his methods, and that these methods are the ordinary methods of his time. Most of his difficulties, however, are due to his own limitations. He was unable to understand clearly either the Christian faith or the Hellenistic philosophies opposed to it. For this reason his books to Autolycus were not influential in the history of Christian theology. Their value lies in their reflection of the beginnings of a learned theology. Theophilus was not successful; but he was a pioneer.

[122] *Altchristliche Städte und Landschaften III. Antiocheia* (Gütersloh, 1930), p. 57.

11

IRENAEUS AND HELLENISTIC CULTURE

THREE RECENT discussions of Irenaeus by Reynders, Audet, and Enslin have examined the thought of Irenaeus almost exclusively in relation to the Christian tradition.[1] This attitude toward his writings is natural, since Irenaeus lives so largely within the tradition; but he lived in the philosophical-rhetorical world of his day as well as in the church. It is the purpose of this paper to examine some of the ideas which he shares with non-Christians of the second century. First we shall consider his use of doxographical materials for the opinions of philosophers, and then we shall turn to his knowledge of other authors and of rhetoric.

A. THE USE OF HANDBOOKS

Early Christian writers commonly take their quotations of Greek philosophical opinions from handbooks. These books consist of lists of the views of philosophers and schools, summarized and arranged under subject-headings. The book commonly employed in the second century goes back to the reign of Augustus, when it was compiled by a certain Aetius and soon used by Philo of Alexandria. In the middle of the second century it was edited and ascribed to Plutarch; another form is that used by Stobaeus in the fifth century. Christian writers employ both

[1] B. Reynders, "La polémique de S. Irénée," *Recherches de théologie ancienne et médiévale,* 7 (1935), 5-27; T. A. Audet, "Orientations théologiques chez S. Irénée," *Traditio* 1, (1943), 15-54; M. S. Enslin, "Irenaeus: Mostly Prolegomena," *Harvard Theological Review,* 40 (1947), 137-65. R. Forni, *Problemi della tradizione: Ireneo di Lione* (Milan, 1939), is concerned exclusively with tradition.

forms. They are eager to arrive at the conclusion expressed by Philo in a fragment preserved by John of Damascus.[2]

> All the different philosophies which have flourished in Greece and barbarian lands have not been able to reach the slightest certain conclusion in their investigation of physical problems. This may clearly be demonstrated by the differences, disputes, and dissensions of those of each sect who are seeking to establish their own views and overthrow those of their opponents.

This is the way in which Philo uses doxographical information.[3]

Both Justin Martyr and Tatian use doxographical collections, but they do not seem to have known the work of Aetius in either Plutarchan or Stobaean form. Athenagoras, on the other hand, writing his *Legatio* in the year 177,[4] makes unmistakable use of Pseudo-Plutarch's doxography, and states that he uses doxographical literature.[5] In his sixth chapter, stock quotations from the *Timaeus* (28c, 41a) are followed by opinions of Aristotle (Aetius 1:7:16) and the Stoics (Aetius 1:7:17), and when in chapter 23 he refers to the views of Thales and Plato on demons, the former opinions are taken, as he implies, from a doxography,[6] and he seems to quote from the *Timaeus*, epistles, and *Phaedrus* of Plato through a commentator like Albinus.[7]

Athenagoras' use of the doxography is not extensive, and we shall have to turn to his successors to find more thoroughgoing quotations from it. At Antioch about 180 it was used by Theophilus in his second and third books *Ad Autolycum*. Unfortunately the way he uses it reveals the slightness of his acquaintance with philosophy. The best example of his method is to be found in *Ad Autolycum* 2:4.

[2] John of Damascus, *Sacra parallela, PG* 96, 472.

[3] *De providentia* 1:22, *De somniis* 1:21 ff.; *Dox.* 1-2; P. Wendland, "Eine doxographische Quelle Philos," *Sitzungsberichte der preussischen Akademie der Wissenschaften zu Berlin* (1897), pp. 1074 ff.

[4] G. Bardy, *Athénagore* (see above, p. 146 n. 78), pp. 10-16.

[5] *Dox.* 4-5; cf. J. Geffcken, *Zwei griechische Apologeten* (see above, p. 147 n. 79), pp. 175-76. I do not agree with the view that a Jewish doxography underlies Athenagoras.

[6] Cf. Pseudo-Plutarch 1:7:11; 1:8:2.

[7] Geffcken, *op. cit.*, p. 212; cf. P. Wendland, *Hippolytus Werke* 3 (Leipzig, 1916), xxi and 19; R. E. Witt, *Albinus and the History of Middle Platonism* (see above, p. 94 n. 21), p. 144.

a) Some of the Stoa deny that there is any God at all, or if there is one they say that God thinks of no one but himself.	Aetius 1:7:1: Some philosophers like Diagoras of Melos and Theodore of Cyrene and Euhemerus of Tegea say there are no gods at all.
b) And the nonsense of Epicurus and Chrysippus set forth these views entirely.	(Theophilus' own idea)
c) But others say that all things are self-moved, the world was uncreated and nature is eternal . . .	Hippolytus *Ref.* 1:22:3: Epicurus
no providence, but God is only everyone's conscience.	[Menander] *Monostichoi* 81 (Jaekel ed., p. 107)
d) Others postulate a divine spirit immanent in everything.	Aetius 1:6:1: Stoics
e) Plato and those of his sect confess God as uncreated and father and maker of all.	Aetius 1:7:31
f) Then they suppose God and matter to be uncreated, and they call matter coeval with God.	Hippolytus, *Ref.* 1:19:4

Theophilus' main source seems to be Aetius, but he does not follow him continuously, and he makes use of other doxographical writers.[8] Elsewhere (3:3) he points out that the philosophers disagree, as one can tell by examining their *dogmata* on the gods, on the origin of the world, and on providence. These are titles taken from Aetius.

Theophilus' contemporary Irenaeus also made use of doxographical materials. Diels observed that in listing the opinions of philosophers (*Adv. haer.* 2:14:1-6, Harvey ed., pp. 287-97) Irenaeus followed Pseudo-Plutarch.[9] There is another passage which Diels does not seem to have observed in which Irenaeus is stressing the complete adequacy of scripture and the impiety of looking for solutions of problems not given there.[10] There are admittedly problems in scripture itself, but they are no greater

[8] *Dox.* 59. Theophilus' mind is so confused on philosophical questions that his sources are difficult to identify.

[9] *Dox.* 171-72.

[10] On this cf. Audet, *op. cit.*, p. 52.

than the insoluble difficulties in science (*Adv. haer.* 2:28:1-2, pp. 349-51). These problems are almost entirely taken from the headings of Pseudo-Plutarch.

a) Cause of Nile's rise	4:1
b) Birds' winter home	(derived from 4:1, mention of winter)
c) Cause of tides	3:17
d) What lies beyond ocean	(derived from 3:17, mention of ocean)
e) Cause of rain, lightning, thunder, clouds, fogs, winds, etc.	3:3—4:7
f) Cause of snow, hail, etc.	3:4
g) Cause of phases of moon	2:29
h) Cause of difference between salt and fresh water	3:16
i) Differences between metals, stones, etc.	(derived from 3:16, differences)

It is interesting to observe that Cicero (*De natura deorum* 2:130-32) had mentioned the overflow of the Nile, the Etesian winds, the tides, and the existence of salt water far from the shore among his proofs for divine providence; elsewhere (*Adv. haer.* 2:30:3, p. 363) Irenaeus' own thought is close to his. But here Irenaeus concludes that "in all these matters we shall not be loquacious in searching for their causes; God alone who made them is truthful."

We may wonder what justification Irenaeus has for so easily dismissing these questions. Some of them had already been answered, but we must remember that answers which seem correct to us might easily have seemed absurd to an ancient writer. There was no clearer criterion of truth in these matters, as Irenaeus insists.

a) The first problem which Irenaeus chooses was notorious in antiquity for its difficulty. Thales, as the doxography notes, had attempted to solve it by the hypothesis that the Etesian winds kept the Nile from flowing to the sea; many later writers, including Philo (*De vita Mosis* 1:115), accepted his theory.[11] But Herodotus had pointed out the fact that other rivers were not affected by these winds (2:20). Anaxagoras, on the other hand, urged that it rose when the winter snow melted, but many writers rejected this view because they did not believe that snow falls in hot countries.[12] Herodotus himself argued that the winds brought rains which filled the Nile (2:24-25); his theory is open to the objection which he had already brought against Thales! (Cf. J. O. Thomson, *History of Ancient Geography* [Cambridge, 1948], pp. 272-73).

b) Aristotle (*De natura animalium* 8:12, 596b20) had already known where storks and cranes went in the winter, but his information had been forgotten by such writers as Pliny (*Historia naturalis* 10:61). Aelian (*De natura animalium* 3:13) knows, however.

c) The cause of the tides was difficult to determine. Aristotle had attributed them to special characteristics of the Spanish coast. While Posidonius visited Cadiz to make observations and correctly concluded that they were related to the phases of the moon, Pseudo-Plutarch does not mention him.[13]

d) What, if anything, lies beyond the world-encircling ocean was a matter of conjecture. Clement of Rome, whom Irenaeus knew, had spoken of "the ocean which man cannot pass and the worlds beyond it" (20:7). Origen (*De principiis* 2:3:6, Koetschau ed., p. 121, 14) understands Clement to refer to the Antipodes, which were regarded as nonexistent by Lactantius (*Divinae institutiones* 3:24) and Augustine (*De civitate Dei* 16:9, Welldon ed., p. 201), as well as by Plutarch (*De facie in orbe lunae* 7, p. 924a).

e, f) These subjects, *ta meteōra*, were discussed in detail by Aristotle, Posidonius, and Seneca; Lucretius devotes his sixth book to them, following the Epicurean Letter to Pythocles (Diogenes Laertius 10:84 ff.). As Bailey observes,[14] these were

[11] A. Wiedemann, *Herodots zweites Buch* (Leipzig, 1890), p. 102.

[12] *Ibid.*, pp. 104 ff.

[13] Strabo, *Geographia* 3:5:8; J. B. Mayor, *M. Tullii Ciceronis De Natura Deorum Libri Tres,* 2 (Cambridge, 1880), 105.

[14] C. Bailey, *Titi Lucreti Cari De Rerum Natura Libri Sex,* 3 (Oxford, 1947), 1551-52.

"phenomena . . . in which the workings of nature showed some apparent element of caprice." Lucretius gives concurrent explanations of them, but non-Epicureans might well think that such explanations were alternative.

g) Most ancient philosophers supposed that the phases of the moon were due to the earth's shadow (Aetius, *Placita* 2:29:6 = *SVF* 2, 676); Pseudo-Plutarch also lists the minority opinions of Anaximander, Berossus, Heraclitus, and "some" Pythagoreans. But Lucretius (5:705-50) had already refused to come to a conclusion.[15]

h) The saltiness of sea water was a problem. Lucretius (5: 269-72) describes how water is purified by the ground and returns through springs to the sea, but he does not explain its saltiness.[16] Irenaeus knows a rhetorical proverb, "He who wants to learn that sea water is salt doesn't need to drink up the whole sea"; this is discussed in the next section.

i) On the genera of metals and stones we may refer to the work of Pseudo-Democritus, *Peri sympatheiōn kai antipatheiōn*, mentioned by Tatian (*Or.* 17, Schwartz ed., p. 18, 12); cf. J. Bidez-F. Cumont, *Les mages hellénisés*, 1 (Paris, 1938), 198 ff.; A. J. Festugière, *La révélation d'Hermès Trismégiste*, 1 (Paris, 1944), 224 ff. *Corpus Hermeticum* 16:4 (Nock-Festugière ed., Vol. 2, p. 233, 12) explains how the three elements of fire, water, and earth come from a single source; cf. *Asclepius* 3 (Nock-Festugière ed., Vol. 2, p. 299, 7) on the origin of species.[17] But we cannot be sure that Irenaeus knew anything about such matters. Is he thinking of "living" and "dead" stones (cf. J. E. Plumpe, *Traditio*, 1 [1943], 8 ff.)?

Irenaeus' attitude is much like that of the Stoa. Strabo tells us that the Stoics, with the exception of Posidonius (who, he says, imitated Aristotle), avoid inquiring into causes because of their obscurity (*Geographia* 2:3:8).[18] But Irenaeus inclines to-

[15] *Ibid.*, pp. 1437 ff.

[16] *Ibid.*, 1359-60.

[17] Geffcken (*op. cit.*, p. 224) suggested that Athenagoras' reference to Hermes Trismegistus (chap. 28) had in view something like *Asclepius* 37.

[18] Compare the old Stoic view: Diogenes Laertius 7:13 = *SVF* 3, 642. Knowledge of such matters requires superhuman inspiration: Virgil, *Georgics* 2:477-82, *Aeneid* 1:742-46; Ovid, *Metamorphoses* 15:69-72; Wisdom 7:17-18. I owe these references to Professor A. D. Nock.

ward skepticism. No one can count grains of sand or stones or waves or stars;[19] even if it were possible, the cause of the resulting number could not be explained (*Adv. haer.* 2:26:3, Harvey ed., pp. 346-47). With the skeptics he would say that there is no evident criterion of truth.[20] They too refrain from making "firm and positive assertions about any of the matters dogmatically treated in physical theory."[21]

In fact, his thought is eclectic, and his philosophical vocabulary is not that of any one school. He uses *katalēmpsis* for "comprehension" (1:2:5, p. 21; 1:8:1, p. 68) but rejects the Stoic *logos endiathetos* (2:12:4, p. 278). He uses *hypolēmpsis* for "opinion," as the Stoics and others use it (3:5:1, p. 19), but he speaks of *hē alēthēs peri tōn ontōn hōs estin hypolēmpsis* (5:2:3, p. 323). The skeptics also speak of the *dogmatikē hypolēmpsis* of Stoics, "the acceptance of a fact which seems to be established by analogy or some form of demonstration" (Sextus Empiricus, *Pyrroneioi hypotyposeis* 1:147). In the skeptical manner he criticizes Plato for introducing the cup of oblivion, *ostensionem nullam faciens, dogmatice autem respondens* (2:33:2, p. 378). Yet in another place (2:32:1, p. 372) he contrasts *doxa anthrōpinē* with the *dogma* of Christ. And finally, as Audet observes,[22] he stresses experience almost in Aristotelian fashion! Irenaeus cannot be classified among philosophical schools. His interest, as we shall see, is more rhetorical than philosophical.

B. RHETORICAL EXAMPLES

At the very beginning of Irenaeus' work against heresies is a passage which has been taken rather too literally by his inter-

[19] Cf. H. V. Canter, "The Figure ΑΔΥΝΑΤΟΝ in Greek and Latin Poetry," *American Journal of Philology,* 51 (1930), 37-38 ("an impossible count or estimate"). The number of the stars or of grains of sand was a skeptical example (Sextus Empiricus, *Adversus dogmaticos* 2:147). Cf. also Sirach 1:2-3; it is a common expression in the Old Testament.

[20] Sextus Empiricus, *Pyrroneioi hypotyposeis* 1:179.

[21] *Ibid.* 1:18.

[22] Audet, *op. cit.,* pp. 26-27. Sometimes, as W. L. Knox observes (*Journal of Theological Studies,* 47 [1946], 181), Irenaeus writes as a historian. He wrote a "very brief and most useful" book *Pros Hellēnas peri epistēmēs* (Eusebius, *H.E.* 5:26). Could Eusebius' notion possibly derive from a hasty perusal of Pseudo-Plutarch, bound among Irenaeus' writings? Cf. H. J. Lawlor, *Eusebiana* (Oxford, 1912), pp. 136 ff., for Eusebius' use of titles.

preters. His disavowal of rhetorical skill is not unrhetorical, and it shows an awareness of a standard from which he is willing to deviate (*Adv. haer.*, 1, praef., 6). Similarly his apology for living in Gaul among the Celts is the statement of one who is accustomed to better things. Rohde has pointed out that the second sophistic movement was militantly Hellenic,[23] and as a matter of fact Gaul was an area where sophists became rich.[24] Let us look at Irenaeus a little more closely.

The fact that he presents his biblical theology in terms of education[25] should encourage us to think that he regarded his own education as not wholly a mistake; and so we are not surprised to find him pointing out to his opponents their lack of education and implying his own thorough training. They do not know music, arithmetic, geometry, astronomy, or any other theoretical arts; nor have they gone on to medicine, the study of herbs, or any other study related to health; nor do they know painting, sculpture, metal-working, or marble-carving, etc.; they are ignorant of these practical arts as well (*Adv. haer.* 2:32:2, p. 373). They are unwilling to apply the effort, the thought, and the perseverance required. When he states that they cannot learn a tenth or even a thousandth part of these studies, he apparently has in mind both their own limitations and the vastness of the educational process. Perhaps he is also considering the fact that he himself does not know it all.[26]

What does Irenaeus know? Education naturally began with the alphabet, and Irenaeus has retained an interest in Jesus' early knowledge of the alphabet, while questioning the apocryphal story (1:20:1, pp. 177-78);[27] he also knows that the alphabet was introduced to Greeks by Cadmus and Palamedes (1:15:4, pp. 152-53).[28] Of course his attention was drawn back to these mat-

[23] E. Rohde, *Der griechische Roman* (Leipzig, 1876), p. 297.

[24] Lucian, *Bis accusatus* 27.

[25] F. R. M. Hitchcock, *Irenaeus of Lugdunum* (Cambridge, 1914), pp. 52 ff. A. Dufourcq, *S. Irénée* (Paris, 1904), pp. 64 ff., claims that this idea is Aristotelian, but as F. Vernet, "Irénée (Saint)," *Dictionnaire de théologie catholique*, eds. A. Vacant-E. Mangenot (Paris, 1899-1950), VII^2, 2508, observes, it is implied in the Bible itself.

[26] Cf. F. H. Colson, "Philo on Education," *Journal of Theological Studies,* 18 (1916-17), 151 ff.

[27] See my note in *Harvard Theological Review,* 39 (1946), 72.

[28] The same story is found in Pliny, *Historia naturalis* 7:192.

ters by Marcosian alphabetism. The boy would next go on to Homer, whom Dio Chrysostom (*Or.* 18:8:2, De Budé ed., p. 317, 13) calls "the beginning and middle and end" of rhetoric; Irenaeus frequently quotes Homer, refers to himself as one experienced in Homeric studies, and perhaps (as Ziegler suggested[29]) made up a cento of verses from various parts of the Iliad and the Odyssey (1:9:4, pp. 86-87). Rhetoric paid considerable attention to Aesop's fables (Hermogenes, *Progymnasmata* 1, Spengel ed., p. 3, 5), and Irenaeus uses the dog chasing his shadow for an illustration (2:11:1, p. 275; cf. Babrius, *Fabulae* 79, Rutherford ed., p. 77). The rhetoricians usually begin their manuals with an analysis of mythology, and Irenaeus is able to refer to the Lernaean hydra (1:30:14, p. 241), the Pandora "of Hesiod" (2:14:4, p. 296; cf. 21:2, p. 325), and the giants (2:30:1, p. 362). Dio Chrysostom recommends the study of Menander and Euripides (*Or.* 18:6:2, De Budé ed., p. 316, 19); Irenaeus refers to Menander (2:18:5, p. 315), paraphrases Antiphanes' *Aphroditēs gonai*, calling it "theogony" (2:14:1, p. 287),[30] alludes to the "tragic Oedipus" of Sophocles (5:13:2, p. 356), and mentions Pindar and Stesichorus (2:21:2, p. 326; 1:23:2, p. 192).

While he calls his opponents "sophists and grammarians" (4:1:1, p. 146), he himself is not ignorant of literary problems. He is aware of textual difficulties (5:30:1, p. 406); he knows what allegorical interpretation is and tries to avoid it;[31] and he knows that the apostle Paul makes use of the rhetorical figures *hyperbaton* and *diastasis* (3:7:1, p. 25).[32] In his anti-Gnostic arguments, as Reynders observes,[33] he relies almost entirely on the dilemma and the question.

The most striking example of Irenaeus' rhetorical training is to be found in his use of examples. These examples or illustrations are scattered through his pages. There are not many

[29] H. Ziegler, *Irenäus der Bischof von Lyon* (Berlin, 1871), p. 17.

[30] See also my article on "Early Christianity and Greek Comic Poetry," *Classical Philology*, 60 (1965), 157-59: not Antiphanes but Aristophanes.

[31] P. Lestringant, *Essai sur l'unité de la révélation biblique* (Paris, 1942), pp. 206-7.

[32] Theon, *Progymnasmata* 4, (Spengel ed., p. 82, 19); Aristides, *De arte rhetoricae* 1:3, p. 464, 16. Irenaeus uses *diastema* (cf. 2:25:1, p. 343) for *diastasis*.

[33] *Op. cit.* (see above, p. 158 n. 1), p. 8.

of them, but they can be classified under several headings and clearly reveal their rhetorical origin. We shall not discuss them in detail but shall simply classify them, adding a few parallels.

a. Art

1:8:1 (p. 67), 2:15:3 (p. 304; from Melito, *Homily on the Passion* 36-37), 19:8 (p. 320), 33:4 (p. 379)

These examples come from the sophistic *ekphraseis* of pictures and statues like the *Imagines* of Philostratus; cf. E. Rohde, *op. cit.*, p. 335 n. 3. The first one seems to be an expansion of Babrius, *Fabulae* 95: 63-64 (Rutherford ed., p. 92).

b. Hunting

1:31:4 (p. 243), 2:14:8 (p. 301)

Philostratus, *Imagines* 1:28, describes a boar hunt, and items similar to these two examples may be found in Xenophon, *Cynegeticus* 10:7-8; 11:2; Oppian (?), *Cynegetica* 4:77 ff., 374 ff.

c. Natural Philosophy and Physical Theory

2:12:2 (p. 277), 12:4 (p. 278), 18:5 (p. 314), 19:6 (p. 319), 28:4 (p. 354), 4:9:2 (p. 169), 39:1 (p. 298), 5:3:3 (p. 327), 27:2 (p. 399)

These examples show Irenaeus to have been a pupil of those who "though they pursued philosophy, had the reputation of sophists." Philostratus (*Vitae sophistarum* 8) expressly distinguishes Dio Chrysostom and Favorinus (W. Schmid, *RE* 6, 2078-84) from real sophists.

d. Music

2:25:2 (p. 343)—lyre

This comparison was very common; cf. P. Lejay, "Le plectre, la langue et l'esprit," *Bulletin d'ancienne littérature et d'archéologie chriétienne,* 2 (1912), 43-45.

e. Medicine

3:5:2 (p. 19), 25:7 (p. 137), 4:38:1 (p. 292)

In discussing the use of Menander and Euripides, Dio Chrysostom (*Or.* 18:7:2, De Budé ed., p. 317, 2) uses a medical example. They are common.

f. Kingship, Gymnastics, Metal Working

1:8:1 (pp. 67-68), 5:13:2 (p. 356), 29:1 (p. 404)

I have omitted one example of military affairs (3:23:2, p. 126), two of kingship (4:34:1, p. 270; 5:24:4, p. 390), and one of either gymnastics or military affairs (5:22:1, p. 385) from my list in the belief that Irenaeus constructed them himself. The others give a picture of his rhetorical environment. One example listed under "natural philosophy" is especially striking. It is the proverb, "He who wants to learn that sea water is salt doesn't need to drink up the whole sea" (2:19:8, p. 320). Athenagoras (*Legatio ad Graecos* 12) says: "Those who appreciate honey and milk in small doses appreciate the whole if it is good." And similarly Philostratus (*Vitae sophistarum* 22) quotes Dionysius of Miletus as saying that honey should be tasted with the finger-tip and not by the handful.[34] Evidently it is a proverb for rhetoricians, and Irenaeus' thought is closely related to it.

Is there any possibility of tracing Irenaeus' teachers? We know one writer familiar to Irenaeus who was interested in works of art, in philosophy, and in animals. Indeed this man has been suggested as the Syrian source of Oppian's *Cynegetica.*[35] This person is Tatian. Two points tell against such a theory of Irenaeus' source. In the first place, Irenaeus disliked Tatian intensely (1:28:1, p. 220; 3:33:7, p. 130). More important, Tatian's slight knowledge of art and his strenuous opposition to it make it impossible for him to have been the writer or speaker who sympathetically explained the artist's mind to Irenaeus. We do not know who his teacher was, just as we do not know who all his Christian teachers were. But we may be sure that in rhetoric as in Christianity he was an apt and intelligent pupil.

A good many years ago, this judgment was made of Irenaeus.[36] "Unlike his master Justin, Irenaeus is no philosopher. He does

[34] Cf. Lucian, *Quomodo historia conscribenda sit* 4.

[35] M. Wellmann, *Der Physiologos* (*Philologus, Suppl.* 22, 1931), 9; cf. Wellmann, "Timotheos von Gaza," *Hermes,* 62 (1927), 189 ff.

[36] G. Bardy, *Littérature grecque chrétienne* (Paris, 1928), p. 36. In spite of Justin's admiration for philosophy, his education lacked such elementary studies as music, astronomy, and geometry (*Dial.* 2; cf. Plato, *Protagoras* 318 e, and the Hermetic *Asclepius* 13, Nock ed., p. 312, 2, with n. 115, p. 369). His advancement in Platonism was insufficient to give him the correct answer to the question whether the soul remembers the vision of God (*Dial.* 4; cf. *Phaedrus* 249 c-d). On this error depends his Christian opponent's victory. See chap. 9 above, and the study by W. R. Schoedel, "Philosophy and Rhetoric in the Adversus haereses of Irenaeus," *Vigiliae Christianae,* 13 (1959), 22-32.

not attack profane wisdom; he is content with disdaining it." Too often we are content with a picture of Irenaeus as orthodox but rather stupid. The camera needs to be refocused and the picture taken over again. Irenaeus is certainly devoted to Christian tradition. But he represents the confluence of Hellenism and Christianity no less distinctly than the apologists do. And he is choosing from the maelstrom of Greek thought what he thinks will be adaptable to the Christian religion. He should not be neglected simply because his results survived.[37]

[37] I have already referred to the article by W. R. Schoedel (p. 168 n. 36) which develops and refines some of the argumentation provided here. In addition, it should be noted that P. Hefner ("Theological Methodology and St. Irenaeus," *Journal of Religion,* 44 [1964], 294-309) presents conclusions in harmony with its main lines (cf. N. Brox, *Offenbarung, Gnosis und gnostischer Mythos bei Irenäus von Lyon* [Salzburg, 1966], p. 11), while R. Wilken has further discussed "The Homeric Cento in Irenaeus, 'Adversus Haereses' I, 9, 4" in *Vigiliae Christianae* 21 (1967), 25-33.

IV
ASPECTS
OF
CHRISTIAN GNOSIS

12

GNOSTIC AND CHRISTIAN WORSHIP

One of the values of the study of Gnosticism, especially the Christian Gnosticism of the second century, is that it permits us to see more clearly and often with some degree of magnification certain tendencies apparently present in late Judaism and early Christianity but not well attested by more "orthodox" evidence. This is the case with certain questions relating to the meaning and purpose of worship. The three principal views held in Gnostic circles are related to views held, if not always clearly expressed, in Jewish and Christian circles generally. The three are these: (1) acceptance of the ordinary Christian pattern of worship with emphasis on baptism and the Eucharist, along with special interpretations of both; (2) movement toward the creation of additional modes of worship, especially sacramental; and (3) rejection of conventional worship as irrelevant and, indeed, mistaken. We shall endeavor to examine the witnesses to each of these viewpoints and to look at some aspects, at least, of their religious backgrounds, although, as one would expect, the viewpoints are not always sharply defined.

A. ACCEPTANCE OF A COMMON PATTERN

The principal witnesses to the sharing of common worship with other Christians are naturally those Gnostics who stand closest to Christian life and thought generally. The primary examples are provided by Marcion and his followers and Valentinus and most of his followers. The Marcionites whom Tertullian knew, for example, used water and oil, and probably milk and honey as well, in baptism (*Adversus Marcionem* 1:14); their practice thus did not differ from that of other Christians. When they admitted only unmarried persons to baptism, they differed from most other Christians, but not from orthodox Christians in Syria.[1] In later times they baptized dead catechumens, but we have no early evidence for this custom. As for the Eucharist, it was a rite which they performed in a manner somewhat different from that followed by orthodox Christians, using water rather than wine. Tertullian says they liked fish (*Adversus Marcionem* 1:14) perhaps because of the fish at the post-resurrection meal in Luke 24:43-44; but Tertullian may just be speaking ironically. They certainly did not regard the bread as becoming the body of Christ, for they explained *Hoc est corpus meum* as *Hoc est figura corporis mei* (*ibid.*, 4:40).

Tertullian complains that they allowed women to baptize (*De praescriptione haereticorum* 41), but it is only from the fourth-century Epiphanius (42:3:6) that we hear of repeated baptisms, three or even more, and of fasting on the Sabbath in opposition to the God of the Jews who rested on that day (42:3:4). It would appear that these liturgical practices developed late and that in the second century Marcionite usage and ordinary Christion usage were much the same.

Among the Valentinians, or many of them, liturgical worship was close to that of ordinary Christians. Thus Ptolemaeus in writing to Flora states that all the rites of the Old Testament were abolished as rites but now are understood in a deeper spiritual sense. He speaks of sacrifices, circumcision, the Sabbath, fasting, and the paschal lamb; but he admits that the actual practice of fasting has been maintained even by Gnostic Christians because of its beneficial effect on the soul.[2] Theodotus clearly tells us that baptism involves the use of water and oil; the Eucharist involves bread, if not wine.[3] According to the *Gospel of Philip* (p. 123, 15) "the cup of prayer contains wine and water."[4]

[1] A. Vööbus, *Celibacy, a requirement for admission to baptism in the early Syrian Church* (Stockholm, 1951).

[2] Epiphanius, *Pan.* 33:5:9-15 (cf. Matt. 6:16-18, 9:15 and parallels).

[3] Clement, *Excerpta ex Theodoto* 82:1.

[4] For "the cup of prayer" compare "the cup of blessing," I Cor. 10:16.

We cannot deny that some Valentinians, at least, belonged to our second group—the liturgical innovators—for the evidence provided by Theodotus and the *Gospel of Philip,* not to mention the Marcosians, clearly points in this direction. But to a considerable extent they retained common Christian rites even though they interpreted them in their own way. In their view baptism, for example, should be primarily an occasion for joy.[5] (Perhaps they were thinking of the joy which, according to John 16:21, follows birth "into the world" and *a fortiori* birth into a new life.) Because unclean spirits are often present at baptism, however, it is necessary to employ fasting, petitions, prayers, laying on of hands, and kneelings (suitable for the confession of sins according to Tertullian and Origen[6]) when a soul is being saved from the world and "from the mouth of lions" (Ps. 21:22).[7] This kind of explanation obviously places the ritual actions on a lower level than the spiritual experience of rebirth—though the various ritual actions are preserved.

While these Valentinians thus interpreted baptism more "spiritually" than did many other Christians, on the other hand the followers of the Syrian Gnostic Menander took it more literally. Irenaeus (*Adv. haer.* 1:23:4) tells us that in Menander's view the disciples who experienced his baptism would not die but would live on, enjoying perpetual freedom from old age. Perhaps this language was itself symbolical, but it would appear that the disciples took it rather literally, since Menander's sect seems to have disappeared in the course of the second century, presumably because the promise was not fulfilled.

B. CREATION OF ADDITIONAL MODES OF WORSHIP

One of the most interesting additions apparently made by Gnostics to the church's patterns of liturgical observance was provided by the followers of Basilides in Egypt. It would ap-

[5] Perhaps this is what the fragmentary passage in *Philip* (p. 122, 24-26) about entering the kingdom "laughing" means.

[6] Tertullian, *De oratione* 23; Origen, *De oratione* 31:2-3.

[7] Clement, *Excerpta ex Theodoto* 83-84.

pear that Easter, the annual celebration of Christ's resurrection, was observed early in the second century in some orthodox communities.[8] We know that the Basilidians tried to date the crucifixion; Clement tell us about four different dates they provided, presumably in an effort to get a precise date for Good Friday. In addition, however, he tells us that they observed the day of Christ's baptism (significant for their theology) and spent the night before it in reading, doubtless liturgical.[9] This sect, therefore, reflects the process of liturgical enrichment which in another way is expressed among the Jewish Christians who, unlike other Christians, observed the Jewish Passover (see Lohse's work cited in note 8). It may be significant that, as Preuschen argued, the date for the baptism came on January 6 (later, Epiphany) according to the Roman-Alexandrian calendar, on December 25 according to the old Egyptian system. If this is so, the Basilidians' holy day anticipated later Christian usage in both regards.

It is difficult to tell just how far back the rites ascribed to the Simonians go; Irenaeus describes their performance of various magical rites and says that they worshiped statues of Simon-Zeus and Helen-Athena, calling Simon *kyrios* and Helen *kyria*.[10] Their claim that a statue of Semo Sancus on the Tiber Island in Rome was really a statue of Simon Sanctus[11] shows that they were accustomed to translate the language of other religions into their own terminology certainly by the middle of the second century. But the Simonians apparently drifted farther and farther away from ordinary Christianity. We hear nothing about their participation in baptism or Eucharist. Their liturgy must have been almost exclusively their own.

The liturgical practices of the Marcosian Valentinians, however, stand fairly close to those of the church. Their baptism took place in water, and the formula they employed is probably based on the reinterpretation of a Christian one. It read thus:

[8] Cf. B. Lohse, *Das Passafest der Quartadecimaner* (Gütersloh, 1953), pp. 117-18.

[9] *Str.* 1:146; see E. Preuschen, "Todesjahr und Todestag Jesu," *Zeitschrift für die neutestamentliche Wissenschaft*, 5 (1904), 1-17.

[10] Irenaeus, *Adv. haer.* 1:23:3.

[11] Justin, *Apol.* 1:26:2.

"into the Name of the unknown Father of all, into Truth the Mother of all, into Him who descended into Jesus, for unity and redemption and fellowship with the powers."[12] This looks like baptism into, or in the name of, the Father, the Son, and the Holy Spirit, along with "one church, the remission of sins, and the communion of saints." Indeed, generally speaking, Christian and Valentinian baptisms were very close to each other, as is shown by the fact that both church writers and Gnostics try to differentiate them. The Marcosians tried to establish a difference by making use of formulas in Hebrew, not in Greek. The clearest picture of the liturgical life of this wing of Valentinianism is presented in a statement in the *Gospel of Philip* (p. 115, 27-29): "The Lord did everything in a mystery: a baptism and a chrism and a Eucharist and a redemption and a bride-chamber."[13] Here the first three rites are essentially Christian in origin, while the last two reflect Gnostic creativity. According to Irenaeus (*Adv. haer.* 1:21:1), there were "as many 'redemptions' as there were mystagogues." Later Marcosians complained that Irenaeus misunderstood their liturgical system, and that a "first washing" was later followed by a second one, called "redemption." This looks like a gradual theological development among Marcosians, an effort to bring order out of chaos, but it may be that they were trying to create something like confirmation in addition to baptism, for Hippolytus says that the redemption formulas were used either in initiation or just before death.[14] Their intepretation of the redemption rites strongly recalls what Jewish writers of the period say about Passover—a rite interpreted by Philo as "a symbol of the migration from body to spirit, the purification of the soul."[15] The "bridal chamber" too may be related to Hellenistic Jewish ideas of the "mystic marriage" of which Philo has so much to say,[16] although the Christian "holy

[12] Irenaeus, *Adv. haer.* 1:21:3, with T. Barns in *Journal of Theological Studies*, 6 (1904-5), 406-8. For Theodotus baptism is in the Name of Father, Son, and Holy Spirit (Clement, *Excerpta ex Theodoto* 80:3).

[13] See E. Segelberg in *Numen*, 7 (1960), 189-200.

[14] *Ref.* 6:42:1; 6:41:2-5.

[15] E. R. Goodenough, *An Introduction to Philo Judaeus* (see above, p. 144 n. 68), p. 208.

[16] E. R. Goodenough, *ibid.*, pp. 190-92, and *By Light, Light* (New Haven, 1935), pp. 235-64.

kiss" has probably contributed something. What we suggest, then, is that among the Valentinians new liturgical developments owe much to Hellenistic Jewish spirituality—concretized into ritual. It may even be that the two rites, "redemption" and "bridal chamber," were brought over together because in mystical Judaism Passover was regarded not only as redemption but also as the wedding day of Yahweh with Israel. We may add that among Jewish Christians of the second century the Christian Passover was called "saving" (*sōtērion*);[17] if our analysis is correct, the Marcosians were not far, at least in their point of departure, from some other Christians.

From the witness of the Basilidians and the Marcosians we conclude that during the second century there was a considerable liturgical development among some Gnostic groups, but that among those we have mentioned this development as such did not constitute a real change. More orthodox Christians, too, were elaborating their ritual, as we see from witnesses like Justin and, especially, Hippolytus. The basic difference lies in the theological outlook, not in the nature of the rites as such.

C. REJECTION OF CONVENTIONAL WORSHIP

In the teaching of Jesus considerable emphasis is laid on the need for reality in worship; this emphasis can be epitomized in the Johannine saying about worship "in spirit and in truth" (John 4:24), in the cleansing of the temple, and in the Matthean sayings about genuine almsgiving, prayer, and fasting (Matt. 6:1-18). Paul rejects the observance of Sabbaths, new moons, annual festivals, and sacred years (Gal. 4:10; cf. Col. 2:16). Outside Christianity there was a theory, set forth by the philosopher Posidonius presumably with some help from Hellenistic Jews, that originally Judaism was a pure, nonritualistic religion; superstitious successors of Moses added the dietary legislation, circumcision, etc., and, by implication, the whole cultic apparatus.[18]

[17] Lohse, *op. cit.*, pp. 50-56.
[18] Strabo, *Geographia* 16:2:35-37; see E. Norden in *Festgabe . . . Harnack* (Tübingen, 1921), pp. 292-301.

There were thus grounds, Christian and non-Christian alike, for a certain hesitancy in relation to liturgical development. Many Greek philosophers had criticized, at least in principle, the employment of prayer, sacrifice, and cultic worship generally.[19]

The earliest Christians, or semi-Christians, we know to have rejected such worship were the Docetists criticized by Ignatius of Antioch early in the second century. "They abstain from Eucharist and prayer because they do not acknowledge that the Eucharist is the flesh of our Savior Jesus Christ which suffered for our sins and was raised by the Father in his kindness" (*Smyrn.* 7:1). Here "prayer" presumably means common worship, as in other Ignatian passages (*Eph.* 5:2; *Magn.* 7:1; 14); but by extension it could easily come to mean "prayer in general," as it did among certain Gnostic groups.

The followers of the Gnostic Prodicus definitely taught that "one must not pray" or "it is not necessary to pray" (*mē dein euchesthai*); Clement of Alexandria claims that their teaching was derived from various philosophers.[20] Origen says that similar Gnostics rejected not only prayer but baptism and the Eucharist as well, because of their abhorrence of anything perceptible to the senses.[21] (Both Clement and Origen insist upon the spiritual nature of prayer, though Origen stands closer to the church's emphasis upon regular ordinary worship.)

It is in the *Gospel of Thomas* that the Gnostic viewpoint is most clearly set forth, although, as S. Giversen has pointed out,[22] something has gone wrong with the question-answer sequence toward the beginning of the book. On p. 81, 14-17 the disciples ask, "Do you want us to fast? and in what way shall we pray and give alms? and what observances shall we keep in eating?" Two pages later comes the answer. "If you fast, you will beget for yourselves a sin, and if you pray, you will be condemned, and if you give alms, you will do harm to your spirits" (p. 83, 14-27; dietary laws are also rejected[23]). Whereas in Matthew

[19] H. Schmidt, *Veteres philosophi quomodo indicaverint de precibus* (Giessen, 1907).

[20] *Str.* 7:41:1.

[21] *De oratione* 5:1.

[22] *Acta orientalia,* 25 (1960), 332-38.

[23] See also the words on washing a cup, p. 96, 13-16.

6:2-18 Jesus rejects ostentation in almsgiving, prayer, and fasting, according to *Thomas* he rejects the practices altogether. This alteration is due to the Gnostic emphasis on the interior life and on the worthlessness of the world and external actions. It is probably significant that all the practices rejected are characteristic both of Judaism and of second-century Jewish Christianity. With these sayings we may compare another (p. 90, 18-23). The disciples ask Jesus, "Is circumcision profitable or not?" Jesus replies, "If it were profitable, their father would have begotten them circumcised from their mother. But the true circumcision in the Spirit has found complete usefulness." The question is Pauline (Rom. 3:1); so is the answer (Phil. 3:3). But the argument looks like an appeal to "nature" rather surprising in *Thomas* and perhaps derived from philosophical criticisms of Judaism made either by outsiders or by the most "liberal" Jews, well to the left of Philo. In any event, *Thomas* vigorously rejects Jewish ritual observances, even when, as in the case of fasting, prayer, and almsgiving, they are practiced by Christians.

Indeed, at one point *Thomas* goes still farther. Presumably quoting the disciples, he has them ask Jesus, "Come, let us pray today and fast." Jesus replies, "What sin, then, have I committed, or in what have I been overcome? But when the bridegroom comes out of the bridechamber, then may they fast and pray" (p. 98, 10-16). Jesus' question is like the one he asks about baptism in the *Gospel of Hebrews:* If baptism is for sins, why should he be baptized?[24] *Thomas* says nothing about baptism; he therefore directs the traditional saying of *Hebrews* (along with some others found in Matt. 9:14, Mark 2:19-20, and Luke 5:34-35) against fasting and praying. The sinless Gnostic simply cannot fast or pray.

Like other Gnostics, *Thomas* is not averse to using traditional language if it is properly reinterpreted. "If you do not fast to the world, you will not find the kingdom; if you do not truly keep the Sabbath, you will not see the Father" (p. 86, 17-20). Verbal parallels to this saying occur in the writings of Justin,

[24] Jerome, *Dialogus adversus Pelagium* 3:2 (*PL* 23, 570).

Clement of Alexandria, and Tertullian,[25] not to mention the letter of Ptolemaeus to Flora.[26] But *Thomas* goes beyond these authors because he absolutely rejects any literal observance of any of the rites involved.

He thus resembles the Valentinian Gnostic radicals mentioned by Irenaeus (*Adv. haer.* 1:21:4); they held that "perfect redemption is the knowledge of the ineffable Greatness," that it has nothing to do with objects of sense-perception, and that only "*gnosis* is the redemption of the inner man." This kind of Gnostic was conspicuous for his rejection of all conventional worship.

D. CONCLUSION

We have now presented evidence for the existence of three kinds of attitudes toward worship among the Christian Gnostics of the second century and have tried to relate them to various tendencies present among Christians and Jews during that period. We began by suggesting that the Gnostic views and practices reflected a certain sharpening or exaggeration of what could be found within the limits of more orthodox Christianity. It is obvious that our first group stood fairly close to Christians in general, and that the second group was enjoying a liturgical enrichment not unlike that characteristic of the worship of other Christians. It is harder to find analogies to the attitudes of the third group, but it may be suggested that in the discussions of spiritual worship by Clement (*Str.* 7:34-49) and Origen (*De oratione)* what is specifically Gnostic is rejected but what is valuable in the Gnostic criticism is utilized and deepened, partly in relation to Platonic and Neo-Platonic ideas about prayer and worship in general. If one compares their views with those of various Neo-Platonists and others, we find that they stand not too far from Plotinus and Porphyry[27] and, indeed, the Hermetic

[25] See R. M. Grant and D. N. Freedman, *The Secret Sayings of Jesus* (New York, 1960), p. 147.

[26] Epiphanius, *Pan.* 33:5:12-13.

[27] See Schmidt, *op. cit.,* pp. 44-48.

authors,[28] whereas on the other hand they are far from the Gnostics who delight in magic or theurgy (perhaps the Simonians, certainly some Marcosians) and from a Neo-Platonist like Iamblichus who favored "not reason but ritual."[29] Both Clement and Origen, and Origen especially, wished to maintain the traditional liturgical worship of the church, but both were aware that it was valuable not in itself but as a concrete manifestation of the Christian's constant inner life. In this sense both of them tried to preserve what was meaningful to Gnostics of the third group.

[28] Cf. G. van Moorsel, *The Mysteries of Hermes Trismegistus* (Utrecht, 1955).

[29] E. R. Dodds, "Theurgy and its Relation to Neoplatonism," *Journal of Roman Studies,* 37 (1947), 55-69.

13

THE MYSTERY OF MARRIAGE IN THE GOSPEL OF PHILIP

A. GOD AND ISRAEL, CHRIST AND THE CHURCH

IN THE Old Testament one of the most striking analogies provided to the relation of God with Israel is derived from human marriage. This analogy does not come as a complete surprise when one recalls the importance of marriage in the patriarchal narratives and in the story of creation. The prophet Hosea did not entirely lack precedents when he acted out a parable of the relation of God to Israel in his marriage to the faithless Gomer. God loves Israel as a husband loves his wife; and in Hosea's parabolic action this love was revealed as established in grace rather than based on works. Among some of the rabbis the covenant at Sinai was treated as God's wedding with Israel.[1] It is significant, however, that in Judaism only God was the husband. Neither Moses nor any messianic figure ever took his place.[2] The Philonic allegories of the union of the soul with the Logos, or even with Wisdom, the "daughter of God," seem to be the product of an individual's exegesis and they refer to individuals, not to a community.[3]

In two Matthean parables, those of the Wedding Banquet (22:2-14) and the Wise and Foolish Virgins (25:1-13), the coming reign of God is portrayed as a wedding, but it is by no means clear that Jesus is the bridegroom. On the other hand, according to Mark 2:19 (and parallels) Jesus referred to himself as a bridegroom and stated that the "sons of the bridechamber" could not fast while he was with them. The Gospel of John

[1] E. Stauffer in *Theologisches Wörterbuch zum Neuen Testament,* ed. G. Kittel (Stuttgart, 1933-), Vol. 1, p. 652.

[2] J. Jeremias, *ibid.,* Vol. 4, pp. 1094-95.

[3] H. Leisegang in *RE* 12, 1076-77; E. R. Goodenough, *An Introduction to Philo Judaeus* (see above, p. 144 n. 68), 90-95.

tells us how Jesus "manifested his glory" at the Wedding in Cana (2:1-11), and we learn that John the Baptist described himself as "the bridegroom's friend," while Jesus himself—"he who has the bride"—was her husband (3:29).

This kind of imagery is clearly intimated in several Pauline epistles and is most fully worked out in Ephesians. In I Corinthians 6:15-17 Paul argues that while union with a prostitute means becoming one body with her, uniting with the Lord means becoming one spirit with him. The analogy of marriage is clearly implicit here, especially since Paul cites Genesis 2:24, "the two shall become one flesh." More explicitly, in II Corinthians 11:2 Paul writes, "I betrothed you to Christ to present you as a pure bride to her one husband." Christ has taken the place of God at Sinai; the apostle has assumed the role of Moses.[4] Again, in a rather confused analogy in Romans 7:2-4 one thing, at any rate, seems to be clear: the community was once wedded to the law and therefore to sin, but with the husband's death she is now free to belong to another, i.e., to Christ.[5] In Ephesians 5:22-33 the prophecy of Genesis 2:24 is described as "a great mystery" and is referred not only to Christ and the church but also to Christian marriage in general. Schlier has argued that this passage is clearly Gnostic in origin, but as Percy points out the parallels from other Pauline epistles suggest that it is Pauline in nature;[6] in turn, Paul's own ideas can be most simply explained in relation to the Old Testament as interpreted in the light of the work of Christ.

In Jewish-Christian apocalyptic the image of Christ as the husband of the church was strongly favored, for in the book of Revelation we frequently encounter "the wedding of the Lamb" (e.g., 19:7-8). And it may be the case that from such circles this image came to be developed in the direction of Gnosticism. The anonymous homily known as *II Clement* treats the church as spiritual and pre-existent, and reflects a semi-

[4] Cf. Jeremias, *op. cit.*, p. 1098.

[5] Cf. C. H. Dodd, *The Epistle of Paul to the Romans* (New York, 1932), pp. 100-101.

[6] H. Schlier, *Christus und die Kirche im Epheserbrief* (Tübingen, 1930), pp. 60-75; E. Percy, *Die Probleme der Kolosser- und Epheserbriefe* (Lund, 1946), pp. 327-28.

Gnostic kind of exegesis when it interprets Genesis 1:27 (God made man male and female) in relation to Christ and the church (*II Clem.* 14).[7] Thus the first creation story in Genesis speaks of the union of Christ and the church; the second one refers to their temporary separation and their eventual reunion.

In circles more fully Gnostic the picture of marriage was still developed in relation to the Old Testament image. Thus the Gnostic writer Justin, retelling the story of mankind, stated that when Elohim "planted a garden" in Eden, what really happened was that he took Eden as a bride—and Eden, he said, was also known as Israel.[8] Other Gnostics may have gone farther in reinterpreting the Old Testament. It may be that when Simon Magus took the ex-prostitute Helena as his bride, he was re-enacting the marriage of Hosea and Gomer. A person who regarded himself as Father, Son, and Holy Spirit could justify his action as the realization of prophecy.[9]

B. THE MARRIAGE THEME IN VALENTINIANISM

It was among the Valentinian Gnostics, however, that most was made of marriage as a mystery. The term "mystery" was, of course, not exclusively Christian in origin; Greco-Roman writers speak of marriage as a mystery in the sense that its hidden rites resemble cultic actions.[10] But the Valentinian ideas seem to be closely related, at least verbally, to New Testament expressions, and their doctrines show us at least one kind of interpretation which was made of the New Testament data.

First of all, the Valentinians retained the idea that perfect marriage was eschatological. At the end of the world-process, when the whole "spiritual seed" is perfected, their mother

[7] J. Daniélou, *Théologie du Judéo-Christianisme* (Paris, 1958), pp. 326-39.

[8] Hippolytus, *Ref.* 5:26:2 and 36; cf. R. M. Grant, *Gnosticism and Early Christianity* (New York, 1959), pp. 19-26.

[9] On Simon cf. Grant, *ibid.*, pp. 70-96.

[10] E.g., Aristaenetus, *Epistulae* 2:7 (Hercher ed., p. 163); Clement, *Paedagogus* 2:96:2; Plutarch, *Amatorius* 23:6; the Hermetic *Asclepius* 21 (Nock-Festugière ed., p. 322, 12, with their note).

Achamoth (Wisdom) will enter the Pleroma and receive the Savior as her bridegroom; there will be a union of the Savior with Wisdom-Achamoth. This, the Valentinians said, is the bridegroom and the bride mentioned in the New Testament; the "bridechamber" is the whole Pleroma (of aeons) above.[11] The destiny of "spirituals" is the same as that of their mother. Their souls are the equivalent of "wedding garments" (Matt. 22:12); they go to the wedding banquet (Matt. 22:2-14), where the master of ceremonies and the friend of the bridegroom are present (John 2:9; 3:29). After they put off their souls and become intelligent or pure spirits, they will be given as brides to the angels about the Savior. Literally, the gospels say that there is no marrying in heaven, but the Valentinians understood that being like or equal to angels (Luke 20:36 and parallels) was really marriage.[12] Such a heavenly, spiritual union will be the Pleroma or Fullness of Joy and Rest: it is obviously the Fullness of Joy because according to John 3:29 John the Baptist said that his joy was made full![13]

Valentinian eschatology is thus based on that of the New Testament but emphasizes ideas which in the New Testament play a subordinate part, combining these ideas with the myth of the fall and restoration of Sophia and the spiritual beings by nature related to her. Because of the Valentinians' concern with eschatological marriage they created a rite of initiation which, whatever it may owe in form to pagan "sacred marriages," was clearly an anticipation of the spiritual marriages to come. Irenaeus tells us that some of them constructed a "bridechamber" and performed a mystical initiation, using special formulas; the rite consisted of a "spiritual marriage after the likeness of the unions above." He quotes one of the formulas used in the ceremony. "Adorn yourself as a bride awaiting her bridegroom, so that you may be what I am and I may be what you are. Place the seed of light in your bridechamber. Receive the bridegroom from me and contain him and be contained by him.

[11] Irenaeus, *Adv. haer.* 1:7:1 (Harvey ed., p. 58); cf. Clement, *Excerpta ex Theodoto* 64; A. E. Brooke, *The Fragments of Heracleon* (Cambridge, 1897), fragment 38, 3.

[12] Clement, *Excerpta ex Theodoto* 22:3.

[13] *Ibid.* 63-65; for "rest" cf. Brooke, *op. cit.*, fragments 12, 3; 31, 5; 32, 9.

Behold, grace has come upon you."[14] New Testament allusions are fairly obvious. The "bride" waiting for the "bridegroom" reminds us of Revelation 19:7 or 21:2. "Behold, grace has come upon you" looks like the words addressed by the angel to the Virgin Mary (Luke 1:28-35), with all the references to the conception of Jesus removed. And it may even be that "the seed of the light" could be justified by the expression "the fruit of the light" in Ephesians 5:9: if there is a fruit, there must be a seed.

Whatever the sources of the formula may be, the nature of the rite is not altogether clear. According to Irenaeus, spiritual marriage was not very spiritual. Some of the female initiates afterwards became pregnant.[15] It is not certain, however, that this was the ordinary result of such an initiation; Irenaeus may be describing isolated cases of abuse rather than the ordinary rite. We can say with some certainty that the rite represented an anticipation of the eschatological union between the spiritual Gnostics and the angels.

But if, as Irenaeus says, the Gnostic was expected to meditate incessantly on "the mystery of union,"[16] we should expect that the line between future realization and present behavior would be somewhat blurred. When these Valentinians stated that "fleshly things are for the fleshly and spiritual things are for the spiritual,"[17] it looks as if they were combining two Pauline phrases (I Cor. 2:13 and 9:11) in a way which left the distinction confused. What was fleshly? What was spiritual? Since the Valentinians were not devoted to asceticism, they had to work out a moral theology in relation to their doctrine of different classes of men.[18]

> Whoever is "in the world" [John 17:11] and has not loved a woman so as to unite with her is not "of the truth" [John 18:37] and will not attain to the truth.

[14] Irenaeus, *Adv. haer.* 1:13:3 (Harvey ed., p. 183).
[15] *Ibid.*, 1:6:3 (p. 56).
[16] *Ibid.*, 1:6:4 (p. 57).
[17] *Ibid.*, 1:6:3 (p. 56).
[18] *Ibid.*, 1:6:4 (p. 56).

> He who is "from the world" [cf. John 8:23] and unites with a woman will not attain to the truth because he possessed the woman with lust [Matt. 5:28].

The Gnostic, who is "from above," experiences love and expresses it in sexual union. The non-Gnostic, who is "from below," experiences nothing but lust. This doctrine is strikingly different from that of the second-century Christian writers whose works we possess. In general, these writers were concerned not with love and marriage but with marriage and reproduction.[19] Perhaps they were reluctant to venture into the more psychological areas in which the Gnostics were so much at home.

C. THE GOSPEL OF PHILIP

Thus far we have been discussing the background in terms of which we now proceed to look at some of the passages to be found in the new Coptic *Gospel of Philip*. This work, found at Nag Hammadi in Egypt about 1945, was published photographically by Pahor Labib in 1956, and a German translation of it was published by H.-M. Schenke early in 1959.[20] Contained in the same codex as the more famous *Gospel of Thomas*, it too contains a few sayings ascribed to Jesus, but much of it is concerned with Gnostic doctrines about the origin and nature of man, the sacraments of baptism, unction, and sacred marriage, and the nature of Gnostic eschatology. Of course all these subjects are often treated together; and the confusion with which Philip presents them may well be intentional. From his mélange we have extracted some sayings about the mystery of marriage in order to relate them to their contexts.[21]

In the first place, the union which is represented in marriage

[19] Exceptions are provided in Theophilus, *Ad Autol.* 2:28, and Clement, *Paedagogus.*

[20] P. Labib, *Coptic Gnostic Papyri in the Coptic Museum* (Cairo, 1956); H.-M. Schenke in *Theologische Literaturzeitung,* 84 (1959), 1-26; cf. H.-C. Puech in W. Schneemelcher-E. Hennecke, *New Testament Apocrypha,* trans. R. McL. Wilson, 1 (Philadelphia, 1963), 271-78.

[21] My thanks are due to W. R. Schoedel for checking the Coptic text.

reflects an archetypal unity. Here the Valentinians doubtless had in mind Genesis 1:26-27, with its statement that God made man after his image and likeness; "male and female he made them." There was an original androgynous unity which it is man's destiny to recover. So we read in *Philip* (p. 116, 22-26; cf. p. 118, 9-17):

> When Eve was in Adam, there was no death. When she was separated from him, death arose. Again, when they reunite and he receives her to himself, death will be no more.

The restoration is related to the indissolubility of marriage in *Philip*, p. 118, 17-20:

> The woman unites herself with her husband in the bridechamber. Those who have been united in the bridechamber cannot be separated again [*ouketi*—an allusion to Mark 10:18 and parallels].

But in the case of Eve there was no real union in the bridechamber, and therefore she was separated from Adam—still further *Philip*, p. 118, 20-22. In other words, an ontological separation was succeeded by an existential one.

> First there was adultery, then the murderer [Cain]. And he was begotten in adultery, for he was the son of the snake (*Philip*, p. 109, 5-8).

Here we find an allusion to the old Gnostic myth, not ordinarily expressed by Valentinians, that the evil Ialdabaoth, in serpent form, actually seduced Eve and was the father of Cain.[22] It does not really seem related to Philip's system, though Gnostic teachers were not always averse to admitting details from the systems of others.

Perhaps Philip treated this old myth allegorically. *Philip*, p. 126, 12-15, seems to point in this direction. "Whomever the woman loves, to him those who are born are like; if her husband, they are like her husband; if an adulterer, they are like the adulterer." Thus far we are in the realm of physiology. But Valentinians naturally preferred to deal with psychological

[22] Hippolytus, *Ref.* 5:26:22-23; Epiphanius, *Pan.* 37:4:4-5; 40:5:3; for a more allegorical version, cf. II Cor. 11:3.

phenomena. "Often when a woman sleeps with her husband, but while her heart is with the adulterer with whom she is accustomed to unite, she bears the one whom she bears so that he is like the adulterer." The problem created by children who do not look like their parents had long ago been discussed by Empedocles, who had given an explanation much like that of Philip, though with a more elaborate psychosomatic theory. His explanation was known in the Greco-Roman world because it was preserved in manuals of philosophical doctrine.[23] We cannot be sure that the Valentinians had read such manuals; presumably this notion is what we call "popular," since we cannot trace its sources exactly. They went on to draw an exhortatory conclusion: "You who are with the Son of God, do not love the world but love the Lord so that what you bring forth may not be like the world but like the Lord!" This injunction means, in relation to *Philip*, that the Gnostic must not love the "unclean spirits" which wish to unite with him in adulterous unions. These spirits will hold him fast if he is not loyal to the Bridegroom and the Bride which he has received from the "mirrored" (*eikonikos*) bridechamber, presumably at initiation.

This bridechamber is both eschatological and actual. It is a "mystery" which has already been received but is to be "fulfilled" in the future. We who are Gnostics have already become "sons of the bridechamber" (*Philip*, p. 124, 5; p. 134, 5), or even "sons of the bridegroom" (*Philip*, p. 130, 17).[24] Therefore our marriages have become symbols of the unions of spiritual beings above. The Matthean parable of the Wise and Foolish Virgins ends with a cryptic eschatological saying: "No one knows the day" (25:13). But Gnostics know what this saying means (*Philip*, pp. 129, 34–130, 8).

> No one knows the day when man and wife unite, except themselves alone. For marriage in the world is a mystery for those who have taken a wife. If even the marriage of defilement is

[23] *Dox.* 423; cf. Soranus, *Gynaeciorum* 1:10.

[24] Matt. 9:15 according to Codex Bezae and Latin; so also Clement, *Excerpta ex Theodoto* 79; on the text cf. A. Jülicher, *Die Gleichnisreden Jesu* (2nd ed.; Tübingen, 1910), pp. 180-81.

> hidden, how much more is the undefiled marriage [cf. Heb. 13:4] a true mystery! It is not anything fleshly; it is pure. It belongs not to lust but to the will. . . .

In its eschatological actuality this heavenly/earthly marriage is a mystery or secret, just as it is in Ephesians 5:32. But its secrecy is related in Philip not only to marriage as such but also to the secret holiness of the temple in Jerusalem. *Philip*, pp. 132, 21–133, 10 combines motives from Matthew and Hebrews in a genuinely allegorical way.[25]

> The bedroom [*koitōn*] is hidden. It is the Holy of Holies [Heb. 9:3, BKL al]. The veil covered it, so to speak, at first while God arranged the creation in order. But if the veil is torn and the inside is revealed, "this house will be left desolate" [Matt. 23:38 D lat Clement]; or rather, it will be destroyed [Matt. 24:2]. But the whole [inferior] Godhead will not depart from these places into the Holy of Holies; for it cannot be mixed with the unmixed Light and the [fault]less Pleroma, but it will be "under the wings" [Matt. 23:37] of the cross and its arms. This Ark [Heb. 9:4] will serve them for salvation, if the deluge gains power over them. If some are in the tribe of the priesthood, these will enter inside the veil together with the high priest [Heb. 6:19-20; 10:20]. For this reason the veil is torn not only above—since otherwise it [the Holy of Holies] would open only for those above—nor will it be torn only below—since otherwise it would be revealed only to those below; but it is torn "from above to below" [Matt. 27:51; Mark 15:38].

It is impossible for us to tell whether these Gnostics were discussing human or spiritual marriage, or whether in their minds there was a significant difference between the two. Similarly it is hard to tell whether a passage which speaks of the union of the Father of the All with the virgin who came down below is historical or eschatological in intention. Probably it is expressed as past but really refers to the future; but we have already seen that in Valentinian thought such distinctions are hard to make. The saying is on p. 119, 3-15, of the *Gospel of Philip:*

[25] Cf. Clement, *Excerpta ex Theodoto* 38:2; Heracleon in Brooke, *op. cit.*, fragment 13, 7.

> Is it permitted to express a mystery? The Father of the All united with the virgin who came down below. And a fire shone for them on that day. It revealed the great bridechamber. For this reason his [the Savior's] body, which arose on that day, came out of the bridechamber [Ps. 18 (19):5-6]. As he originated from the Bridegroom and the Bride, so Jesus directed the All into it [the bridechamber] through them [the Bridegroom and the Bride]. And it is necessary that each of the disciples enter into his rest.

In the very last part of the *Gospel of Philip* the result of this realized eschatology is clearly portrayed. *Philip*, p. 134, 4-18 shows what it means to be a Gnostic.

> If anyone becomes a "son of the bridechamber" he will receive the Light. If anyone does not receive it while he is in these places, he cannot receive it in the other place [cf. Luke 16:26]. He who receives any light will not be seen nor can he be held fast. No one will be able to trouble him in this way, whether he lives in the world or leaves the world. He has already received the Truth in images, and the world has become the Aeon. For the Aeon already exists for him as Pleroma [fulfillment], and he exists in this way. It is revealed to him alone, since it is not hidden in darkness and night but is hidden in a perfect Day and a holy Light.

What the *Gospel of Philip* reveals to us is a highly significant picture of salvation as equivalent to marriage and of marriage as an archetype of salvation. The way of initiation was, of course, not for everyone. "The bridechamber will not be shared by animals or by slaves or by defiled women" (*Philip*, p. 117, 1-3); and "animals" are men controlled by material souls,[26] just as "slaves" are those who have no part in Gnostic freedom. Such a picture of redemption seems to have been confined to Gnostics in the early second century, though after it was, so to speak, baptized (or rebaptized) by Clement and Origen it flourished among Christians in various modified forms.[27] Though the date of *Philip* is doubtful, the picture of the mystery of marriage certainly goes back to second-century Valentinianism,

[26] Clement, *Excerpta ex Theodoto* 50:1.

[27] For Origen cf. A. Lieske, *Der Theologie der Logosmystik bei Origenes* (Münster, 1938), pp. 5-7, 61-67, 147-53.

and it provides a valuable supplement to what we knew from the Fathers.

Perhaps the most remarkable supplement is given in what *Philip* says about the Lord and Mary Magdalene. Many Christian and Gnostic writers were impressed by what they found in the gospels about this Mary, who by the end of the second century was being identified with the sister of Lazarus (John 11:3) and with the woman who in Luke 7:36-50 expressed her love for Jesus.[28] They recognized that according to Matthew 28:9 and Mark 16:9 (a verse apparently part of Mark by Justin's time) she was the first witness to the resurrection. Obviously, then, Jesus loved her more than the other disciples; he often kissed her (*Philip*, p. 111, 34-37); she constantly accompanied him (*Philip*, p. 107, 6-9; cf. Mark 15:40-41). She became spiritually pregnant and perfect (*Philip*, p. 107, 1-4).

Schenke has used these passages about Mary Magdalene in support of his claim that the basic mystery of *Philip* and of the Valentinians consisted of a holy kiss which the initiate received from the mystagogue.[29] He says that the rite cannot have been a "sacred marriage" because of the rejection of marriage, called "the marriage of defilement" in *Philip*, p. 130, 4. The evidence of Irenaeus seems to contradict this theory, as we have already suggested. It is obvious, however, that the holy kiss must have been included in the ceremony. Like other aspects of Valentinianism, this one was taken over from the church. We first encounter it in the Pauline epistles and in I Peter.[30] None of the Apostolic Fathers mentions it, but this silence is accidental, for it reappears in Justin's first apology and flourishes thereafter.[31] We also find an allusion to it in the Odes of Solomon (28:6-7), which are probably Valentinian, or at least Gnostic, in origin. "Immortal Life embraced and kissed me; from him the Spirit which can never die, since it is Life, originated in me."

[28] Cf. Origen, *In Iohannem commentarius,* fragment 78 (Preuschen ed., pp. 544-45).

[29] *Op. cit.* (p. 188 n. 20), p. 5.

[30] I Thess. 5:26; I Cor. 16:20; II Cor. 13:12; Rom. 16:16; I Pet. 5:14.

[31] *Apol.* 1:65:2; cf. K. M. Hofmann, *Philema Hagion* (Gütersloh, 1938), pp. 94-144.

Gressmann aptly entitled this Ode "the kiss of life," since the kiss transmits the Spirit.[32]

Should we wish to trace this practice back behind Christianity we should encounter a great deal of difficulty. Many older commentators cite two passages in Philo's *Questions on Exodus* which, in their opinion, proved that it came from the synagogue.[33] Now that we have Ralph Marcus's translation of these passages, we can see that they have nothing to do with the subject.[34] There is no evidence for a Jewish origin of the practice. Perhaps, as Hofmann suggests, it was a unique contribution made by the Christian church itself. The new relationship of fellowship and love in the community was expressed in the holy kiss of peace.

Once more, the Valentinians were making use of Christian materials but were exaggerating some elements and neglecting others. They were laying unusual emphasis on the uniquely Christian doctrine of the union of Christ with his church and were "literalizing" the metaphors used by Christians.[35] With this emphasis they combined the uniquely Christian practice of the holy kiss, and thus produced a result quite out of harmony with the mind of the church as a whole. In this respect their attempt reminds us of the Marcionite stress on what was novel in Christianity, at the expense of what was not so novel. Both sects emphasized the newness of the new and neglected the continuity of the old. This is one reason for the appeal which documents like the *Gospel of Philip* can make. It presents a fascinating picture of one aspect of early Christianity—perhaps neglected by others but here pushed to an extreme.

[32] E. Hennecke, *Neutestamentliche Apokryphen* (2nd ed.; Tübingen, 1924), p. 461; cf. Hofmann, *op. cit.*, p 87.

[33] *Quaestiones in Exodum* 2:78 and 118.

[34] *Philo, Supplement II, Questions on Exodus* ("Loeb Classical Library" [London, 1953]), pp. 128, 169.

[35] For an excellent discussion of "bridal mysticism in Christian tradition" see O. Perler, *Ein Hymnus zur Ostervigil von Meliton?* ("Paradosis," 15; Freiburg [Switzerland], 1960), pp. 37-62.

14

GNOSTICISM AND THE PROBLEM OF METHODOLOGY

TWO PROBLEMS are involved in the analysis of Gnosticism. First comes the criticism of the sources. Since most of our information about gnosis still comes from the church Fathers, we must try to determine how reliably such writers as Irenaeus, Hippolytus, and Epiphanius have reproduced their sources. In this connection Sagnard's *La gnose valentinienne et le témoignage de saint Irénée* (Paris, 1947), is especially useful since it establishes Irenaeus' essential trustworthiness. Second comes the interpretation of the Gnostic text once it has been established. At this point there is much disagreement among modern scholars.[1] In general the older way of looking at Gnosticism, set forth by such scholars as De Faye, Leisegang, Casey, Nock, and most recently Sagnard, is based on description and historical investigation, with emphasis laid on the search for sources and interrelations. Ideally, proof of the existence of these sources and interrelations is offered, and the proof is based on historical probabilities.

A newer way of approach was set forth in 1934 by Hans Jonas, a pupil of Rudolf Bultmann, in his *Gnosis und spätantiker Geist*, Part I. Jonas' method, like his master's, is partly philological and partly intuitional. He believes that by apprehending the "form" of a Gnostic system and filling in missing links one can come to understand the system from within. Chronology and source-criticism become partly irrelevant. To some extent Jonas builds on the foundations laid by Wilhelm Bousset.

An offshoot of Jonas' method is to be found in the understanding of Gnosticism as ancient psychology, based on Gnostic experience. Such a method was employed to some extent by Hans

[1] See R. M. Grant, "The Earliest Christian Gnosticism" in *Church History*, 22 (1953), 81-98.

Leisegang in *Die Gnosis* (Leipzig, 1924), but it has been carried much further by H. C. Puech in *Le manichéisme* (Paris, 1949) and by Gilles Quispel in various studies. Sometimes this method is employed cautiously, as in Quispel's analysis of Basilides' doctrine of man, in *Eranos-Jahrbuch* (1948); sometimes it is presented without qualifications. In *Gnosis als Weltreligion* (1952) Quispel states flatly that "Gnosticism is the mythical projection of the individual's experience."

Both Puech and Quispel believe that gnosis is based on and expressed in "tragic myth." At this point they rely on the patristic criticism of Gnostic mythology. They do not always recognize, however, that when the Fathers, usually trained in literary criticism, call something a "tragic myth" they mean only that it is an untrue story such as one would see presented in a tragedy. Their analysis is literary, not psychological, and it cannot be transmuted into a ground for psychological treatment. The only ancient writer who really refers to the "tragic" content of the Gnostic myths seems to be Plotinus (*Enneads* 2:9:13).

The basic question is this: Can we dispense with the older historical criticism of Gnostic thought and simply translate gnosis into psychology or any other modern philosophical-theological construction, or do we have to keep digging away at sources and interrelations? It is my contention that the modern short cut method results only in a short circuit. In many instances, to understand the sources is to understand the system; at any rate, the system cannot be understood apart from the sources. In other words, often the "form" of a Gnostic system is given it not so much by the psychological experience of its author (easier to mention than to find) as by the sources he uses.

The example which can be used in testing this view is the book *Baruch* by a Gnostic named Justin. He wrote this treatise, along with others totally lost, at the end of the second century or the beginning of the third. Our only direct evidence concerning it is given in fairly full excerpts cited by Hippolytus in his *Refutation of all heresies* (5:24:2–27:5). At a later time it seems to have influenced Marcionites known to the Syrian Eznik (cf. Harnack, *Marcion: das Evangelium vom fremden Gott* [see above, p. 59 n. 9], p. 374*).

A. THE MYTHOLOGY OF JUSTIN'S "BARUCH"

Before approaching Justin's mythology we must clear away several misconceptions ancient and modern. Hippolytus himself is baffled by Justin. He prefixes to his account a story of Heracles and the Echidna taken from Herodotus 4:8-10. This story actually has nothing to do with Justin's myth, for the three sons of Heracles and the Echidna are certainly not the three cosmic principles of Justin. It is a story intended to demonstrate Hippolytus' scholarly ability. He gives similar prefaces, usually equally irrelevant, for other Gnostic systems. At another point he says that Justin's system is like that of Basilides (*Ref.* 10:15:1). It is not. Finally, what is apparently a marginal gloss calls the whole fifth book "Naassenes–fifth." It is the fifth book, but Justin is not a Naassene.

The most recent study of Justin is that of Ernst Haenchen in the *Zeitschrift für Theologie und Kirche*, 50 (1953), 123-58. Haenchen combines a great deal of valuable information with readiness to eliminate difficult passages as insertions, along with zeal for finding a primary "Gnostic myth." He refuses to look for earlier written sources and prefers to speak of motifs. This refusal is too vigorous.

Let us turn to Justin. In his view the universe owes its origin to three principles, two male and one female. The first is the Good, the only one who can be so called (Mark 10:18, a favorite Gnostic text). He possesses foreknowledge of everything and dwells in light above the heaven; he is identical with the cosmic Priapus (Haenchen rejects this). The second is the Father of everything generated or created, Elohim; he does not possess foreknowledge and is unknown and invisible. The third is the female principle, Eden. Like the Father, she lacks foreknowledge. She is irascible, double-minded, and double-bodied. In fact, she is half virgin and half viper; thus she is the Echidna of Orphic cosmogony. Her role is essentially that of matter.

As a result of the love of the Father Elohim and the female Eden, twenty-four angels were produced; "Elohim planted a paradise [the angels] in Eden" (Gen. 2:8). Twelve of the angels resembled their father. These were Michael, Amen, Baruch, Gabriel, and Essadaeus (El-Shaddai), as well as seven more whose names have been lost. Twelve resembled their mother. These were Babel, Achamoth, Naas, Bel, Beliar, Satan, Sael (Sheol), Adonai, Kauithan, Pharaoth, Karkamenos, and Lathen.[2] These angels are the equivalent of the trees in the garden of Eden; the tree of life is Baruch, while the tree of the knowledge of good and evil is Naas. The twelve angels of Elohim formed man from the earth, or rather from the human portions of Eden; Elohim gave him the spirit, Eden the soul. Adam and Eve were fashioned as eternal images of the marriage and love of Elohim and Eden ("our image and likeness," Gen. 1:26). They commanded Adam and Eve to "increase and multiply and inherit the earth" (Gen. 1:28)–i. e., Eden. Human marriage and love are a continual memorial of the relation of Elohim and Eden.[3]

The twelve angels of Eden, on the other hand, were divided into four groups (the seasons) after the four rivers flowing from Eden. They are the twelve signs of the Zodiac, constantly circling about the earth and bringing various tribulations upon it.[4]

The origin of evil is not directly due to them, even though they are called a "flow of evil."[5] Elohim ascended to contemplate the universe and to see if it lacked anything. When he had ascended above the heaven he saw a light brighter than that which he had made,[6] and recognizing that he was not the Lord,[7] he appealed for admission through the gate.

[2] In Manicheism the second of the twelve zodiacal "virgins of light" is sometimes called Wisdom (= Achamoth); cf. A. V. W. Jackson, *Researches in Manichaeism* (New York, 1931), p. 241, and H.-C. Puech, *Le manichéisme* (Paris, 1949), p. 79. Compare also the twenty-four deities made by Ahuramazda (Plutarch, *De Iside* 47) and the twenty-four stars of the Chaldaeans (Diodorus Siculus 2:31:4).

[3] On sacred marriages as archetypes among the Valentinians, Clement, *Str.* 3:1:1, and Quispel's note on Ptolemaeus in Epiphanius, *Pan.* 33:4:4.

[4] Zodiacal angels in Irenaeus, *Adv. haer.* 1:17:1 (Harvey ed., p. 168). On the soul's passage through the Zodiac cf. Clement, *Str.* 5:103:4-5; Gruppe in *RE* Suppl. 3, 1104.

[5] On disease and the zodiac cf. Boll-Bezold-Gundel, *Sternglaube und Sterndeutung* (3rd ed.; Leipzig, 1926), pp. 54-55, 134-35.

[6] De Faye (*Gnostiques et gnosticisme* [Paris, 1913], p. 191) derives this idea from the *Phaedrus* (247b-c) of Plato.

[7] This is a common Gnostic theme; cf. Ialdabaoth in Irenaeus, *Adv. haer.* 1:30:5 and in the *Apocryphon Iohannis;* the Demiurge in Basilides (Hippolytus, *Ref.* 7:26:1), Ptolemaeus (Irenaeus, *Adv. haer.* 1:7:4) and Heracleon (cited by Origen, *In Iohannem commentarius* 13:60). Ialdabaoth is stupid and malevolent; the Demiurge, like Elohim, recognizes his superior.

> Open the gates for me so that I may enter and acknowledge the Lord; for I thought that I was the Lord.

A voice replied,

> This is the gate of the Lord; the just enter through it.[8]

Therefore, since Elohim was just, the Good admitted him and seated him at his right hand. Overcome by remorse, the Father Elohim wanted to overturn the universe and recover his spirit from men (Gen. 6:3), but the Good reminded him that the world and men were good (Gen. 1:31), for they originated in the mutual love of Elohim and Eden. The Good's statement is curiously reminiscent of John 21:22.

Let Eden have the creation as long as she wishes; you stay with me.	If I wish him to remain till I come, what is that to you? you follow me.

It also recalls God's word to Moses in Deuteronomy 5:31: "You stand with me, and I will tell you the commandments and the ordinances and the judgments which you shall teach them."[9]

Evil was not due precisely to Elohim's departure but to Eden's consequent frustration. In her grief she gathered her angels around her and adorned herself attractively so that Elohim would desire her again and return.[10] When this attempt failed, she ordered Babel (Aphrodite) to bring about adultery and divorce among men so that Elohim's spirit might suffer the same torment as Eden herself.[11] At the same time she empowered Naas to punish Elohim's spirit in men for his abandoning her and breaking his marriage compact. Naas seduced both Adam and Eve (thus originating both pederasty and adultery)[12] and transgressed the first law, to increase and multiply. Elohim had sent

[8] Ps. 117:19-20; cf. *I Clem.* 48:2-5; against Ps. 23:7-8 (cf. Justin, *Apol.* 1:51:7).

[9] Philo, *Quod Deus immutabilis sit* 20-23, uses this verse to prove divine immutability.

[10] Perhaps the mention of adornment (*kosmos*) is based on exegesis of Gen. 2:1 (LXX): "The heaven and the earth and all their *kosmos* were completed." Similar exegesis occurs in *I Clem.* 33:7.

[11] Divorce grieves Elohim; Mal. 2:15-16.

[12] The serpent seduces Eve in Irenaeus, *Adv. haer.* 1:30:7 and Epiphanius, *Pan.* 40:5; cf. L. Ginzberg, *Die Haggada bei den Kirchenvätern* (see above, p. 136 n. 35), p. 59.

his third angel, Baruch, to command men not to eat of Naas, the tree of knowledge. He could eat of the other trees, for although like their mother they had passions, they did not transgress the law. Passion in itself is not evil.

In this way Elohim brought about both evil and good. By leaving Eden he became the ultimate cause of evil (cf. Isa. 45:7), but by ascending he showed men how to ascend. Elohim has sent Baruch to contend with Naas on four other occasions. The first mission was to Moses, but Naas "overshadowed" the commandments of Baruch and made his own commandments heard. Thus the soul was set against the spirit and the spirit against the soul. The second was to the prophets, so that the spirit might escape from the evil creation;[13] but Naas seduced the prophets and men did not follow Baruch's words. The third was to Heracles, a prophet from the uncircumcision, who performed twelve labors against the twelve angels of Naas.[14] Unfortunately, when he seemed to be victorious he was seduced by Omphale (Babel-Aphrodite), who took away his power, the commandments of Baruch. She exchanged clothing with him and put on him the power of Eden.[15] Thus his work became ineffective.

Finally, "in the days of king Herod,[16] Baruch was sent to Nazareth, where he found Jesus, the twelve-year-old son[17] of Joseph and Mary, feeding sheep.[18] He told him the Justinian gospel and said to him, "Jesus, son of man, do not be seduced but proclaim this message to men and tell them about the Father and about the Good, and ascend to the Good and sit there with

[13] Cf. the Marcionite view in Clement, *Str.* 3:12:1 (Harnack, *Marcion: das Evangelium vom fremden Gott* [see above, p. 59 n. 9]), p. 276*.

[14] Most of the monsters were the offspring of Typhon and the Echidna (Hesiod, *Theogony* 306:327-28; Apollodorus, *Bibliotheca* 2:74; Hyginus, *Fabulae,* praef. 39, Rose ed., p. 5). According to Titus 1:12 Epimenides was a pagan prophet, while Theophilus (*Ad Autol.* 2:36) views the Sibyl as a prophetess for the Greeks and other gentiles.

[15] According to Diodorus Siculus 4:31:8, this exchange meant that Omphale took the courage of Heracles.

[16] Matt. 2:1; Luke 1:5; or the *Gospel of the Ebionites* (Klostermann ed., fragment 1).

[17] According to Josephus, *Antiquitates* 5:348, Samuel began to prophesy at the age of 12; cf. Luke 2:42 (and Valentinian exegesis in Irenaeus, *Adv. haer.* 1:20:2).

[18] David also fed sheep (I Sam. 17:15) and killed lions and bears (17:34).

Elohim, the Father of us all."[19] Jesus replied, "Lord, I will do all [these] things," and kept his promise by remaining faithful to Baruch in spite of the attempt of Naas to seduce him. In anger Naas had him crucified, but he left his body to Eden by the cross ("Woman, you have your son," John 19:26), committed the Father's spirit into his hands (Luke 23:46), and ascended to the Good.[20]

With this key one can understand Greek mythology and the Old Testament. The swan is Elohim, Leda Eden; the eagle is Naas, Ganymede Adam; the gold is Elohim, Danae Eden. "Hear, heaven, and give ear, earth; the Lord has spoken" (Isa. 1:2); in this verse heaven is Elohim's spirit in men, earth is the soul given by Eden, and the Lord is Baruch. "Israel did not know me" (Isa. 1:3): Israel is Eden; if she had known that Elohim was with the Good she would not have mistreated the spirit in men through her ignorance of the Father. The fornication of the earth in Hosea 1:2 refers to Eden.

The statement that in Hosea 1:2 the prophet has expressed the whole mystery[21] illuminates the biblical relations of Justin's system. Married love and its frustration is a symbol of the relation between God and his people in the first two chapters of Hosea, as well as in some of the later prophets. Similarly in early rabbinic exegesis the Song of Songs was understood to refer to God and Israel;[22] and in the Song we read of the search of the girl for her beloved, whom she cannot find because he has left her (5:6), and of her identification with a garden (4:12–5:1). In this connection it is significant that one of Eden's angels is called Karkamenos, presumably a Greek form for *karkom*, the "saffron plant" in the garden of Song of Songs 4:14. Other angels include Pharaoth (Pharaoh), called a tree in Eden in Ezekiel 31:9, 18;

[19] This call resembles such passages as Ezek. 2:1-8; 3:4-11, etc.

[20] Cf. the Gospel of Peter 19, where "the Lord" is taken up immediately after he says, "My Power, my Power, you have abandoned me." Cf. L. Vaganay, *L'évangile de Pierre* (Paris, 1930), pp. 255-57. It appears that like Marcionites (Harnack, *op. cit.,* p. 236*) Justin omits Luke 23:43 ("Today you will be with me in paradise").

[21] A similar expression is ascribed to Naassenes in Hippolytus, *Ref.* 5:7:9.

[22] Cf. R. H. Pfeiffer, *Introduction to the Old Testament* (New York, 1941), p. 714; J. Bonsirven, *Exégèse rabbinique et exégèse paulinienne* (Paris, 1939), pp. 215-25. In *Bereshith Rabbah* 22 the garden of Song of Songs is identified with Eve; cf. L. Ginzberg, *op. cit.,* p. 58.

Kauithan (Leviathan), identified with him in Ezekiel 29:3 (32:2); Sael (Sheol), associated with him in Ezekiel 31:16-17 (cf. Isa. 5:14; 14:9), and Babel, found not only in Genesis 11:9 but also in Isaiah 14:4, where its king is brought down to Sheol (14:9). Lathen may be a variant for Leviathan. The other angels are Achamoth (wisdom), Naas (the serpent), Bel, Beliar, and Satan, as well as Adonaios (Adonai). It is obvious that all this comes from the Old Testament or from Jewish apocryphal literature. In the Psalms of Solomon (14:3) the trees in the garden of Eden are identified with the holy ones of God.

Christian exegetes were naturally accustomed to allegorize the "fornication of the earth" in Hosea 1:2.[23] Such allegorization also prepared the way for Justin.

B. ROOTS OF THE SYSTEM

Now we must ask what the foundation of the system really is. Is it Greek or oriental? Is is Jewish or Christian or Gnostic? The answer to this question can be given at once. Undoubtedly Justin's expression of the myth is Jewish, Christian, and Gnostic. Undoubtedly it has oriental and astrological coloring. But the myth itself is a Greek cosmogonic myth taken from the ancient treatise of Pherecydes of Syros, highly valued in the second century of our era.[24]

Pherecydes spoke of three primal principles, Zeus, Chronos (Kronos), and Chthonié. When Zeus was about to create the universe, he "changed into Eros" and married Chthonié (earth)—a marriage which was the archetype of all human marriages.[25] His union with her produced gods and men. Later there was a conflict between Kronos and the forces of Ophioneus, the "snaky one." Maximus of Tyre says that Pherecydes described "Zeus and Chthonié and the Eros in them and the birth of Ophioneus

[23] Cf. Irenaeus, *Adv. haer.* 4:20:12; Clement, *Eclogae propheticae* 3:3.

[24] Isidore, son of Basilides, in Clement, *Str.* 6:53:5; Numenius (Leemans ed., *testimonium* 48); Tatian, *Or.* 3:2; 25:2; Celsus in Origen, *Contra Celsum* 6:42; Maximus of Tyre, *Dissertationes* 10:4; Clement, *Str.* 1:62:4; 5:50:3.

[25] In his edition of Hippolytus, P. Wendland notes only this parallel to Justin.

and the conflict of the gods." E. Wüst points out[26] that Maximus is a little confused, but his confusion brings us even closer to Justin. After Kronos had defeated the forces of Ophioneus he received a crown, presumably from Zeus.[27]

Pherecydes also taught, or was regarded as teaching, that there were two kinds of spirits in men, a divine and an earthly. He apparently used the words "soul" and "spirit" without differentiation, but we cannot be sure. According to Porphyry, he used such expressions as "doors" and "gates" to refer to the births and rebirths of souls.[28] With these we may compare the "gates" of Justin.

Obviously a highly developed myth of this sort lies at the base of Justin's system. How can we account for the translation of Pherecydes into Jewish-oriental terminology? The connecting link seems to lie in the statement of Philo of Byblos that "Pherecydes took his point of departure from the Phoenicians."[29] The same Philo mentions the Phoenician god El-Kronos,[30] and the identification of Kronos with Elohim was not uncommon.[31] Justin has combined Zeus with Kronos and assigned the highest place of all to Priapus, the Good. The twelve angels of Elohim are probably the twelve Olympian gods, while those of Eden are the Titans, who follow Ophioneus.

The Good is Priapus, the life-principle,

> who created before [*prinpoiesas*] there was anything; he is called Priapus because he prefabricated everything. For this reason he is erected in every temple, is honored by all creation, and before him on the roads carries fruits, i.e., the fruits of creation, of which he was the cause, prefabricating the creation before there was any.

This is the god who dwells in light above. We know that in the Roman period Priapus was often identified with other gods,[32] and his cosmic significance was recognized. The Stoic Cornutus (*Theologiae graecae compendium* 27) speaks of his generating

[26] In *RE* 18^1, 646.
[27] Tertullian, *De corona* 7 (*Vorsokr.* B4).
[28] *De antro nympharum* 31 (*Vorsokr.* B4).
[29] Eusebius, *Praeparatio evangelica* 1:10:50 (*Vorsokr.* B4).
[30] *Ibid.* 1:10:16.
[31] M. Pohlenz in *RE* 11, 2000.
[32] H. Herter, *De Priapo* (Giessen, 1932), pp. 297-309.

and preserving what he generates. In the second century Arrian identifies him with Helios, the sun God. Justin goes a little further and treats him as the cosmic source of all life. This notion is Stoic.[33]

Haenchen argues that Justin's system has room only for "the Good," who does not love the world but remains far from it in self-sufficiency. Since "the Good" is not said to be entirely unknown (though Haenchen says he is), and since "the Good" actually restrains Elohim from overturning the world and allows the just to enter to the light above, he cannot be called entirely self-sufficient and he could easily be identified with the cosmic Priapus, the *élan vital* to which earthly life owes its existence. Elohim is not independent of the Good (though Haenchen says he is); Elohim gradually comes to recognize the Good Priapus as Lord.

The myth begins, then, with the origin of the universe and relies on an allegorical exposition of Pherecydes for its framework. Pherecydes gives the form and most of the content, but the terminology is largely derived from the Old Testament and Jewish apocryphal literature.

The story of redemption is based largely on the Old Testament as a kind of negative preparation for the New, though Heracles is introduced as almost a prototype of the apostle Paul. It may be worth recalling that in *I Clement* Paul had already been treated as an archetypal Christian athlete. Here Heracles is important because his twelve (zodiacal) labors (cf. Clement, *Str.* 5:103:5; "philosophers" in Lydus, *De mensibus* 4:67, Wünsch ed., p. 121) and his seduction by Omphale could be fitted into Justin's system.

But what is redemption? The human situation involves the opposition of soul to spirit, as expressed in I Corinthians 2:14; the angel of Eden dwelling in Moses overshadowed the commandments of Baruch and made Moses hear the commandments of Naas; *therefore* the soul is set against the spirit and the spirit against the soul. We may compare Galatians 5:21, and for the relation of the Mosaic law to this, Romans 7.

[33] *Ibid.*, pp. 237-39.

Such an opposition of soul to spirit is also found among the Valentinians. The spirituals put off their souls and become intelligible spirits, to be given as brides to the angels about the Savior.[34]

Is it oriental, as modern scholars have often claimed? The presence of an analogous doctrine in Pherecydes should remind us of its Greek origin, and Haenchen rightly observes that Justin does not regard matter as essentially evil. The notion of evil matter is often oriental, but Justin does not share it. His idea seems more akin to Greek philosophy.

The redemption of the spirit comes by following the preaching of Baruch's messengers and by following the example of the Father Elohim and especially Jesus—by being washed in the waters above the firmament (Gen. 1:6-7), as the Father was washed, by drinking from the living water (John 4) as the Father drank. For spiritual being there is a spiritual baptism (John 3:3-5). This doctrine too is Valentinian.[35] When the spiritual man is redeemed he takes an oath; he swears "by the one above all, the Good, to keep these mysteries and to tell them to no one and not to return from the Good to the creation."

Justin's notion of redemption is at once Gnostic and Christian. He takes his point of departure from Pauline theology as set forth in Romans, Galatians, and I Corinthians, and tries to make this theology intelligible in a world where Pherecydes meant something, or anything.

Can we then say that his sources are unimportant? On the contrary, his use of Pherecydes is highly significant, since it reveals the cosmogonic atmosphere of Greco-Roman syncretism in which he works. To Justin, Pherecydes gives the true symbolical picture of "creation." With this picture he must correlate the narrative in Genesis. He understands Genesis in the light of Pherecydes. And since he knows that Pherecydes wrote allegory he is free to interpret the allegory by relating it to Jewish apocryphal literature, not to mention other stories of Greek

[34] Irenaeus, *Adv. haer.* 1:7:1; other references in W. Bousset, *Kyrios Christos* (Göttingen, 1913), p. 241; cf. G. Verbeke, *L'évolution du doctrine du Pneuma* (Louvain, 1945), pp. 301-3.

[35] Cf. J. Thomas, *Le mouvement baptiste en Palestine et Syrie* (Gembloux, 1935), p. 401.

mythology. On the other hand, Pherecydes does not give him an understanding of redemption. Therefore he turns to Pauline-Valentinian Gnosticism for an analysis of human nature.

The essential feature of human existence he finds in love, not the *agapé* of Paul but the *eros* of Plato and others. Sexual love is the source of all life. It has its origin in Priapus, the Good, and is expressed in the universe which is the result of the mutual love of Elohim and Eden. Nevertheless, sexual love, at least on earth, is subject to frustration. Elohim leaves Eden, and from her frustration arise the evils of the world. In Justin's system the female principle is primarily responsible for this disorder. Eden is too emotional for her own good, or for the good of mankind.

What is evil? Evil is disobedience to the basic command, "Increase and multiply." It is expressed in sins which frustrate the purpose of marriage, such as adultery, fornication, and pederasty. What Baruch wants men to do is turn from human marriage and love, which though good are subject to frustration, to the higher heavenly marriage and love to be found with the Good (cf. Eph. 6:13).

'Tis Love that makes the world go round; but true love is to be found only with the Good Priapus. Eden loves Elohim, but is frustrated; Elohim loves Eden, but leaves her to ascend to something (someone) beyond and above himself, to a love he had not known before. Only the highest love lasts. We might be reading a romanticized version of I Corinthians 13. Striving to pass beyond one's limitations brings frustration. Naas, bad though he may now be, is the tree of knowledge of good and evil and thus represents man's striving to know more than he can. Babel means man's striving to ascend to the Good by his own efforts without revealed gnosis. Babel is also the earthly (Eden-like) Aphrodite, not the heavenly Priapus.

The psychological origin of Justin's system lies in the experience of love and frustration; it represents an externalization of man's inner psychological drama. (We thus agree at this point with Puech and Quispel.) Man loves, but in his love *surgit amari aliquid* (Lucretius, *De rerum natura* 4:1134). He desires to come to the Good, but in his desire he causes frustration for others. The only solution for him is to understand his nature as a child of love and frustration and to transcend his limitations by coming to the Good and remaining there. When he is with the Good, the Good will bring him to acceptance of himself and his past. He will not wish to destroy the memory of his earlier love, though the creativeness of the Good is far higher than the creativeness of the earth.

We have reached an interpretation of Justin's mythology as psychological theology. But we cannot dispense with our historical investigation of his sources and his setting. Without such analysis we get a picture not of Justin but of modern psychology. Both elements are absolutely necessary, but historical investigation must come first. Otherwise we jump from ancient documents to modern theology or psychology as if they were entirely homogeneous. These currencies are not so easily convertible. The documents of the past bear the image of the past and to neglect this image is to deny the reality of time.

Just as in the study of the Bible or of early Christianity we cannot take a leap of faith without breaking our chronological bones, so in the study of gnosis we must always remember that the Gnostics were not modern theologians or psychologists. They were men of antiquity whose ideas can be understood only by beginning with their historical context.

15

TATIAN AND THE GNOSTICS

THE MOST difficult passage in Tatian's *Oration to the Greeks* is a section in the thirtieth chapter which, he says, is addressed to *hoi hēmōn oikeioi*—a group which he contrasts with *humeis hoi Hellēnes.* One might suppose that the *oikeioi* were Christians (cf. Gal. 6:10; Eph. 2:19), but the mysteriousness of the passage suggests that it contains secret doctrines not addressed to all, even among Christians. The two principal problems which arise out of the passage are (1) how to translate it and (2) in what context to interpret it.

I

In the twenty-ninth chapter Tatian has been discussing the consequences of conversion. When the soul is instructed by God, man's slavery in the world is terminated and he is freed from many rulers *(archontes)* and countless tyrants. He is given not what he had not received but what he had received and, by error, had been prevented from holding—presumably the divine Spirit or the "inner man." "Therefore," Tatian continues, "after comprehending these matters I desire to strip myself like newborn infants. For we know that the essence of evil is like that of the tiniest seeds; it grew from a small beginning and will be dissolved again if we obey the Word of God and do not scatter ourselves." The subject of the next verb is not stated, but since the last noun of the preceding one was "Word" we use this as the subject. "The Word gained power over what is ours through a hidden treasure; when we dug it up we were filled with dust but gave it opportunity to exist. For he who receives the All as his possession has gained control over precious wealth."[1]

[1] *τούτων οὖν τὴν κατάληψιν πεποιημένος βούλομαι καθάπερ τὰ νήπια τῶν βρεφῶν*

In making this translation we have rejected two conjectures of E. Schwartz. (1) He believed that there was a lacuna between *brephōn* and *apodusasthai* (p. 30, 17) and tentatively inserted *genesthai kai ton choïkon anthrōpon.* This is unnecessary because *apodysasthai* can be used absolutely. (2) In the last sentence he substituted *pas ὁ* for *pan.* This does not seem to suit the sense.

While the translation is not absolutely certain, we shall try to show that it is the most probable one.

II

We have already noted two New Testament parallels for *oikeioi.* It should be added that the Valentinian Heracleon speaks of men who are *oikeioteroi* to the Demiurge and are *allotrioi* because they are a *sperma ponēron kai anomon* (fragment 34/40). This statement implies that there are men who are *oikeioi* to the one whom Tatian calls "the perfect God" (Schwartz ed., pp. 5, 12; 13, 26; 16, 20; 19, 18; 27, 5) and possess "the perfect Spirit" (p. 22, 12).

As such a man, Tatian desires to strip himself (actually of the "old man," as Schwartz suggested) to the state of the newborn infant. His language recalls that of Hermas (*Similitudes* 9:29:1-3), who speaks of newborn infants and then says: "Blessed are you who put away wickedness from yourselves and put on innocence; you will be the first of all to live to God."[2] It also recalls the *Gospel of Thomas* (pp. 87, 27–88, 2): Jesus will appear "when you undress yourselves and are not ashamed and take your clothing and lay them under your feet like little children."[3] "Little children" or "little ones" are mentioned elsewhere in *Thomas;* they represent "the ideal for Gnostic asceticism."[4] The

ἀποδύσασθαι. τὴν γὰρ τῆς πονηρίας σύστασιν ἐοικυῖαν τῇ τῶν βραχυτάτων σπερμάτων ἴσμεν ἅτε διὰ μικρᾶς ἀφορμῆς τούτου κρατυνθέντος, πάλιν δ' αὖ λυθησομένου, ἡμῶν πειθομένων λόγῳ θεοῦ καὶ μὴ σκορπιζόντων ἑαυτούς. διά τινος γὰρ ἀποκρύφου θησαυροῦ τῶν ἡμετέρων ἐπεκράτησεν, ὃν ὀρύττοντες κονιορτοῦ μὲν ἡμεῖς ἐνεπλήσθημεν, τούτῳ δὲ τοῦ συνεστάναι τὴν ἀφορμὴν παρέσχομεν. τὸ γὰρ αὐτοῦ πᾶν [*πᾶς ὁ* conj. Schwartz] *ἀποδεχόμενος κτῆμα τοῦ πολυτιμοτέρου πλούτου τὴν ἐξουσίαν ἐχειρώσατο.*

[2] On the expression "live to God" see F. Barberet in *Recherches de science religieuse,* 46 (1958), 397-407; on being "like children," my note in *Harvard Theological Review,* 29 (1946), 71-73.

[3] Compare also Hippolytus, *Ref.* 5:8:44 (Naassenes).

[4] E. Haenchen, *Die Botschaft des Thomas-Evangeliums* (Berlin, 1961), p. 52.

disciples are like little children who dwell in a field that is not theirs (p. 85, 1). Little ones who receive milk are like those who enter into the kingdom (p. 85, 21).

Tatian next proceeds to discuss what the newborn infant knows. First we should say that his language recalls that of several Matthean parables of the kingdom: (1) the grain of mustard seed, very small in size (13:32, cf. *Thomas,* p. 84, 26-33); (2) the hidden treasure (13:44; cf. *Thomas,* pp. 98, 31—99, 3); and (3) the pearl "of great price" (13:46, cf. *Thomas,* p. 94, 13-22). There may also be an allusion to the parable of the tares, where we obviously find bad seeds (13:24-30, explained in 13:36-43; cf. *Thomas,* pp. 90, 32—91, 7).

In other words, Tatian's statement contains reminiscences of these parables found both in Matthew and in Thomas; and he provides a kind of exegesis of them which is found among Valentinian and Naassene exegetes. From Theodotus (Clement, *Excerpta ex Theodoto* 52-53) we learn that the tares which grow up with *(symphyes)* the good seed (the soul) represent the flesh or the "seed of the devil." And while for orthodox writers like Irenaeus (*Adv. haer.* 4:26:1) or Origen (*In Matthaeum commentarius* 10:8) the hidden treasure is Christ, for the Naassenes it is the kingdom of heaven "within us" (Hippolytus, *Ref.* 5:8:8; cf. *Thomas,* pp. 98, 31—99, 3). The idea of digging to find the kingdom is clearly set forth in *Thomas* (p. 85, 6-19): "If the householder knows that the thief is coming he will . . . not let him dig into his house of his kingdom" (see also p. 99, 2). And the dust mentioned by Tatian may well be that of which Theodotus (3:2) speaks: "After the resurrection, breathing the Spirit into the disciples [John 20:22], he blew off and separated the dust [Gen. 2:7] like ashes but he inflamed the spark and made it live." The "dust" is the fleshly element in man. Finally, Tatian's mention of wealth is paralleled in several sayings in the *Gospel of Thomas,* where we learn that knowledge of the true self is wealth and freedom from poverty (pp. 80, 10—81, 5; 86, 31—87, 2; 95, 15-17, 29-34; 99, 4-5). By means of this knowledge the Gnostic receives back what was originally his.

This analysis of Tatian's text confirms, in my opinion, the

claim that when he wrote the *Oration* he was influenced by Gnostic—especially Valentinian—ideas.[5]

Therefore we should proceed to paraphrase what he says as follows:

> He wishes to strip off his fleshly or material element and become like infants, the models of Gnostic asceticism. For this evil material element is comparable to a mustard seed; it is itself the seed of the devil, and though it grows it will be dissolved again if we obey the Word (Logos) of God and as good seeds do not scatter ourselves; we will be collected by the Logos-Savior. The Logos-Savior got power over what belongs to us (our spark) by means of the hidden treasure (the inner man). We searched for this treasure. Although in the course of the search we came under the power of the flesh, we also gave the spirit or inner man the opportunity to exist and to become effective. If we receive the whole of our spiritual nature again as our authentic possession (Gnostics claim to have grace "intrinsically" [*idioktēton*], Irenaeus, *Adv. haer.* 1:6:4), we have obtained authority over the most valuable thing there is.

Even if, or when, the body is destroyed, we are laid up in the treasuries of a rich master (*Or.* 6, Schwartz ed., p. 6, 2-3).

Elze suggests[6] that "*ktēma* here means possession of land, i.e., the field [of the parable of the Treasure in the Field], and Tatian is here referring to the whole man—his body and soul—in which the spark of the *pneuma* is hidden." This is an attractive suggestion, but does not quite do justice to Tatian's notion of the badness of the dust.

III

We have indicated that parallels to the parables Tatian uses, and to his language in paraphrasing them, are to be found in the *Gospel of Thomas.* Should we infer that he actually used *Thomas?* We know that in the *Oration* he used the Gospel of John, for he quotes "what is said" in John 1:5 (p. 14, 18) and gives an almost exact quotation of John 1:3 (p. 22, 5-6).[7] Use of a canonical gospel does not exclude use of an uncanonical one

[5] See *Journal of Theological Studies,* N.S. 5 (1954), 62-68.

[6] M. Elze, *Tatian und seine Theologie* (Göttingen, 1960), p. 99.

[7] See *TU* 68, 297-306.

(compare the Naassenes). The parallels are not quite close enough to prove actual use, but they certainly make it possible.[8]

But the *Gospel of Thomas* is not the only Gnostic document to provide parallels to what Tatian says. His rejection of "scattering" may be illustrated by a quotation from what Epiphanius calls the Gospel of Philip (*Pan.* 26:13:2, Holl ed., Vol. 1, p. 292, 14-20).

> The Lord revealed to me what the soul must say during its ascent into the heaven and how it must make a response to each of the powers above. "I have known myself, and I have collected myself from everywhere, and I did not sow children for the Archon; but I uprooted his roots and I collected the scattered members. . . ."

The mention of "children" and "scattered" suggests that the formula is based, at least in part, on exegesis of John 11:51-52: Jesus was going to die in order to gather the scattered children of God into one (cf. also Matt. 12:30; Luke 11:23; John 16:32).

Still more significantly, the Coptic *Gospel of Philip* offers a passage strikingly similar to Tatian's remarks. I quote from the translation by R. McL. Wilson.[9]

> So long as the root of wickedness is hidden, it is strong. But when it is recognized it is dissolved. That is why the logos says: Already the axe is laid at the root of the tree. . . . As for us, let each one of us dig down after the root of evil which is within him, and let him pluck it out of his heart to the root. But it will be plucked out if we recognize it. But if we are ignorant of it, it strikes root in us and brings forth its fruit in our hearts. It is master over us and we are its slaves. It takes us captive, so that we do what we do not want and what we want we do not do. It is powerful because we have not recognized it. While it exists it is active . . . (p. 131, 8-13, 18-29).

Here we find "wickedness" being "dissolved," the "logos" or Word, "digging," and the question of the "existence" of evil. In addition, there are two mentions of "possessing the All" or "receiving the All" (p. 124, 17–18, 33).

[8] See G. Quispel in *Vigiliae Christianae,* 16 (1962), 40. He considers only Tatian's *Diatessaron.*

[9] *The Gospel of Philip* (London and New York, 1962), pp. 59, 185.

The conclusion we should draw from Tatian's similarity to passages in the gospels of Thomas and Philip is that he was acquainted with both or with the kind of teaching set forth in both. The doctrine which he expounds to his *οἰκεῖοι* is Christian only to the extent that Valentinianism was Christian.

EDITIONS CITED

AELIUS ARISTIDES, *Orationes.* B. Keil, editor. Berlin, 1898.

ALBINUS, *Eisagogē.* C. F. Hermann, *Plato,* Vol. 6. Leipzig, 1892.

ALEXANDER OF APHRODISIAS, *Quaestiones.* I. Bruns, editor. Berlin, 1892.

Apocrypha and Pseudepigrapha of the Old Testament. R. H. Charles, editor. 2 vols. Oxford, 1913.

ARISTAENETUS, *Epistulae.* R. Hercher, *Epistolographi Graeci.* Paris, 1873.

AUGUSTINE, *De civitate dei.* J. E. C. Welldon, editor. 2 vols. London, 1924.

BABRIUS, *Fabulae.* W. G. Rutherford, editor. London, 1883.

CLEMENT OF ALEXANDRIA. O. Stählin, editor. (GCS.) Leipzig, 1905-09.

CORNUTUS, *Theologiae graecae compendium.* C. Lang, editor. Leipzig, 1881.

Corpus Hermeticum. A. D. Nock and A. J. Festugière, editors. 4 vols. Paris, 1945-54.

De sublimitate. O. Jahn and P. Vahlen, editors. Leipzig, 1905.

DIO CHRYSOSTOM, *Orationes.* Guy de Budé, editor. Leipzig, 1916, 1919.

DIONYSIUS OF ALEXANDRIA. C. L. Feltoe, *The Letters and Other Remains of Dionysius of Alexandria.* ("Cambridge Patristic Texts.") Cambridge, England, 1904.

EPIPHANIUS, *Panarion.* K. Holl, editor. *(GCS.)* Leipzig, 1915-33.

GALEN, *De usu partium.* G. Helmreich, editor. Leipzig, 1907-9.

Gospel of the Ebionites. E. Klostermann, *Apocrypha,* 2. ("Kleine Texte," 8.) Bonn, 1910.

Gospel of Philip. Translated by R. McL. Wilson. New York, 1962.

Gospel of Thomas. Translated by W. R. Schoedel, in R. M. Grant with D. N. Freedman, *The Secret Sayings of Jesus.* New York, 1960.

GREGORY OF NYSSA, *Opera.* Werner Jaeger, editor. 8 vols. Leiden, 1952-64.

HERMOGENES, *Opera.* H. Rabe, editor. Leipzig, 1913.

HIPPOLYTUS, *On the Theophany.* H. Achelis, editor. *(GCS.)* Leipzig, 1897.

HYGINUS, *Fabulae.* H. J. Rose, editor. Leiden, 1934.

IRENAEUS, *Adversus haereses.* W. W. Harvey, editor. 2 vols. Cambridge, 1857.

LYDUS (Johannes), *De mensibus.* R. Wünsch, editor. Leipzig, 1898.

[MENANDER], *Menandri Sententiae.* S. Jaekel, editor. Leipzig, 1964.

The Mishnah. H. Danby, editor and translator. Oxford, 1933.

MUSONIUS RUFUS. O. Hense, editor. Leipzig, 1905.

NEMESIUS, *De natura hominis.* C. F. Matthaei, editor. Halle, 1802.

NUMENIUS. E. A. Leemans, *Studie over den wijsgeer Numenius van Apamea met uitgave der fragmenten.* (Académie Royale de Belgique, Classe des Lettres, Mémoires, 2e série, tome 37, fasc. 2.) Brussels, 1937.

ORIGEN, *De principiis.* P. Koetschau, editor. *(GCS.)* Leipzig, 1913.

ORIGEN, *In Iohannem commentarius.* E. Preuschen, editor. *(GCS.)* Leipzig, 1903.

ORIGEN, *In Matthaeum commentarius.* E. Klostermann, editor. *(GCS.)* Leipzig, 1935 ff.

ORIGEN, *Homiliae in Jeremiam.* E. Klostermann, editor. (TU.) Leipzig, 1894.

ORIGEN, *Commentarius in Canticum Canticorum.* W. A. Baehrens, editor. *(GCS.)* Leipzig, 1925.

PHILO, *Opera.* L. Cohn and P. Wendland, editors. Berlin, 1896-1915.

PHILO, *Quaestiones in Genesin.* Translated by J. B. Aucher. Venice, 1826. Translated by R. Marcus, *Questions and Answers on Genesis.* London, 1953.

PLUTARCH, *Opera.* G. N. Bernardakis, editor. Leipzig, 1888-96.

STOBAEUS, *Eclogae.* C. Wachsmuth and O. Hense, editors. 5 vols. Berlin, 1884-1912.

STRATO OF LAMPSACUS. F. Wehrli, *Die Schule des Aristoteles,* Vol. 5. Basil, 1950.

TATIAN, *Oratio ad Graecos.* E. Schwartz, editor. (*TU* 4^1.) Leipzig, 1888.

THEON, *Progymnasmata.* L. Spengel, *Rhetores Graeci,* Vol. 2. Leipzig, 1854.

THEOPHILUS, *Ad Autolycum.* J. C. T. Otto, editor. Jena, 1861.

INDEXES

Biblical References

OLD TESTAMENT

OLD TESTAMENT APOCRYPHA AND PSEUDEPIGRAPHA

NEW TESTAMENT

Ancient Authors

Jewish Authors and Writings

Early Christian Authors

Gnostic Authors and Groups

Gnostic Documents

Modern Authors